Thinking Clearly

Cases in Journalistic Decision-Making

EDITED BY

TOM ROSENSTIEL AND AMY S. MITCHELL

COLUMBIA UNIVERSITY PRESS

New York

Columbia University Press
Publishers Since 1893
New York   Chichester, West Sussex

LIBRARY OF CONGRESS CATALOGING-IN-PUBLICATION DATA

Thinking clearly : cases in journalistic decision-making / edited by Tom
  Rosenstiel and Amy S. Mitchell.
        p.   cm.
    Includes bibliographical references.
    ISBN 0-231-12588-7 (cl. : alk. paper) — ISBN 0-231-12589-5 (pbk. : alk. paper)
    1. Journalistic ethics—Case studies.   2. Reporters and reporting—Case
  studies.   I. Rosenstiel, Tom.   II. Mitchell, Amy S.
  PN4756 .T49   2003
  174′.9097—dc21

                                                              2002041138

Printed in the United States of America

c 10 9 8 7 6 5 4 3 2 1
p 10 9 8 7 6 5 4 3 2

—— CONTENTS ——

—— EDITORS' NOTE ——

These case studies are not intended as a manual of ethics. They are about real-life moments in which those who work in the news had to make critical decisions. In such instances—as we hope readers will discover for themselves —questions of craft, ethics, competition, and commerce intertwine. Ethics, to some extent, forces one to draw artificial distinctions; when taught separately, it can make the subject of professional responsibility seem subordinate or even superfluous.

These cases are designed to encourage readers to think more deeply about the reasoning behind and the implications involved in the journalistic choices they illustrate.

In developing this project, we first consulted those who use the case study method in other fields, principally law and business. Next, we assembled a team of respected journalism teachers, editors, and reporters to help in the initial planning phase. We began by identifying a list of critical issues and journalistic skills to be addressed. It included such categories as private life versus public good, economics versus the public interest, verification and best practices, and the role of journalism and newsroom culture. Each of these broad themes was then broken down into more specific categories, such as the question of timing and the role of technology.

The group then selected cases from a range of topics, localities, and media types that would address those issues. For instance, the McCarthyism case study involves issues of competition and verification. The Minnesota basketball cheating case considers the public's right to know coupled with questions of verification and timing.

The authors spent months researching, writing, and editing their cases. Unlike traditional reporting, case studies are not written with the key findings at the top—just the reverse. The authors do not give away the final outcomes or implications until the end. In this way, readers can think through the decision-making process themselves without having the final outcome already in mind.

Next came development of the teaching notes, a process that began with the authors raising the questions they considered important. The academic advisers then added the perspective of their teaching experience. Finally, each case was "lab taught" at several different journalism schools to take account of feedback from teachers and students.

Our team of designers, writers, and editors is a large one. In addition to the authors, whose biographies appear at the back of the book, James W. Carey, CBS Professor of International Journalism at the Columbia University Graduate School of Journalism, and Richard Roth, associate dean of the Medill School of Journalism at Northwestern University, were academic advisers to the project. Jim Dickenson, former political editor of the *Washington Post,* and Cleve Matthews, former reporter at the *New York Times* and news director at National Public Radio, served as editorial advisers.

We also wish to thank the numerous teachers who have taught the cases and shared their insights. We are grateful to Tom Avila at the Project for Excellence in Journalism, who helped with the graphic design of the cases as they were initially presented on the Web and in written form.

This book would not have been possible without the financial support of the Pew Charitable Trusts, which funded the effort, and the continuing faith and support of Rebecca Rimel and Don Kimelman at Pew.

Finally, we remember Eileen Shanahan, a design team member whose enthusiasm and intellect helped inform the effort and who passed away during its final stages.

Thinking Clearly

Introduction

>⊷─○─⊶⊰

JAMES W. CAREY

The case study method of inquiry, and the Socratic dialogue that goes along with it, have a long and distinguished history. We generally identify them today with training in the law. Indeed, the subject matter of the law comes predigested in the form of cases, and thus the method fits as naturally into the classroom as into the courtroom. The case study method has also been used in schools of business, where the cases must be created (sometimes hypothetically, but more often by virtue of the pioneering efforts of the Harvard Business School) through the distillation of actual commercial and industrial experiences into a realistic case format.

Yet the case study method has not been widely used in journalism schools, with the exception of teaching press or communications law and, to a lesser extent, in classes in advertising or media management. One area that lends itself naturally to the case study method and Socratic dialogue is the teaching of ethics, a subject often subsumed under the heading of "critical issues" or "contemporary problems" in journalism. The case study method can also be used to teach news judgment, editing, and a number of other subjects. However, journalism issues and problems, unlike legal ones, do not deliver themselves neatly packaged as teachable cases. They must be created from scratch. This can be done hypothetically, a method pioneered by the Fred Friendly seminars on the Public Broadcasting System. Yet such cases frequently suffer from a studied lack of reality, or else age quickly—or both. Instructors can, of course, create their own cases—real or hypothetical—but faculty are quick to point out that they lack the time, resources, and, sometimes, access to original materials that are necessary to make such cases definitive. Valuable ethics books exist that pose cases or, less satisfactorily, stage arguments on opposing sides of controversies. However, the cases presented are brief and contain only modest detail. Staged arguments suffer from the problems common to, well, staged arguments: they are a little too neat, and no obvious means are available for reconciling the conflicting views.

Because I have long felt the need for a book of journalism case studies, I was delighted when the Project for Excellence in Journalism decided to undertake the preparation of one. Yet these cases, as carefully developed as they are, still do not teach themselves. Unlike cases in law, cases in journalism do not have a clear procedure for adjudication; unlike business cases, they do not have an obvious and quantifiable goal in view, namely the maximization of profit. Thus, while valuable instructional notes are included in a separate volume of teaching notes, teachers of the cases that follow must add two things to the mix from their own experience: knowledge and reading. First, they must add a standard of judgment against which to test proposed solutions to the cases, or else classroom discussion will collapse into mere opinion or an unprincipled relativism. Second, these cases demand that careful thought be given to the procedures for reasoning them through, from the initial facts to the principles governing their resolution.

What standard of judgment is appropriate in journalism cases? Clifford Christians, in *Media Ethics: Cases and Moral Reasoning,* has outlined the most important and traditionally invoked of such standards: the Golden Mean and the Golden Rule, otherwise known as the Categorical Imperative—for example, the greatest happiness of the greatest number. However, I suggest that the standard of judgment to be used in attacking these cases is the ethics of democracy. Without a free press there can be no political democracy. It is equally true that without the institutions of democratic life there can be no journalism. No journalism, no democracy. And equally: no democracy, no journalism. Journalism and democracy share a common fate, for journalism is identical with or simply another name for democracy. When democracy falters, journalism falters, and when journalism goes awry, democracy goes awry.

This is a controversial principle, for it seems to commit journalists to the defense of something—to compromise their valued independence or nonpartisanship. The principle claims that journalists can be independent or objective about everything but democracy, for to do so is to abandon the craft. About democratic institutions, about the way of life in a democracy, journalists are not permitted to be indifferent, nonpartisan, or objective. It is their one compulsory passion, for it forms the ground condition of their practice. Without the institutions or spirit of democracy, journalists are reduced to propagandists or entertainers. The passion for democracy is the one necessary bond journalists must have with the public.

We do not need much evidence to support the principle. There were people in the former Soviet Union who called themselves journalists, who worked for things called newspapers, broadcast stations, and magazines. Such people were not journalists but propagandists; their organizations did not constitute a press but the apparatus of a state and a party. Soviet journalism was an oxymoron. Without the institutions of democracy—including freedom of expression protected by law and tradition—it was a sham. However, forces other than the Totalitarian State can destroy journalism; the Entertainment State can also destroy it. When journalists measure their success or their ethics by the size of their readership or their audience, by the profits of their companies or by their incomes, status, and visibility, they have caved in to the temptation of worshipping false gods. They have sold their heritage for pottage, as completely as those who cynically convinced themselves they were serving democracy by acting as the mouthpiece of a putatively revolutionary party.

Democracy requires more than a free press. It also requires a high level of trust among citizens, a healthy judiciary, an effective legislature, a strong presidency, and a balance of powers among these institutions. The ethics of journalism is a matter of judging the consequences of stories, actions, and investigations for the vitality of these institutions and the continued capacity of people to act as citizens.

Doing good journalism, like writing good prose, is always a matter of judgment. What is right may change from situation to situation. Still—as anyone who has done journalism or who has read or watched closely knows—there are good choices and bad choices.

The key for journalists and for democratic societies is the process those who produce the news go through in making their decisions. Once a journalist begins to develop a disciplined, thoughtful way of making choices, he or she will build on it and refer to it over and over again, much the way a musician continues to practice scales or an athlete continues to perform calisthenics. Like most valuable talents, the ability to make intelligent choices is refined through continued practice. Without an inbred process of critical decision-making, journalists in the minute-by-minute world of news are doomed to lean on less reliable pillars: peer pressure, fashion, convention, the fear of being scooped, the toss of a coin, or, most damagingly, the pressure of competition.

This book and the concept of learning by case study is about how to make reasoned decisions when reason is tied to the needs of a democratic polity. In preparing it, journalists and teachers joined together. We thought about what decision-making areas we could cover in ten or so cases. The cases might be taught as a single course or used individually as elements in several different courses. On our list we included such areas as the discipline of verification, competitive pressure and commercial influence, political imperatives, the timing of stories, the use of sources, and the impact of new technology. We sought out distinguished journalists to serve as authors, for we believed that the creation of cases that would ring true depended on deep and systematic reporting to retell as fully as possible the thinking of the journalists in the case. Though any of these cases may raise various issues, each of them was designed to focus on one or two key ideas. Once written, each case was "lab taught" at journalism schools around the country before being edited again.

Some of these cases raise questions concerning such practices as the mutual manipulation of press and government that leaves citizens as increasingly powerless and cynical spectators. Other cases lend themselves to discussion of some very general issues: What is the role of the press in a democracy? Is it to be a watchdog? Where does such a concept come from? Who enunciated it? How well does the press play the role of watchdog? Are there other roles, even more ennobling, that the press can play?

There is no mystery behind the case study method. The point of it is to get students to think through problems in a public forum, to make and defend judgments against the criticisms brought to bear by the instructor and other students. Each case is subject to multiple interpretations, and each raises more than one issue and advances more than one principle. The creativity emerges in laying out the questions that take the student from the facts to the principle and to the debate that ensues about the validity of the principle and the degree to which it fits the facts in question. Others who teach by the case study method in different fields offer other advice. Professor Robert Bruner, distinguished professor of business administration at the University of Virginia, claims the following advantages for the case study method:

- Students learn best the lessons they teach themselves.
- The case study method builds the capacity for critical thinking.
- It helps students weigh the practical implications of their decisions.
- It teaches risk taking, respect, trust, and tough-mindedness.
- It helps establish inductive, continuing learning habits.

The skills enumerated are precisely those desperately needed in modern journalism: critical thinking rather than habitual reaction; trust and respect rather than cynicism and contempt; tough-mindedness rather than sentimentality, timidity, and closed-mindedness; and most of all the realization that journalism is a craft depending on lifelong cultivation of intelligence and discipline.

Beyond that, the case study method is a pleasure to use in the classroom—a pleasure for both teacher and student. Enjoy!

— 1 —

McCarthyism, 1950–1954

John Herbers

EDITORS' NOTE

In the early years of the cold war between the United States and the Soviet Union, Senator Joseph R. McCarthy, Republican of Wisconsin, rose to prominence by making charges, most of them unsubstantiated, that the United States government had been widely infiltrated by Soviet spies. Critics accused the American press of allowing the senator to manipulate the coverage, giving birth to the term *McCarthyism.*

As a reporter for the Southern newspapers' United Press during the McCarthy era, author John Herbers brings personal knowledge to this case. He also spent twenty-four years reporting for the *New York Times,* where he covered, among other stories, civil rights, the Kennedy presidential campaign, and the Watergate years.

In this narrative, Herbers focuses on two of the many issues suggested by coverage of McCarthy. First, the case explores the difference between reporting the facts and reporting the truth about the facts. It touches on how, in practical terms, a journalist can navigate between the two. Second, it examines the issue of speed—the pressure to get the story.

During the McCarthy era, journalists operated according to a strict code of factual reporting and avoided analysis. They nonetheless felt the pressure of their own morning and afternoon deadlines, as well as those of several wire services.

Today, whereas journalists have more freedom to analyze, the pressure of the 24-7 news cycle, the frequency of live broadcasts, the sophistication of sources, and an increase in the number of news outlets all create difficulties surprisingly similar to those faced in the 1950s.

Could McCarthyism happen today?

Following the Allied victory of 1945 that ended World War II, the world was polarized between the western democracies and the communist blocs of Russia and Asia, both seeking global domination. Deep divisions evolved in the United States over how best to deal internally with the threat now posed by the nation's wartime ally, the Soviet Union. There was a broad consensus that persons loyal to the communists should not be allowed to work in sensitive positions within the federal government. But a strong movement developed among certain political leaders and opinion makers that the government and others had been too lax in demanding loyalty to the United States.

The dispute had its roots, in part, in the Great Depression of the 1930s, when unemployment reached 25 percent. People were starving, and the economy seemed to have collapsed. Many intellectuals and others (although still only a small minority) turned to the American Communist Party in search of a more just and equitable system. During the war, when conditions improved and the United States fought with the Soviets against the fascist powers, those who had shown sympathy for communism were integrated into the American military and the work force. Most of them severed any ties they may have had with communist ideology.

But so great was the fear of communism sweeping the world in the aftermath of the war that both political parties sought ways to block communist influence, especially in government. President Harry S. Truman, a Democrat, established a security program within the executive branch in which staff members had to sign a loyalty oath, despite the opposition of civil libertarians who charged that loyal Americans could be fired simply for being suspected of having sympathy for "subversive" groups.[1] But this was not enough to keep conservative Republicans from charging the Democrats with being "soft on communism."

This charge contributed to the GOP victory in the Congressional elections of 1946. Future President Richard M. Nixon, for one, was first elected to the House after a campaign in which he accused his opponent, a Democratic incumbent, of holding communist sympathies. In Washington, the House Un-American Activities Committee (HUAC) held hearings in which it searched for communists and their sympathizers, not only in government, but throughout American society. One of its major targets was the entertainment industry. Producers, actors, and directors were blacklisted, their careers damaged or ruined, if they refused to cooperate with the committee. Lillian Hellman, for one, complained that she lost her cherished farm because she experienced a drastic reduction in income once the committee labeled her as a suspect.[2] Others in Hollywood could no longer work at all. Several writers were forced to work under false names.

As Thomas C. Reeves observed in *The Life and Times of Joe McCarthy*, politicians were not alone in charging the Soviet Union with infiltrating American society. The United States Chamber of Commerce distributed publications associating postwar labor demands with Kremlin conspiracies. The Hearst and Scripps-Howard newspaper chains devoted large headlines to spy accusations.

Roman Catholic leaders supported FBI director J. Edgar Hoover in his charges that American communists had made deep inroads "in practically every phase of our national life, infiltrating newspapers, magazines, books, radio, movies, unions, churches, schools, colleges and fraternal orders."[3]

The conflict was further inflamed by the emergence of the Soviet Union as a nuclear power. Then, in 1949, Alger Hiss, a former high-level official in the Roosevelt and Truman Administrations suspected of passing American secrets to the Soviets during the war, was convicted of perjury when he denied knowing communists in the 1930s. An array of politicians and columnists charged that, despite the Truman loyalty program, the government was protecting many subversives.

After Truman's 1948 electoral victory, Republicans sought an issue that would help them win back the White House after almost two decades of Democratic rule. The communist issue seemed tailor made for that purpose. After all, the alleged infiltrations had occurred on the Democrats' watch. The national Republican Party assigned the junior senator from Wisconsin, Joseph R. McCarthy, to a routine speaking tour in 1950. Because he was not well known and had little authority in Congress, McCarthy was directed to small, obscure cities. His subject, he decided after careful consideration, would be communists in government. His first stop, on February 9, was Wheeling, West Virginia, where he addressed the Women's Republican Club. Before a small audience, his remarks followed the standard Republican line on subversion, except that McCarthy added the following shocker: "While I cannot take the time to name all the men in the State Department who have been named as active members of the Communist Party and members of a spy ring, I have here in my hand a list of 205 names that were known to the Secretary of State as being members of the Communist Party and who nevertheless are still working and shaping policy in the State Department."[4]

The Role of Newspapers

McCarthy's Wheeling speech was covered only by the *Wheeling Intelligencer* and the *Chicago Tribune,* the latter a McCarthy supporter. The Associated Press bureau in Charleston, West Virginia, obtained the story from the managing editor of the Wheeling paper, an AP stringer. At 2 A.M. on February 10 the bureau routinely filed over its wires a 110-word story containing the charge that 205 communists had infiltrated the State Department.

Relatively few newspapers printed, or even noticed, the AP story. But when McCarthy arrived in Denver the next day en route to Salt Lake City, several reporters were at the airport, demanding that he supply the names of those accused. He replied that he had left the list in a suit on the plane, but if the Secretary of State would call him in Salt Lake City, he would be glad to read him the list. The reporters filed just what he said.

Secretary of State Dean Acheson responded that he had no idea what McCarthy was talking about and denied that any known communists or sympathizers were in his department. Yet McCarthy, in further speeches, kept repeating the charge, changing the numbers, dodging and bluffing as he went, and promising to reveal his list at some point in the future. The newspapers by that time were prominently displaying his charges, thus giving credence to long-standing charges by a number of prominent Republican leaders that the Democrats were soft on communism. Within a matter of days, McCarthy was no longer unknown; he had gained a large national following of supporters who flooded his office with supportive letters, telegrams, and telephone calls—just what the senator wanted.[5]

McCarthy never produced any list of names. Later that year, when his charges were under investigation by a Senate committee, he went to one of his supporters, the newspaper publisher William Randolph Hearst Jr., for help. "Joe never had any names," Hearst later recalled. "He came to us. 'What am I gonna do? You gotta help me.' So we gave him a few good reporters" to help him find names.[6]

It is helpful at this point to understand how Americans got their news in 1950 and the framework within which reporters and editors operated. Television was then in its infancy; it was still largely an entertainment medium, as was radio. Daily newspapers were by far the major source of information about national and foreign affairs. Weekly magazines were becoming more important, both in providing analysis and in shaping public opinion. But their impact was overshadowed by the daily barrage of news and opinion from the newspapers. *Time* magazine, for example, was dubious from the beginning about McCarthy's charges, but its coverage seemed to have little impact as McCarthy's popularity soared. The dailies proliferated in cities across the country, and the news they offered from outside their circulation areas came largely from the three wire services: the Associated Press (AP), United Press (UP), and International News Service (INS). (UP later acquired INS and became United Press International [UPI].)[7]

The enforced standard for the wire services, as well as for most reporters writing directly for newspapers, was strict objectivity. News stories were to contain no opinion from the writer. That was the sole province of the editorial page and columnists. Reporters could not write about private transgressions of public officials or what was said in private meetings without the permission of those involved. News analysis, so prominent today in the news columns, written by reporters and intended to help readers understand the meaning of a news event, was a rarity.

The demand for strict objectivity was, in part, a reaction to the undisciplined journalism, in which readers could not tell fact from opinion, that had been prominent during much of American history. The wire services also had practical reasons for adhering to a strictly factual approach. The newspapers themselves owned AP through an association, and on issues such as subversion in government they were sharply divided editorially. Rival UP was owned by the Scripps-Howard chain, and INS by the Hearst newspapers. But both services sold their feeds to papers across the board and so did not want to appear biased in any way.

All three wire services sought to produce stories that would be selected for publication by as many papers as possible. They put high priority on being first to report a news event, even if only by minutes. When McCarthy became hot copy after his Wheeling speech, they raced to get his performances on the wire, usually without any idea as to whether or not his charges were true. Editors allowed stories to run in their papers with a comparable lack of scrutiny. UPI was particularly pressed to beat the AP to the wire because it sold its service at a flat rate. The AP billed its member papers in proportion to their circulation size and was on much sounder financial footing. UPI was under enormous economic pressure, for it was basically a secondary service for the big papers; many of its clients were smaller papers, because it was cheaper than AP. The large number of afternoon editions (which meant that papers replated their front pages throughout the day) kept time pressure on the wires all day long.

"JUST A POLITICAL SPEECH"

In the early 1950s some reporters covering McCarthy had evidence that he could not back up his claims—evidence that never got into their stories. McCarthy was gregarious and a heavy drinker who talked freely to reporters. For example, he told two newsmen who were pressing him in his office for names, "Look, you guys, that was just a political speech to a bunch of Republicans. Don't take it seriously." Neither reported what he said. In another incident, reporters overheard McCarthy pressuring his office by telephone to give him names of suspected subversives at a time when he was publicly claiming to have all the names. But this, too, was never disclosed to readers. Edwin R. Bayley, himself a reporter for the *Milwaukee Journal,* wrote in his 1981 book *Joe McCarthy and the Press* that such incidents, had they been reported at the time, could have had an important effect. "But reporters covered politics then as if it were a stage play; only what happened in public counted."[8]

With the truth about him kept from the public, McCarthy continued making charges that were headlined in papers across the country. His staff dug up the names of some suspects in the government, but none proved to be a communist sympathizer, or even in a position to influence American policy. Back in Washington, McCarthy promised to expose the "top Soviet agent in the State Department." Called into a closed committee hearing by dubious Democratic senators, he claimed that the agent was Owen Lattimore, a scholarly expert on Asia who had advised the State Department but had never been an employee of the government. McCarthy could offer no proof in support of his charge, which Lattimore adamantly denied. He had been publicly lambasted as a traitor by McCarthy's conservative allies because he believed (realistically as it turned out) that the nationalist government of China, America's ally in the war, could not be restored. He felt the United States would do better to work with the emerging communist government, to encourage it to remain independent of communist Russia—a strategy that Richard Nixon, a friend and supporter of McCarthy, would follow twenty years later when he became president.[9]

With McCarthy unable to support his charges, it seemed to many that his star would soon fade. But just the opposite happened. The polls showed his popularity to be rising. Many Americans believed that somehow what he said had the ring of truth. In addition he had the editorial support of many important newspapers, columnists, and commentators, including Fulton Lewis Jr. of the Mutual Radio Network and Walter Winchell of the NBC Blue Network, as well as such spiritual leaders as the politically powerful Roman Catholic Francis Cardinal Spellman of New York.[10]

LEADER OF A CRUSADE

The truth or falsity of McCarthy's charges no longer seemed to be the chief issue. Most of his Republican colleagues in the Senate disregarded his tactics and cheered him on as the leader of a crusade that could win them the next election. The issue of subversives in government had been totally politicized, and McCarthy went on to win reelection in his home state in 1952. While editors and reporters across the country bitterly debated what to do about him, their system of gathering and disseminating news remained unchanged for the moment.[11]

William Theis, then Senate correspondent for INS, told Edwin Bayley, in an interview in 1976,

> All three wire services were so goddam objective that McCarthy got away with everything, bamboozling the editors and the public. . . . We let Joe get away with murder, reporting it as he said it, not doing the kind of critical analysis we'd do today. The public in those days was accustomed to believe damn near anything. It was just a big lark to Joe. He was like a kid in a candy store, trying to grab everything he could. . . . As a reporter you did what you could, but things never solidified. He'd talk you blue in the face. . . . The main trouble was in the climate of the country. People were ready to believe anything about communism. . . . Editors and editorial writers refused to believe that McCarthy would make such charges without having the evidence to back them up. . . . It was the most difficult story we ever covered. I'd go home literally sick, seeing what the guy was getting away with.[12]

Reporters for the other wire services were equally embittered. One of them was George Reedy, who left UP in disgust at having to cover McCarthy and went to work for Senator Lyndon B. Johnson, later becoming his presidential press secretary. "We had to take whatever McCarthy said at face value," Reedy told Bayley. "Joe couldn't find a communist in Red Square—he didn't know Karl Marx from Groucho—but he was a United States senator."[13]

BUT HE KNEW THE NEWS BUSINESS

McCarthy may have been ignorant about communism, but he was clever about the news business. He knew all the deadlines of the major newspapers, enabling him to make a charge just before deadline and get it into print before the papers could check it out. He especially knew how to manipulate the wire services. He knew they operated on two cycles, one for the morning papers and one for the afternoon papers. If a story broke in late afternoon it would make the morning papers. But the afternoon papers would want a fresh angle—and McCarthy would always supply it to them, offering a lead serving his purposes. Often the story with the new angle would not appear on the wires until the middle of the night, when reporters could not check it out. The early editions of the afternoon papers would then go to press with McCarthy's charge as the lead.

It is hard to find anyone who even tried to buck the system. One who did was Allen Alexander, then an AP editor in Charlotte, North Carolina, responsible for relaying national stories to newspapers in the Carolinas. He recalled how it was on the morning cycle:

> It was quite apparent that many of Senator McCarthy's headline-catching statements were deliberately timed so that they would be bulletined out of Washington around 10 A.M. This assured him of reaching the first editions of the Eastern time zone press, including 25 to 30 afternoon dailies in the Carolinas.
>
> The 10 A.M. bell ringer usually would be followed by a new lead at noon, which would come closer to giving more balance to the original pronouncement. That is, instead of the original unvarnished "Senator Joe McCarthy declared today that John Doe is a lousy, no-good communist" it would state "John Doe denied today that he is or ever was a lousy, no-good communist." By 2 P.M., in time for final afternoon editions, the semblance of a balanced, fair story on the senator's charges might be available. All too often, however, this did not take place during the same news cycle.

Alexander recalled that, if the first story were "blatantly irresponsible," he would on occasion try to delay filing it, knowing that a fairer lead was expected. But some papers complained that UP and INS were beating the AP, and Alexander's boss would come after him: "The competition wires got all the play on McCarthy Wednesday. How come? What time did our Washington trunk story come in? What time did you relay it?" Alexander could not argue in such cases, because every story carried the date and time it had moved.[14]

It would be difficult to exaggerate how competitive both the wire services and the newspapers were in those days. In 1950 there were 322 morning dailies with a combined circulation of twenty-one million and 1,450 evening papers with a combined circulation of more than thirty-two million. The larger cities had several competing papers, each publishing as many as eight or nine editions a day. All of the papers were struggling to retain readers and advertising against the rising tide of television, which was beginning to come into its own as a purveyor of news.[15] *Time* magazine ran a cover showing McCarthy against a backdrop of newspaper headlines screaming "Threatens, Charges, Defies, Accuses, Warns, Hunts, Demands, Brands" and a caption reading "Senator McCarthy: Opportunity keeps knocking."

The Challenge of Fairness

The question raised in some newsrooms at the time was whether McCarthy was an honorable senator concerned with the nation's security, a shameless fraud, or something in between. The problem for many conscientious journalists was how to report about the man fairly without letting him manipulate the coverage, as he clearly was doing. The following are some of the approaches that were tried or discussed:

- Send one or more reporters to Wisconsin to do a profile of McCarthy in his early years in politics, to give readers a better opportunity to judge his character. For example, few people knew that McCarthy had lied in his first successful run for office, telling voters that the incumbent judge he was trying to unseat was 76 years old and ripe for retirement. The judge was actually 65, and McCarthy knew it. He had also grossly exaggerated his war record, but these incidents were little known outside his home state.

- Because of the rule against opinion or analysis in the news columns, assign a reporter to write background and details of previous developments in the case to run alongside each breaking story of a McCarthy accusation, or to bracket the same material into the running story. The *Washington Post* had success with this strategy, assigning Murray Marder to the task. On some days Marder's stories ran for two columns. This approach, though rare, was important because the breaking story almost always covered only the events of the day in almost every newspaper.

- Adopt a rule never to run a McCarthy accusation until the paper could contact the accused and put the events into focus, and to ask the wire services to do the same. Reputations were ruined as the truth seldom caught up with the lie. This proposed rule, however, would have been difficult to enforce because of the intense competition among wire services and newspapers. It is interesting in this respect to compare McCarthy-era excesses in a highly competitive field to those common today, when there are so many competing outlets for news that an unfounded report in a less disciplined publication, or on the Internet, finds its way into the public arena and must then be dealt with by the responsible press (for an example of this, see Chapter 2 on the Starr investigation).

- Come clean with readers and report what goes on behind the scenes as a way to understand events in the public forum. For example, shortly after McCarthy's Wheeling speech, he and two reporters and an editorial writer for the *Milwaukee Journal* met for lunch and got into a shouting match about McCarthy's refusal to provide any names of the alleged spy ring in the State Department. The journalists left convinced that McCarthy had no names. That meeting started the paper on its long crusade against McCarthy—but only on the editorial page.

Quite a few stories were circulating around the country that together would have cast grave public doubt on the senator and his charges. There is often a surface story and a background story. And the background story, with hard work, can often be written well within the boundaries of strict factuality.

THE ROLE OF BROADCASTERS

When McCarthy won reelection to another six-year term in 1952 and the Republican party took control of the Senate, he was assured of a long run, bashing alleged communists. He became chairman of the Senate Committee on Government Operations, a post from which he conducted extensive hearings into alleged communist influence on the Voice of America, the State Department's radio outlet in countries around the world, and later in the U.S. Army. His power was further increased by reports that he had been responsible for the election of at least eight other Republicans in the Senate who ran on the subversive issue.[16]

At the same time there was a rapid increase in the number of Americans who got their news from television. In 1950 alone, the number of television sets in American homes increased from little more than three million to ten million, receiving broadcasts from 106 stations in sixty-five cities. It did not take McCarthy long to learn how to manipulate both newspapers and broadcasting at the same time.[17]

In the 1950s a fairness rule was adopted by the Federal Communications Commission, which required broadcasters to give persons airtime to reply to charges made against them on broadcast stations. (The fairness rule was repealed in 1987, because the FCC felt it put too much of a burden on broadcasters, but an "equal time" law pertaining only to candidates for public office remains in effect.) McCarthy was quick to demand time to respond to anyone making accusations against him, however vague, and the networks, then novices at political jousting, were usually quick to give it to him. Further, he kept the broadcast media—which, unlike newspapers, were federally regulated —on the defensive by charging that there were vast numbers of communists and their sympathizers within broadcasting.

The senator repeatedly charged that all journalists who disagreed with him were espousing the communist line and took their orders from the *Daily Worker,* an organ of the American Communist Party. This charge was ludicrous on its face. Both the party and its newspaper were weak and did not even pretend to order straight journalists around. But Republican leaders, although fully aware of McCarthy's methods, made no effort to rein him in as long as he was not damaging them.

McCarthy used his Senate hearings to advance his own views while shutting out opposing ones. "After rehearsing a witness—friendly or hostile—in closed session, he arranged for the testimony he wanted the public to see and hear to testify during the two hours a day that the hearings were covered by television," Edwin Bayley wrote.

For example, one witness, Reed Harris, acting director of the Federal Information Administration (who had written a book twenty years earlier advocating the right of professors to teach atheism and communism), was accused by McCarthy of never having been cleared for loyalty and security. Harris tried to protest that indeed he had been cleared six times, but McCarthy cut him off. He was promised time for rebuttal while the hearing was being broadcast by ABC, which was carrying the hearing two hours a day. McCarthy used most of the two hours that day for witnesses hostile to Harris and said he understood that ABC would extend its broadcast for the Harris testimony. ABC replied that there was no such understanding, and Harris had only begun to testify when ABC switched to a commercially sponsored giveaway show. What viewers were left with was an overwhelmingly hostile portrait of a public servant who had broken no law and had never shown disloyalty during his federal service. A short time later Harris, thoroughly humiliated, resigned. McCarthy, expressing satisfaction, said he hoped some of his associates would follow him out of the government.[18]

The broadcast media were even slower than the press to try to come to terms with McCarthy, in part because all stations were federally regulated and broadcasters did not want to be drawn into political battles. One of the few exceptions was Martin Agronsky, a commentator for ABC, who had been critical of the methods used by HUAC as well as those of McCarthy. Agronsky had a daily radio program, sponsored by businesses and other institutions in each city where it was carried. After he discovered that he was losing sponsors around the country, Agronsky learned that McCarthy and his staff were putting pressure on his sponsors to end their support. The program began losing money, and a number of local station owners demanded that ABC fire him. Robert Kitner, the network's president, refused, and even encouraged Agronsky to continue his criticism.[19]

A 1954 broadcast by Edward R. Murrow attacking the senator's methods has been widely heralded as one of the chief factors resulting in McCarthy's censure by the Senate later in the year. But as Edwin Bayley pointed out, Murrow's commentary was not nearly as strong as a number of newspaper editorials that had appeared much earlier, and it came only once McCarthy had become vulnerable.[20]

As McCarthy's power grew, so did his ambition. His Republican colleagues never dreamed that he would challenge the popular Eisenhower Administration in the way he had President Truman and the Democrats. But he soon let it be known that, although he thought Eisenhower had done more than Truman to rid the government of communists, the new president had not done enough. He took on the U.S. Army as another area of suspect loyalty, and publicly browbeat Secretary of the Army Robert Stevens and senior Army officers. By this time, he talked as if he, not the president, were the real leader of the Republican Party. Eisenhower, who had been reluctant to criticize McCarthy openly, finally did so by publicly praising Stevens and the Army officers under attack.[21]

It was the extensively telecast Army hearings of 1954 that had the most negative effect on the senator.[22] The Army, chafing under McCarthy's abuse, charged that McCarthy and his chief counsel, Roy M. Cohn, had pressured the Army to give preferential treatment to G. David Schine, a committee staff member who had been drafted and stationed at Fort Dix despite Cohn's efforts to have him remain on McCarthy's committee. A bipartisan subcommittee opened televised hearings on the Schine dispute. McCarthy only redoubled his abusive behavior and tactics. As the hearings ground on, drawing ever larger audiences, McCarthy's public support began to slip away.

The scene best remembered by many came on June 9, 1954, when McCarthy accused Joseph Welch, a Boston lawyer who was the Army's counsel for the hearings, of having a suspected communist sympathizer in his law firm. Welch, a flamboyant speaker, explained that the young lawyer, Frederick Fisher, indeed had belonged to the Lawyer's Guild, once affiliated with the American Communist Party, but had since become active in Massachusetts Republican politics. Fisher had been recommended by another member of the law firm, but Welch, knowing the sensitivity of the hearings, had not taken him on and had instead sent him back to Boston.

But McCarthy kept at his accusations. Finally Welch interrupted and, before millions of Americans watching on television, said, "Let us not assassinate this lad further, Senator. You have done enough. Have you no sense of decency, sir? At long last, have you no sense of decency?" The hearing room burst into loud applause.

Did it require prolonged television coverage to demonstrate what was now so apparent to many? Could not editors and reporters have found a way under existing practices to define the real McCarthy—especially since it had long been believed in journalism circles that McCarthy cared little about the communism issue, that he was only interested in increasing his own political power?

Later in the year, after the Democrats regained control of Congress in the 1954 elections, the Senate voted 67–22 to "condemn" McCarthy for violating due process and the rules of the Senate. Thereafter his colleagues simply turned their backs on him, walking off the floor when he rose to speak or declining to acknowledge his presence in a crowded elevator. Reporters no longer hung on his every word, and he did not make page one news again until he died, on May 2, 1957, of cirrhosis of the liver brought on by heavy drinking.[23]

THE DEBATE OVER THE IMPACT OF MCCARTHYISM

Scholars have long debated the impact of "McCarthyism," of which Joseph McCarthy himself was the chief—but certainly not the only—practitioner.[24] Even before he was censured, the term McCarthyism had entered dictionaries. It has been in constant use for half a century, defined as the use of indiscriminate (often unfounded) accusations, sensationalism, and inquisitorial investigative methods toward such ends as the suppression of political opponents.[25] Yet the controversy continues, not only about McCarthy himself, but also about the extent of communist infiltration in American society and what impact it may have had on the nation's politics and culture.

Probably no institution felt the impact of the McCarthy phenomenon more than the news media. Murray Marder of the *Washington Post,* who covered McCarthy extensively, remembers well one aspect of the period when McCarthy was flourishing. From his position at the center of the controversies, the period appeared to be one of "national turmoil, at least as serious as the reaction to the Vietnam War. Careers and families were destroyed; people committed suicide. Fear was in the atmosphere: you always had to know who you were talking to. It threw into jeopardy all the great American attributes— freedom of speech, thought, and association. Anybody who had been in public life was vulnerable, and you had to think back [on] all your associations. It was the closest we ever came to a real totalitarian atmosphere."[26]

More than in any other period, the press was a major contributor to shaping the character of the times. Yet the events of the times also exposed flaws in how journalism was practiced, and they ultimately led to major changes in the way news is gathered and presented in this country. What changes in the practice of journalism during the twentieth century, in your opinion, can be attributed in whole or in part to the events of the McCarthy period?

Discussion Questions

1. Who are some contemporary McCarthy-like figures, able to control and dominate the news?

2. How should you as a journalist respond if a senator makes an accusation like McCarthy's and then says he or she will turn the names over to the authorities at the proper time? Are there new rules of evidence for journalists today, rules that did not exist during the McCarthy era? If so, what are they?

3. How did journalists reporting the McCarthy accusations justify their coverage? How did it serve the public interest, if at all?

SOURCES

This case study was based on a variety of books and articles about the era, which are cited in the notes. All other quotations and additional information come from personal interviews with Allen Alexander and Murray Marder in December 1999 and from the first-hand knowledge of the author, who reported for the Southern newspapers' United Press from 1949 to 1963.

NOTES

1. Edwin R. Bayley, *Joe McCarthy and the Press.* Madison: University of Wisconsin Press, 1981, pp. 6–7.
2. Lillian Hellman, *Pentimento.* Bergenfield, N.J.: Signet/New American Library, 1973, pp. 164–65. Miss Hellman elaborates on her blacklisting in other writings.
3. Jim Tuck, *McCarthy and New York's Hearst Press.* New York: University Press of America, 1995, pp. 1–21.
4. Bayley, pp. 17–18.
5. Ibid., pp. 18–38.
6. Daniel Cohen, *Joseph McCarthy: The Misuse of Political Power.* Brookfield, Conn.: Millbrook Press, 1996, p. 54.
7. Bayley, p. 66.
8. Ibid., pp. 36, 29.
9. Thomas C. Reeves, *The Life and Times of Joe McCarthy.* New York: Madison Books, 1997, pp. 267–83.
10. John Cooney, *The American Pope: The Life and Times of Francis Cardinal Spellman.* New York: Times Books, 1984, pp. 218–22.
11. Bayley, pp. 39–65.
12. Ibid., pp. 67, 68.
13. Ibid., p. 68.
14. Ibid., pp. 70, 71. In a telephone interview with the author in December 1999, Alexander provided additional information about the wire services.
15. *The New York Times Almanac,* 1993, p. 401.
16. Bayley, p. 182.
17. Ibid., p 176
18. Ibid., pp 182–94; Reeves, p. 483.

19. Bayley, pp. 194–95.
20. Ibid., p. 193.
21. Ibid., p. 188.
22. Reeves, pp. 595–637.
23. Ibid., pp. 662, 671, 672.
24. Jacob Weisberg, "The Rehabilitation of Joe McCarthy," *New York Times Magazine*, November 28, 1999, p. 116, describes "the latest offensive in the nasty, never-ending battle over American Communism."
25. *Webster's New World Dictionary*, Third Edition.
26. Interviews with Bayley, pp. 148–51, and with the author.

Appendix

M'Carthy Charges Reds Hold U.S. Jobs; Truman Blasted for Reluctance to Press Probe; Wisconsin Senator Tells Lincoln Fete Here "Chips Down"

FRANK DESMOND, *Intelligencer* Staff

Joseph McCarthy, junior U.S. Senator from Wisconsin, was given a rousing ovation last night when, as guest of the Ohio County Republican Women's Club, he declared bluntly that the fate of the world rests with the clash between the atheism of Moscow and the Christian spirit throughout other parts of the world.

More than 275 representative Republican men and women were on hand to attend the colorful Lincoln Day dinner of the valley women which was held in the Colonnade room of the McLure hotel.

Disdaining any oratorical fireworks, McCarthy's talk was of an intimate, homey nature, punctuated at times with humor.

But on the serious side, he launched many barbs at the present setup of the State Department, at President Truman's reluctance to press investigation of "traitors from within," and other pertinent matters.

He said that recent incidents which brought traitors to the limelight [are] the result of an "emotional hangover" and a temporary moral lapse which follows every war. However, he added:

"The morals of our people have not been destroyed. They still exist and this cloak of numbness and apathy needs only a spark to rekindle them."

Referring directly to the State Department, he declared:

"While I cannot take the time to name all of the men in the State Department who have been named as members of the Communist Party and members of a spy ring, I have here in my hand a list of 205 that were known to the Secretary of State as being members of the Communist Party and who, nevertheless, are still working and shaping the policy in the State Department."

The speaker dwelt at length on the Alger Hiss case and mentioned the names of several others who, during the not so many years, were found to entertain subversive ideas but were still given positions of high trust in the government.

"As you hear of this [Hiss] story of high treason," he said, "I know that you are saying to yourself[,] well, why doesn't Congress do something about it?

"Actually, ladies and gentlemen, the reason for the graft, the corruption, the disloyalty, the treason in high government positions[,] the reason this continues is because of a lack of moral uprising on the part of the 140 million American people. In the light of history, however, this is not hard to explain.

Wheeling Intelligencer, February 10, 1950. Obtained from the West Virginia Archives and History Web site, History Center: http://www.wvculture.org/history/mccarthy.html.

"It is the result of an emotional hangover and a temporary moral lapse which follows every war. It is the apathy to evil which people who have been subjected to the tremendous evils of war feel.

"As the people of the world see mass murder, the destruction of defenseless and innocent people and all of the crime and lack of morals which go with war, they become numb and apathetic. It has always been thus after war."

At another time, he declared:

"Today, we are engaged in a final all-out battle between Communistic atheism and Christianity. The modern champions of Communism have selected this as the time and, ladies and gentlemen, the chips are down[,] they are truly down."

In an informal quiz with his audience, the Senator answered a number of questions dealing mostly with the plan of Secretary of Agriculture Brannan to destroy millions of tons of potatoes, eggs, butter and fruits; he gave forthright views on the old age and social security problems and a number of other topics.

McCarthy was introduced by William Callahan, executive director of the Ohio Valley Republican organization. Mrs. A. E. Eberhard, president of the women's group, presided, while [the] program director, Mrs. Robert J. Harshman, introduced Callahan. State Senator William Hannig led the group singing.

The invocation was delivered by the Rev. Philip Goertz, pastor of the Second Presbyterian church, and the benediction was pronounced by the Rev. W. Carroll Thorn, of St. Luke's Episcopal church.

Senator McCarthy arrived by Capital Airlines at the Stifel airport late yesterday afternoon and was greeted by former Congressman Francis J. Love and Tom Sweeney, Jr., who drove him to the Fort Henry Club.

—2—

Internet Journalism and the Starr Investigation

J. D. LASICA

EDITORS' NOTE

The Internet, as it is known and used today, has evolved over the course of many years. Like radio and television, the Internet first caught on among those with a degree of technological savvy and only later developed into a form of communication accepted and used by the general public. In 1995 only 14 percent of the public went on line, according to a public opinion survey carried out by the Pew Research Center for the People and the Press. By 1997 that number had risen to 37 percent, but it was not until the late spring of 1999 that half of those questioned reported that they used the Internet.[1]

A pivotal moment in the Internet's coming of age was an eight-month investigation of the president of the United States during 1998. The investigation, led by independent counsel Kenneth Starr, focused on whether President Clinton had had a sexual affair with a 24-year-old White House intern named Monica Lewinsky and had lied about it under oath to a federal grand jury. The highly political scandal ended in the president's impeachment by the House of Representatives, although he avoided conviction or removal from office by the Senate. More important for journalism, it forced the traditional media to overhaul their ways of presenting news on line in order to meet the needs and demands of Internet users.

The new technology was used to break the news of the scandal, to voice new allegations, and to release in its entirety Starr's final report on his investigation. Coverage of the Clinton-Lewinsky scandal provided the first detailed look at the differences in character between the Internet and traditional broadcast and print media.

The scandal itself lasted more than a year. Journalist J. D. Lasica, who has worked in the online world and also written about it for other media, focuses on three specific events:

1. The breaking of the story by Matt Drudge through his online newsletter.
2. Reports, based on shaky sourcing, in the *Dallas Morning News* and the *Wall Street Journal* that the president and the intern had been seen together in a compromising situation.
3. The final report issued by investigator Kenneth Starr and widely carried in full on the Web.

Lasica asks readers to ponder the advantages and potential disadvantages of reporting on line. The Internet may help journalists disseminate the news faster and in greater depth, but does it also have the potential to compromise accuracy and fairness? How can journalists approach this medium in a way that upholds the fundamental principles of journalism?

The issues at play in this case include sourcing, verification, timing, and weighing the public interest in the age of Internet reporting.

The Story Is Born

By January 1998 *Newsweek* correspondent Michael Isikoff had spent months pursuing tips and rumors about the sexual activities of the president of the United States. He had covered the suit in Arkansas brought by Paula Corwin Jones, who accused Bill Clinton of propositioning her in a Little Rock hotel room when he was governor. He had also followed the investigation by Kenneth Starr into Clinton's activities in Arkansas. Now—back in Washington and with the help of Linda Tripp, who had formerly worked in the White House, and her literary agent friend, Lucianne Goldberg—he was working on a detailed story about Clinton's affair with Monica Lewinsky.

Shortly after midnight, in the early hours of January 17, Tripp's lawyer arrived at the Washington offices of *Newsweek* with two tape recordings made by Tripp of conversations she had had with Lewinsky. Tripp and Lewinsky had both been transferred from the White House to the Pentagon, where they became acquainted. After hearing the tapes, evaluating their contents, and weighing Starr's entreaties that they wait a week, *Newsweek*'s editors decided against running the story—partly in exchange for a promise that Starr's office would give them a complete account for the following week's edition.[2]

About five hours after *Newsweek* decided to hold off, Matt Drudge—a one-man Internet gossip and news agency—was tipped off about the piece. He promptly reported it, without verifying the facts. His story appeared on his *Drudge Report* Web site, in an e-mail alert sent to 85,000 newsletter subscribers, and later in his column on America Online. Here is his report:

Web Posted: 01/17/98 21:32:02 PST—NEWSWEEK KILLS STORY ON WHITE HOUSE INTERN

   BLOCKBUSTER REPORT: 23-YEAR OLD, FORMER WHITE HOUSE INTERN, SEX RELATIONSHIP WITH PRESIDENT

      World Exclusive

      Must Credit the DRUDGE REPORT

At the last minute, at 6 P.M. on Saturday evening, NEWSWEEK magazine killed a story that was destined to shake official Washington to its foundation: A White House intern carried on a sexual affair with the President of the United States!

The DRUDGE REPORT has learned that reporter Michael Isikoff developed the story of his career, only to have it spiked by top NEWSWEEK suits hours before publication. A young woman, 23, sexually involved with the love of her life, the President of the United States, since she was a 21-year-old intern at the White House. She was a frequent visitor to a small study just off the Oval Office where she claims to have indulged the president's sexual preference. Reports of the relationship spread in White House quarters and she was moved to a job at the Pentagon, where she worked until last month.

The young intern wrote long love letters to President Clinton, which she delivered through a delivery service. She was a frequent visitor at the White House after midnight, where she checked in the WAVE logs as visiting a secretary named Betty Curry, 57.

The DRUDGE REPORT has learned that tapes of intimate phone conversations exist.

The relationship between the president and the young woman became strained when the president believed that the young woman was bragging about the affair to others.

NEWSWEEK and Isikoff were planning to name the woman. Word of the story's impending release caused blind chaos in media circles; TIME magazine spent Saturday scrambling for its own version of the story, the DRUDGE REPORT has learned. The NEW YORK POST on Sunday was set to front the young intern's affair, but was forced to fall back on the dated ABC NEWS Kathleen Willey break.

The story was set to break just hours after President Clinton testified in the Paula Jones sexual harassment case.

Ironically, several years ago, it was Isikoff that found himself in a shouting match with editors who were refusing to publish even a portion of his meticulously researched investigative report that was to break Paula Jones. Isikoff worked for the WASHINGTON POST at the time, and left shortly after the incident . . . for the paper's sister magazine, NEWSWEEK.

Michael Isikoff was not available for comment late Saturday. NEWSWEEK was on voice mail.

The White House was busy checking the DRUDGE REPORT for details.

Drudge had earlier broken an Isikoff story being held by *Newsweek* about a White House volunteer, Kathleen Willey, who said Clinton had fondled her. That story had not attracted much attention, but this one, about a White House intern, set off intense journalistic competition.

THE STORY GOES MAINSTREAM

The next morning, Drudge's report was mentioned by conservative commentator Bill Kristol on ABC's *This Week* with Sam Donaldson and Cokie Roberts. By Monday, January 19, the Washington bureaus of the major news organizations knew about the report. Drudge's e-mail dispatch had been seen by a number of influential news managers who subscribed to his newsletter, such as Doyle McManus, Washington bureau chief of the *Los Angeles Times*. Journalists of all stripes were chasing the story.

Although many mainstream news reporters found the sexual underpinnings of the episode distasteful, there was little disagreement that it was a legitimate news story. The office of the independent counsel was investigating whether the president had obstructed justice by encouraging Monica Lewinsky to lie under oath about their relationship. The fact that the oath had been taken for a deposition in a separate sexual harassment case against Clinton made it no less newsworthy.

"When you use the words *president, sex,* and *intern* in the same sentence, you're going to get everyone's attention," says Leah Gentry, former director of new media for the *Los Angeles Times*. "For an online journalist, the story was a lot of fun to work on because it had constantly breaking developments, lots of Web storytelling challenges, opportunities for multimedia, and high reader interest. All the lights were green. If stories were holidays, this story was Christmas."

The public airing of the charges dimmed the independent counsel's hope of eliciting tape-recorded corroboration of the allegations, and suddenly Starr and his staff made themselves more accessible to journalists. *Newsweek* had lost its scoop.

In the early evening hours of Tuesday, January 20, Dave Willman, the investigative reporter at the *Los Angeles Times* covering the Whitewater story (allegations surrounding the Clintons' connection with real estate transactions while he was governor of Arkansas), walked into the office of his boss, McManus. Willman informed the bureau chief that Starr's mandate had just been broadened to include investigation into allegations of the affair and whether Clinton had told Lewinsky to lie and commit perjury. *Times* reporters immediately went to work on the story—and found that they had heavy competition. "The *Washington Post* had the story the same evening; ABC News had the story the same evening," McManus recalls. "So there was clearly a lot of leakage."[3]

Late Tuesday night, the story hit the mainstream media. In its early edition, the *Washington Post* announced in a four-column headline across the front page:

CLINTON ACCUSED OF URGING AIDE TO LIE;
STARR PROBES WHETHER PRESIDENT TOLD WOMAN
TO DENY ALLEGED AFFAIR TO JONES'S LAWYERS

The article, by Susan Schmidt (who had been working the same territory as Isikoff), was attributed to "sources close to the investigation." Minutes after midnight, ABC News broadcast a piece recapping the *Post* story on its radio network. ABC's Jackie Judd had also been covering the Arkansas angles along with Schmidt and Isikoff. And the *Los Angeles Times* broke the story in its Wednesday edition with a front-page story headlined:

STARR EXAMINES CLINTON LINK TO FEMALE INTERN

None of these stories named a single source.

THE STORY BUILDS

A media feeding frenzy followed public disclosure of Starr's investigation. Revelation piled upon revelation, each more sensational than the one before. Journalists scrambled to confirm the allegations, but often ended up running them with only anonymous sourcing. During the first week alone, various newspapers and networks reported the following, most of which in the end proved false:

- That White House staff members once saw Clinton and Lewinsky in an intimate encounter.
- That the two had engaged in phone sex.
- That Clinton had left a message on Lewinsky's answering machine.
- That Clinton may have had sex with a second White House intern.
- That Clinton had said he did not consider oral sex to be adultery.
- That he claimed to have had sex with "hundreds" of women.
- That in his sealed deposition he had admitted under oath to having an affair with another woman, Gennifer Flowers.
- That he might have had an affair with a distant cousin.
- That he had had an affair with the widow of a former ambassador to Switzerland, who had been exhumed from Arlington National Cemetery and reburied in another site when it was discovered that he had fabricated his military record.

On top of the leaks came declarations from journalists that Clinton would be forced from office. Four days after the story broke, the prospect of impeachment or resignation was a major topic of discussion on the Sunday talk shows.

Sam Donaldson, ABC's White House correspondent, asserted on *This Week* that "Mr. Clinton, if he's not telling the truth and the evidence shows that, will resign, perhaps this week."

The public disagreed. A *Washington Post* poll taken ten days after the story broke found that 56 percent of those surveyed believed that the news media were treating Clinton unfairly, and 74 percent said that the media were giving the story "too much attention." A Freedom Forum poll found that the top two adjectives used by Americans to describe the coverage of the story were "excessive" and "embarrassing." But the potential for impeachment and the constant stream of rumors and allegations remained powerful lures for journalists covering the developing story.

Nearly all news organizations had established their own home pages on the Web by this time, but few were taking advantage of the online medium's inherent potential for immediacy, interactivity, and depth. The vast majority of newspapers still updated their sites once a day, following the print cycle, thus preventing the Web site from "scooping" the printed paper. Most news sites relied almost exclusively on "shovelware"—content that had the twin disadvantages of being written for a different medium (print) and being yesterday's news. Breaking news, if covered at all, was left to a wire service feed on the site. Interactivity was a novelty. Some Internet news sites associated with television, such as CNN Interactive and MSNBC.com, were experimenting with multimedia strategies, but most news sites continued to use video and audio sparingly or not at all. For the most part, the experience for users remained a tame one: they came, they clicked, they yawned. It seemed that newspapers considered the Web a reluctant obligation rather than the future of their business.

Perhaps inspired by competition to get the story first—or even by Drudge's wide readership—many news organizations set about expanding their online presence during the Clinton-Lewinsky scandal. Immediate delivery of information on the Web suddenly caught on as a way not only of offering background or analysis but also of breaking news to the public. This case study looks closely at two early incidents in the coverage: A report in the *Dallas Morning News* and a report in the *Wall Street Journal*, each of which could have dealt a crippling political blow to Clinton's presidency.

THE EYE OF THE STORM: THE *DALLAS MORNING NEWS*

The publication that found itself most squarely in the eye of the storm during early press coverage of the Clinton-Lewinsky matter was the *Dallas Morning News*.

On Sunday, January 25, ABC News reported on *This Week* that Starr was looking into claims that in the spring of 1996 the president and Lewinsky had been "caught in an intimate encounter" by either Secret Service agents or White House staffers, according to "several sources." The following day, David Jackson, a veteran member of the *Dallas Morning News* Washington bureau, received a tip from a source who put more meat on the story. Jackson's source, a well-connected Washington lawyer, said he had knowledge that a federal employee had seen Clinton and Lewinsky in a "compromising situation" in the White House and had agreed to testify as a government witness. The report, if true, dramatically escalated the stakes for the president.

On Monday the *News* spoke with the source again and amended the story to report that Starr's staff had spoken with a Secret Service agent—a level of detail that added gravity to the charge. The paper's executive vice president and editor, Ralph Langer, says the source confirmed the story after it was read to him.

But a *News* official would later claim that the source's law partner called Jackson at 5 P.M. to warn the paper off the story. Longtime Washington bureau chief Carl Leubsdorf acknowledged that he learned of the call around midnight Washington time but minimized the reservations expressed by the law partner.

At a meeting of senior editors early that evening, the story was discussed at length. John Cranfill, managing director of the dallasnews.com Web site, recalls expressing doubts about the story's accuracy. "I was skeptical of the story. It raised chill bumps on my arms. I lobbied to wait on the story. But the others felt we had it solid, and the decision was made to run it in the first edition."[4] The story was then sent out to the Associated Press and Knight Ridder wires and posted on the paper's Web site.

On Monday night the paper ran in its bulldog edition (which hit the streets that night but carried the next day's date) and on its Web site a story with this lead: "Independent Counsel Kenneth Starr's staff has spoken with a Secret Service agent who is prepared to testify that he saw President Clinton and Monica Lewinsky in a compromising situation in the White House, sources said Monday."

All hell broke loose. Wire services sent the story worldwide. Cable networks, radio shows, and local television newscasts led with the report. Larry King interrupted his program to read the story live. Ted Koppel led *Nightline* with the news. The story was so explosive that Clinton's attorney, David Kendall, called *Nightline* and denied the story on the air.

"THERE'S A PROBLEM WITH THE STORY"

By the end of the *Nightline* broadcast the original source had called the *News* and backed off his claim, saying, "I don't think I really said what you're reporting."[5] (Both Langer and Cranfill suggest that White House pressure led to the source's turnabout, but journalists reconstructing the piece for the *Dallas Observer* conclude it is more likely that one of Starr's staff members called the source to retract the claim—because it was not true.)[6] A flurry of phone calls ensued. Recalls Cranfill: "At 11:30 P.M. I got a call from the national editor, who said, 'There's a problem with the story; Ralph Langer says to take it off the site.' We put up an explanation that the source had changed his statement."

Langer pulled the story out of Tuesday's second edition. The *News* later substituted a story that said in part, "The source for the story, a longtime Washington lawyer familiar with the case, later said the information provided for Tuesday's report was inaccurate."

The Associated Press carried the newspaper's report on the wire for nearly four hours that night before filing a "bulletin kill" at 1:02 A.M. Tuesday. Darrell Christian, Associated Press managing editor, says that the news service tries to be cautious about repeating allegations supported only by unidentified sources. He had no reason to doubt the Dallas paper's account, based on its trustworthy track record: "We take into account the news organization, the nature of the report, and the qualifications they give to the report," he says. "It's hard to fault anyone for picking up that report. It passed the smell test."[7]

Just a few hours passed between the *Morning News* story and its retraction, but that was more than enough time for the news to circle the globe. Dozens of newspapers—including the *Washington Post, Wall Street Journal, Los Angeles Times,* and *Chicago Tribune*—carried the report the next day. (The *New York Post*'s front page headline blared: "I SAW THEM DO IT"; the *New York Daily News* screamed: "CAUGHT IN THE ACT.") The papers were then forced to publish an account of the *Morning News's* quasi-retraction the next day.

RETRACTION OF A RETRACTION

Yet a third version of the story appeared on the *Morning News* Web site late Tuesday and in its print edition the next day. This time, the paper partly reasserted its original claim—now seemingly based on multiple sources— saying that the first story had been "essentially correct." Quoting two sources, the paper reported that "one or more witnesses" had seen Clinton and Lewinsky in "an ambiguous incident" rather than "a compromising situation." It also said that an "intermediary for one or more witnesses"—and not a Secret Service agent—had "talked with independent counsel Kenneth Starr's office about possible cooperation."[8]

Later on Wednesday, the newspaper assembled more than 200 editorial employees in a ballroom at the Hyatt Regency Hotel to discuss the fiasco. Langer fielded questions from staffers with the aid of a wireless microphone while Leubsdorf chimed in from a speaker phone. Langer told the employees that the *News* had unwittingly relied on only one source to publish its original story, violating the paper's two-source standard. Senior editors mistakenly believed that a second source existed because of a "miscommunication" between Dallas and the Washington bureau.[9]

Pundits, politicians, and press critics immediately pounced on the paper's retraction. The *New York Times* devoted a story to the debacle under the headline, "RETRACTING A RETRACTION, SELF-DEFENSE AND REVELATION." Reporter Janny Scott wrote: "The *Dallas Morning News,* the newspaper that made news by becoming the first news-gathering organization to officially retract a front-page story on the White House sex scandal, went itself one better yesterday and retracted the retraction. Sort of."

THE *WALL STREET JOURNAL'S* REVISIONS

About three weeks after the story first broke, on February 4, a *Wall Street Journal* reporter approached Joe Lockhart, the White House deputy press secretary, shortly before 4 P.M., according to Lockhart. The reporter was asking for a reaction to accusations that a White House steward had once seen Clinton and Lewinsky alone in a study next to the Oval Office.[10] The reporter said he needed the information quickly because the paper planned to publish the story on its Web site. According to Lockhart, he and the reporter agreed that Lockhart would get back to the reporter within 30 minutes unless the reporter paged him to say that he had less time. A few minutes later, the reporter paged him to say that the story had already gone up on the *Wall Street Journal's* site.

The *Journal's* online story reported that Bayani Nelvis, a White House steward, had testified before Starr's grand jury that he had seen Clinton and Lewinsky alone together. The story claimed that the steward "found and disposed of tissues with lipstick and other stains following a meeting between Mr. Clinton and Ms. Lewinsky," and that he had recounted the episode to the Secret Service because he was "personally offended" by it. The report was attributed to "two individuals familiar with" the steward's testimony. Within minutes after the story was posted, the *Journal's* Washington bureau chief,

Alan Murray, appeared on the cable news channel CNBC—the *Journal's* new television partner—discussing the scoop. His remarks were later picked up by MSNBC and posted on its Web site.

Less than 90 minutes after the *Journal* first posted the story, Nelvis's attorney issued a statement calling the report "absolutely false and irresponsible." Later that afternoon, the *Washington Post* and other news organizations sought to verify the original allegations, but the *Post* reported that its sources close to the grand jury strongly denied that Nelvis had given any such testimony.

At 6:40 P.M., the *Journal* posted a revised version of the story in which it added the strong denials from the steward's lawyer—who had refused to comment when the *Journal* was preparing its initial report. The softened story contained a second change as well: the steward reportedly spoke to Secret Service personnel, and not necessarily the grand jury, about what he had seen. In the meantime, both the original report and the revised version had flashed to news outlets across the country.

Brian Duffy, who shared a byline on the story, justified the online publication this way: "We heard footsteps from at least one other news organization and just didn't think it was going to hold in this crazy cycle we're in."[11]

The following morning, February 5, yet another version appeared in the *Journal,* this time in the print edition. The story, with a few small modifications, ran on page A24 under the headline "CONTROVERSY ERUPTS OVER TESTIMONY TO GRAND JURY BY WHITE HOUSE STEWARD." Hours later, at his daily press briefing, Lockhart noted that in its haste to post the story, the *Journal* had not waited for a response from the White House. "The normal rules of checking or getting a response to a story seem to have given way to the technology of the Internet and the competitive pressure of getting it first," he said. "I understand the competitive pressure that everybody is under. But I do think it's a significant lowering of standards when getting it first supersedes getting it right."

Richard Tofel, a spokesman for the *Journal,* denied the White House's assertion of declining journalistic standards and said that the newspaper had merely updated a breaking news story, a standard practice for news organizations. "In the wire service business, this happens all the time," he noted. Paul Steiger, the paper's managing editor, released a statement saying, "We stand by our account of what Mr. Nelvis told the Secret Service." He said that the *Journal* had posted the story when the editors "felt it was ready." The *Journal* did not wait for a response because the paper felt that the White House had made it clear it would not answer questions about the case.

On Monday, February 9, the *Journal* reported that, contrary to its earlier story, the steward had not told the grand jury he had seen Clinton and Lewinsky alone. In fact, far from seeing something, Nelvis turns out never to have seen the two alone and had testified to that before the grand jury.[12] "We deeply regret our erroneous report of Mr. Nelvis's testimony," the *Journal* quoted Steiger as saying.

During the week, while several wire services filed reports about the *Journal* story and its later retractions, the Associated Press did not touch it. Darrell Christian, the managing editor who had earlier picked up the *Dallas Morning News* story, said this time: "We went to our own sources and tried to check it out and were pretty much convinced that there were enough doubts about the accuracy of the report that we would not go with it."

As it turns out, no eyewitness to an intimate act by Clinton and Lewinsky has ever come forward. Supporting documents to the Starr report show that White House steward, Bayani Nelvis, had complained to the Secret Service about having to collect towels that had lipstick on them. This is the closest thing there is to evidence that there was a witness. The Starr report, in the end, was mute on the subject.[13]

THE SCARS REMAIN

Nearly two years later, it is apparent in the newsroom of the *Dallas Morning News* that scars from the episode remain. "The conventional wisdom is that the *Dallas Morning News* really screwed up," John Cranfill says, a bit brusquely. "But it was the witness who changed his story. During those early weeks there was a lot of rumor and innuendo flying around, and a lot of news organizations were put in the position of trying to sort out the truth. We had sources swearing to us up and down that certain events happened, and it turned out it wasn't true. There was a lot of pressure to put the next revelation up without as much confirmation as we needed."

While it may sound like a convincing argument to go slow on a big story and not worry about scooping the competition, Cranfill does not see it that way. "News coverage is always sloppy. You don't have the luxury of being able to pore over the documented facts like a historian and say, 'Here's what really happened.' When you're in the heat of the moment, you're at the mercy of what people who step forward tell you. We're especially vulnerable on the Web."

Cranfill, who became the Web site's news projects editor in 1999, adds: "Most Internet-based breaking news stories advance faster than television, much faster than newspapers, and at least as fast as radio. Anyone who has had any experience reading wire service bulletins learns quickly that the initial reports on the wire are partly right and partly wrong, and only time will tell which is which. Now, if you're running a news Web site, are you going to sit on what you've got, or are you going to report it? If you hold off, I'll guarantee you people will pick up the phone and ask us why we're not publishing the news."

THE ISSUE OF SOURCING

During press coverage of such past scandals as Watergate in 1974 or the Iran-Contra controversy in 1987, perhaps the biggest challenge facing journalists had involved news gathering—teasing out enough information from reluctant sources to build a solid story. In the Clinton sex scandal, information flowed like floodwaters. Thanks to the Internet, it was everywhere—but much of it was murky or polluted. One news organization might cite another organization as its source, or link to another's Web site story. Once a story made it onto the public airwaves, it was difficult if not impossible to slow it down. A study commissioned by the Committee of Concerned Journalists found that in the early stages of the Starr investigation, 21 percent of the reporting was based on anonymous sources, and almost half of those stories were based on only one source.[14]

Sandy Grady, Washington columnist for the *Philadelphia Daily News,* dubbed the early coverage "Monica Meltdown Week." He wrote: "This was the worst performance by the American press my eyes and ears witnessed since I began covering Washington in 1974. I've never seen so many stories flying through the ether disconnected from sources, stories flatly wrong, over-dramatized hype, hypothesis disguised as fact, and toxic stuff circulating through the Internet, cable, and mainline press."[15]

The real challenge came in filtering out fact from rumor.

News organizations covering the story firsthand had to determine the reliability of the information obtained. Some sources had political motives: many participants had Republican ties and a visceral hatred of President Clinton, dating back to the outset of his 1992 presidential campaign or even earlier. Certain sources in the independent counsel's office were using the press, selectively leaking information to gain tactical advantage with reluctant witnesses like Lewinsky. Faced with the possibility that any given source might have such mixed motives, reporters and editors made the call based on their experiences, news judgment, and gut feelings.

News organizations, especially those in small and medium-size markets, were forced to wade through the digital data stream pouring through the newsroom from outside channels each day to decide what to publish. Even established news providers like the *Wall Street Journal* and *Dallas Morning News* were stumbling, while newcomers like cyber-columnist Drudge seemed handily wired to knowledgeable—if anonymous—sources.

Editors had an especially difficult time determining what was fit to print. They were often troubled by the endless leaks and the constant parade of unidentified sources, particularly when they had to rely on the judgments of other news organizations.

Dan Berko, online content editor for the *Daily Camera* of Boulder, Colorado (daily circulation 35,000), recalls: "We didn't have correspondents in Washington; we didn't have sources in Kenneth Starr's office; we didn't know anything firsthand. We were somewhat at the mercy of the big news outfits and the wire services. We trusted them to get it right, and I'm not sure they always got it right. But if we limited our coverage, were we doing a disservice to our readers?"

Large news organizations also wrestled with the sourcing problem. The editors at the *New York Times* were particularly wary of passing along reports based on unidentified sources. At one point the *Times'* Washington bureau had four hearsay sources asserting there was indeed a witness to an intimate encounter between Clinton and Lewinsky. Executive editor Joseph Lelyveld says the *Times* came close to running a story, but it could not nail down the account to its editors' satisfaction. "We got quite a coherent story from one person, and fragments supported by others. Then we got some very stiff denials of key elements from people said to be involved. In the end, it just didn't seem good enough. It's easy to slip up and make mistakes. It takes a lot of self-discipline to keep asking the question: 'How do we know this?' We've all heard the same stuff. We're trying very hard to anchor what we put in the paper on our own reporting, but it's a difficult standard. We're all swimming in the same murky sea."[16]

Eric Owles, national producer for the *New York Times on the Web,* says it would have been easy to publish the allegations by attributing them to another news source, such as the Dallas paper. But he says the paper's Web editors decided early on not to report any new development unless they had independently confirmed the report with the paper's Washington bureau. "While the Starr investigation put new media in the spotlight," Owles says, "we didn't want the pressure of 24-hour news to be used as an excuse to rush stories into print on the basis of unverified, unnamed sources."

Other media followed the same approach. A wire editor at CNN was responsible for reconciling conflicting information on the scandal that came in from outside news providers. The *Los Angeles Times* sought to stick to its two-source rule and assigned a copy editor to see that stories were acceptably sourced before they appeared in the paper or on the Web site. As a result, some big stories—such as the initial reports about the now-famous stained blue dress worn by Lewinsky during one encounter—did not appear in the *Times.*

The Starr Report

On September 9, 1998, the House of Representatives received special prosecutor Starr's report. The report—formally titled "Referral From Independent Counsel Kenneth W. Starr in Conformity With the Requirements of Title 28, United States Code, Section 595(c)"—was a document without precedent in U.S. history. It contained graphic accounts of Clinton's sexual affair with Lewinsky and alleged that the president had committed perjury, obstructed justice, tampered with witnesses, and abused his constitutional powers. The report laid the foundation for Clinton's impeachment by the House along party lines that December; he was acquitted in his Senate trial two months later. Two days after it got the report, the House voted to release it—on the Internet—and for one improbable, and historical, afternoon and evening, the Net had the spotlight all to itself.

In the online melee that ensued, journalists scrambled to get a copy—but so did millions of ordinary Americans. Congress had made no provisions to handle the crush of traffic on the three official government Web sites posting the report. Its servers were hopelessly jammed. To compound the problem, legislative techies had posted the 445-page report in a clunky format that required users to download the entire document without being able to peek at its contents.

At 2:45 P.M. on September 11, CNN.com became the first news site to post the report, beating the competition by 15 minutes because of "good connections inside the Capitol," says Scott Woelfel, general manager and editor in chief of CNN Interactive. By midafternoon the free-for-all was in full swing. CNN.com's front page was getting 300,000 hits per minute. MSNBC reported 1.94 million visitors to its site that day, a record. Across the entire Web, traffic was up 175 percent over the previous day. All told, 20 million Americans read parts of the report on line within 48 hours of its release.

The release of the Starr report was widely seen as the single most important event in the history of the Internet up to that point. "The real milestone of the Starr report," Woelfel observes, "was that if you weren't on the Net, you felt like you were missing part of the story."

Journalists new to the Internet are sometimes surprised by how much nuts-and-bolts technical tinkering goes on in new media newsrooms, and this was never truer than on September 11, 1998. At the *Los Angeles Times,* the entertainment staff joined the entire new media department in cutting and pasting text documents into smaller file sizes to enable users to scan through Web-friendly HTML pages. CNN placed the report on an internal server so television correspondents could access it immediately while sitting at computer terminals. And at the *Daily Camera* in Boulder, Colorado, the 23-year-old Berko went to heroic lengths—working 27 straight hours—to download the report from an FTP server, upload it to the local site, and then send it on to Scripps-Howard's corporate site.

Many came to the same conclusion as an editor at the *Providence Journal:* "It's clear to us that many readers want to get their hands on the raw data as opposed to information that has been filtered through editors and reporters. These are people who want to make their own judgment, and giving them the actual report is the only way to do that."

Certainly the Starr report's availability on the Internet changed the dynamic of the deliberations inside newsrooms. Some decided to pass on the report because of its wide availability elsewhere. Others saw posting the full report on the news publication's Web site as a civic responsibility. The fact that users had to access the report proactively on the Web, rather than having it enter their living rooms through the airwaves or a family newspaper, was a decisive factor for them.

A nationwide survey of daily newspaper editors by *Presstime,* the magazine of the American Newspaper Publishers' Association, found that, three days after the report's release,

- 17 percent published the full report in print.
- 70 percent ran excerpts.
- 64 percent ran the full text online, and these sites saw an average 80 percent increase in traffic.

THE REPORT TAKES SHAPE ON THE WEB

Once online news publications had a copy of the report in hand and had crafted an appropriate warning about its explicit content, they got down to the business of making it web friendly. "It's not enough to just put up a 445-page document and say, 'Here it is, everyone,'" says CNN's Woelfel. "Our online staff had to figure out how to tame this multi-tentacled creature." News organizations faced a number of decisions:

- How to handle the explicit language and descriptions of lascivious conduct described in the report.
- Whether to print excerpts or the full text of the report.
- Whether to publish it on line in the same format in which it had first been released by the White House.
- Whether the report's contents should be filtered by the traditional news role of "gatekeepers."

While dozens of non-news sites, ranging from search engines like Lycos to financial services sites like the Motley Fool, also made the report available online, some news sites provided a full complement of Web tools to help in dissecting the report.

At the *Boulder Daily Camera* web site, the Starr report was wrapped into the site's "Clinton in Crisis" package, including an archive of past stories relating to the scandal and a biographical cast of characters that sketched out the major players and their role in the affair. The *Dallas Morning News* Web site added the Starr report to its ongoing scandal package. The paper's dallasnews.com gave the report context by assembling in one place scores of staff-written stories, press conference transcripts, biographical sketches, and background profiles, as well as a slide show of photographs of the key players, video footage, reader forums, a list of e-mail addresses of members of Congress, and links to other sites. "I don't know of anything written or said or photographed about this event that was not up on our site," says online editor Cranfill.

At latimes.com, the release of the Starr report gave editors an opportunity to cover multiple elements of the story and allow readers to engage in "personal storytelling," as former new media director Leah Gentry likes to call it. "The personal nature of the Web allows you to move through information at your own pace, access the material at multiple entry points, and seek out the elements you're most interested in. The Web is a nonlinear experience, and no two people move through the Web the same way."

The latimes.com site interwove the Starr report with the deep content of its "Clinton Under Fire" package: an interactive timeline of the major events, including video of the major participants; an archive of staff-written articles, columns, and op-ed commentaries on the Clinton-Lewinsky matter; video-taped testimony and transcripts of testimony dating back to the Whitewater affair; e-mail addresses of members of Congress (which thousands of readers

made use of); and lively discussion forums—which were now closely monitored because of a death threat made against the president on the "Clinton
Under Fire" bulletin board on February 27, 1998. (The FBI and Secret Service
were alerted and tracked down the culprit.) On the day of the report's release,
the *Los Angeles Times* broke with tradition when its Washington bureau filed
midday off-cycle news stories to its online site. The online reports included a
reporter's notebook, a Q&A on the Starr report, and another first for the site:
several audio filings throughout the day in which an online editor interviewed
various *Times* political reporters.

At CNN.com, a team of four staff members worked nonstop over three
days to index the report and cross-reference the document with links from
participants' names to thumbnail sketches. Reporters from CNN and *Time*
magazine's joint AllPolitics team filed breaking news stories with congressional, White House, and public reaction. Links were added from both the
report and supporting materials to the site's "Investigating the President"
package, including photos of key players; a video of Clinton's admission of an
affair; transcripts of interviews, press conferences, and remarks by congressional leaders; discussion forum postings; polls; editorial cartoons; and
dozens of online stories, archived by month. A search engine allowed users to
browse the Starr report by table of contents, name, date, or keyword. The
resulting package set the standard for how to treat primary source material on
the Web.

The Starr report raised questions about what content is suitable for family newspapers and live broadcasts. Many news organizations resolved this
dilemma by heavily editing its content in print and on air and then making the
entire report available on their Web sites, accompanied by prominent warn-
ings about the report's graphic content.

Some of the oddest moments in the media's coverage of the Starr investigation came when broadcast journalists read excerpts of the report live on the
air. CBS News correspondent Bob Schieffer reported that the president and
Lewinsky had engaged in "a sex act of a kind," and he edited himself as he
thumbed through the report. CNN correspondent Candy Crawford, reporting
live in front of an office computer, warned viewers that the report was explicit
and then read excerpts off the Internet that described various sex acts.

"When you had broadcast journalists sitting down at a computer screen
and showing the viewer passages from the report on the Web, it demonstrated
vividly how completely reliant television journalists were on the Web for this
story," says James Naughton, president of the Poynter Institute, a media think
tank.

A Role for Analysis, Synthesis, and Context

On the day the Starr report swooped into cyberspace, news sites saw their online usage surge. A poll by the Pew Research Center for the People and the Press found that the public turned to Internet sites in large numbers as a news source during the scandal.[17] Journalists should be heartened by the knowledge that online users gravitated to the major national news sites: MSNBC.com, CNN Interactive, USAToday Online, nytimes.com, washingtonpost.com.

But they should not be smug or complacent about their role in cyberspace either, for millions of users accessed the report directly—without the filter of the news media. As late as 1995, such a document could have been conveyed to the public only by journalists. Now it was instantly available to anyone with an Internet connection to read, dissect, forward to others, debate in an online forum, or print out and share with friends and neighbors.

Online columnist Katz says he received 25 or 30 copies of the report that people had e-mailed to him within a span of five minutes. "This was the first time in American history that millions of citizens were given access to a critical document at the same time as their elected representatives and the news media," he says. "People reached their own conclusions about the document fairly quickly, without the Washington press corps, the pundits, and Beltway politicians telling us what to think. People in positions of power have been rattled by the Net because they sense they're losing control over the civic agenda. The Net spreads the agenda-setting around."

Still, although millions perused the report online, few read the full 445-page document. Fewer still read the hundreds of pages of supporting materials. Does this mean there is still a need for journalists to divine the significance of news and put events into perspective? Or can people get what they want for themselves? Is there no longer a need for the kind of work the *Los Angeles Times* produced for its paper and later posted on its Web site—a comprehensive look at the Starr report's most significant findings, coverage of congressional reaction and local public sentiment, an examination of how the media covered the report on television, a story on how to answer children's questions about the scandal, a business piece on the stock market's reaction to the Starr report (stocks were up because the report contained no bombshells), and an editorial on the scandal?

The release of the report draws attention to another interesting aspect of the Internet. The report of the Watergate investigation, which predated the widespread development of the Internet, has never been released. Nor was it written as a narrative, according to Jim Doyle, former special assistant to the

Watergate special prosecutors. It was an index to the documents—all of which were sealed from public view by congressional order. In the current case, Starr apparently expressed chagrin at the release of the report. But some Republican lawmakers told reporters that it was released for political reasons: they felt that its contents would so disgust the public that Americans would come to favor impeachment and conviction, after having opposed them for nearly a year.[18] If that is true, then the Internet—which made the wide and immediate release of the report so easy—takes on a new political role. It has the potential to lift closely held documents out of the hands of the favored few in government and place them squarely within the arena of direct democracy.

In the end, this attempt at direct democracy, to change public opinion, backfired. The public did not change its mind and the president was not convicted. What then does the Internet mean for democracy? Does it in fact move us toward direct democracy?

The Report's Aftermath

The Starr report remained newsworthy for far longer than just the week it came out. CNN's Woelfel observes: "As more materials became public and as the impeachment process moved forward, we were able to link new stories back to the Starr report to add context to what was happening. It became a living document that we used over and over. It's still up on our site for that reason and we plan to keep it up indefinitely."

At the outset of the scandal, the Internet was still in its infancy. By the time the Starr report was released eight months later, the tables had turned: the Internet largely dictated how the story played out, and online news organizations responded with respectful, restrained, serious coverage.

By late 1998 Internet news had turned into a mass phenomenon. The washingtonpost.com site saw its traffic jump from 25 million page views in December 1997 to about 70 million a month one year later. Other news sites reported similar gains. But perhaps more important than the phenomenal growth in visitors are the new questions journalists must address as they continue to deliver the news.

Epilogue: A Still-Evolving Medium

Ten days after the online stampede for the Starr report, a new round of Web mania erupted as visitors flocked to watch video of Clinton's August 17, 1998, testimony before Starr's grand jury. The House Judiciary Committee voted to make public the four hours of ostensibly sealed testimony the president had given before a federal grand jury the previous month. That day latimes.com saw a significant bump in traffic. "We were frankly amazed at the tens of thousands of people who demonstrated they will use even low-quality video when something is of interest to them," Gentry says. The site was able to provide both the live feed of the prerecorded event as it was released by the House and RealVideo snippets of key highlights.

Remarkably, several cable news operations reported wider viewership on their Web sites than on their cable channels, tapping into the thousands of workplaces with PCs and high-speed Net access but no television sets. Because bandwidth-hogging video travels far slower over modem lines than does text, CNN.com removed all its other video from the site so that users could call up the grand jury video segments at a reasonably brisk pace. August 17, 1998, remained the site's busiest day until Election Day 2000.

News sites flexed their multimedia muscles again 11 days later when they posted audiotapes and transcripts of Linda Tripp's phone conversations with Monica Lewinsky, released by the House Judiciary Committee. Until the Starr investigation, few news sites had gone through the trouble of producing video or sound files.

As 1998 drew to a close, multimedia had become another weapon in the arsenal of many news sites. Internet usage had risen to 43 percent, according to a survey by the Pew Research Center for the People and the Press. More striking was the extent to which the credibility of online news had risen. In fact, among the better-known news organizations, the public often awarded more credibility to the organization's Web site than to the organization itself. For example, 44 percent of respondents rated ABCNews.com highly credible while only 29 percent gave that rating to the network itself. Fully 54 percent gave CNN.com a high believability rating, compared with only 40 percent for CNN's cablecast.

By June 2001 a Pew Research Center survey reported Internet usage at 62 percent of the general public. At least for the time, the public seems to value the Internet as a source for unfiltered, unanalyzed information. Whether that trust grows or dwindles to the levels enjoyed by print and broadcast news has yet to be seen.

DISCUSSION QUESTIONS

1. What advantages does the speed of the Internet offer citizens in spreading news? Are there drawbacks? Is so, how can the conflicts be resolved?

2. If you were the editor of a newspaper and your Web site ran the Starr report verbatim, would you edit out certain sections? How would you explain your decision to readers?

SOURCES

The information in this case study is based on a thorough reading of the news coverage during the investigation as well as on books, transcripts, other publications, and personal interviews. The books and other publications are cited in the notes. Other quotations came from telephone interviews with John Cranfill on December 6, 1999, and Eric Owles on December 27, 1999.

NOTES

1. Pew Research Center for the People and the Press, "Optimism Reigns, Technology Plays Key Role," October 24, 1999, available at www.people-press.org.
2. Tom Rosenstiel and Bill Kovach, *Warp Speed* (New York: Century Foundation, 1999), p. 11.
3. Committee of Concerned Journalists forum transcripts, "The Clinton Story and the Press," National Press Club, Washington, D.C., February 18, 1998. A summary of the forum is available at www.journalism.org.
4. Jim Schutze and Christine Biederman, "Poop on the Scoop: DMN editors spin the truth," *Dallas Observer,* February 5, 1998, p. A1.
5. Rosenstiel and Kovach, *Warp Speed,* p. 57.
6. Schutze and Christine Biederman, "Poop on the Scoop."
7. David Foster, "Media Challenged by Clinton Crisis," *AP Online,* January 29, 1998.
8. Schutze and Christine Biederman, "Poop on the Scoop."
9. Ibid.
10. Janny Scott, "Testing of a President: Media Notebook," *New York Times,* February 6, 1998, p. A20.
11. Howard Kurtz, "*Wall Street Journal* Story Is Rushed onto the Web: Response Follows, Disputed Report Is Softened," *Washington Post,* February 5, 1998, p. A12.
12. Thomas Oliphant, "The Witness Who Wasn't," *Boston Globe,* February 17, 1998, p. A15.
13. Rosenstiel and Kovach, *Warp Speed,* p. 166.
14. Committee of Concerned Journalists, "The Clinton Crisis and the Press: A New Standard of American Journalism?" February 18, 1998, available at www.journalism.org.
15. Sandy Grady, "Press Performs Poorly in Monicagate," *Buffalo News,* February 3, 1998, p. 3B.
16. Foster, "Media Challenged by Clinton Crisis."
17. Pew Research Center for the People and the Press, "Event-Driven News Audiences: Internet News Takes Off," June 8, 1998, p. 3, available at www.people-press.org.
18. Robert A. Jordan, "Hey, You in the Glass House! Handle Those Stones Carefully," *Boston Globe,* September 20, 1998, p. F4.

Appendix

Clinton Accused of Urging Aide to Lie; Starr Probes Whether
President Told Woman to Deny Alleged Affair to Jones's Lawyers

SUSAN SCHMIDT, PETER BAKER, and TONI LOCY, staff writers

Independent counsel Kenneth W. Starr has expanded his investigation of President Clinton to examine whether Clinton and his close friend Vernon E. Jordan Jr. encouraged a 24-year-old former White House intern to lie to lawyers for Paula Jones about whether the intern had an affair with the president, sources close to the investigation said yesterday.

A three-judge appeals court panel on Friday authorized Starr to examine allegations of suborning perjury, false statements and obstruction of justice involving the president, the sources said. A Justice Department official confirmed that Attorney General Janet Reno had forwarded Starr's request to the panel that oversees independent counsels after Starr had asked her for "expeditious" consideration of his request.

The expansion of the investigation was prompted by information brought to Starr within the past few weeks by a former White House aide who surreptitiously made tape recordings of conversations she had with the former White House intern describing a relationship with Clinton.

The former intern, Monica Lewinsky, began work in the White House in 1995 at age 21 and later moved to a political job at the Pentagon, where she worked with Linda R. Tripp, who had moved there from an administrative job at the White House.

Sources said Tripp provided Starr with audiotapes of more than 10 conversations she had with Lewinsky over recent months in which Lewinsky graphically recounted details of a year-and-a-half-long affair she said she had with Clinton. In some of the conversations—including one in recent days—Lewinsky described Clinton and Jordan directing her to testify falsely in the Paula Jones sexual harassment case against the president, according to sources.

Lewinsky gave an affidavit in connection with the Jones case Jan. 7 and sources who have seen the sworn statement said she denied having an affair with Clinton. She is scheduled to be deposed by Jones's lawyers Friday. In his own deposition in the Jones case Saturday, Clinton was asked about Lewinsky and denied under oath having a sexual relationship with her, according to a source familiar with the testimony.

White House officials said they were unaware of the expansion of Starr's investigation and referred calls to Robert S. Bennett, the president's lawyer in the Jones case.

"The president adamantly denies he ever had a relationship with Ms. Lewinsky and she has confirmed the truth of that," Bennett said. "This story seems ridiculous and I frankly smell a rat."

Neither Bennett nor White House officials would comment on whether the president had conversations with Lewinsky about her testimony. Efforts to reach both Lewinsky and Tripp this week were unsuccessful.

William Ginsburg, an attorney for Lewinsky, confirmed that Starr is investigating his client's involvement with Clinton and said he has talked with Starr's staff. He would not discuss the substance of the case but portrayed his client as an innocent young victim of the political system. He would not comment on whether Lewinsky had a sexual relationship with Clinton.

"If the president of the United States did this—and I'm not saying that he did—with this young lady, I think he's a misogynist," he said. "If he didn't, then I think Ken Starr and his crew have ravaged the life of a youngster."

He added that a young person like Lewinsky can be devastated "if you're not terribly sophisticated and you're misled by the people at the center of the political system, and that includes the president and his staff and the special prosecutor."

William Hundley, who represents Jordan, said he was unaware of the investigation and declined to discuss it. "It's all news to me," he said. "I'm not disputing what you're telling me, but at this time I'm certainly not going to comment and I can assure you that Mr. Jordan would not comment. . . . You can rest assured that we're going to cooperate with the authorities."

On the tape recordings made by Tripp, sources said, Lewinsky described her sexual relationship with Clinton and said the president advised her not to worry about the Jones case because Jones's lawyers would not find out about the relationship. Lewinsky said that when she was notified by Jones's lawyers in mid-December that they wanted her testimony, she called the president and he advised her to deny the affair, the sources said.

She said that Clinton then told Lewinsky that Jordan would help figure out what to say, the sources said.

Jordan, a prominent Washington lawyer and civil rights figure, has been a regular Clinton golfing partner and among the president's closest advisers outside the White House.

He has come to Starr's attention before for helping another Clinton friend, former associate attorney general Webster L. Hubbell, line up lucrative consulting fees while Hubbell was under investigation for fraud and tax evasion. Starr wants to determine whether any of that money was intended to encourage Hubbell's silence about Whitewater matters.

While Starr's original mandate was to look at the complicated Whitewater real estate deal, it has been expanded several times by the court over the years to cover other incidents involving the president, including the firing of White House travel office employees and the improper collection of FBI background files on former Republican White House officials.

It was unclear last night how the new Starr inquiry might affect the Jones case, which has been moving toward a public trial scheduled for May.

In her suit, Jones alleged that Clinton crudely asked her for sex in a Little Rock hotel suite in 1991 while she was a state worker and he was governor. For several months, Jones's lawyers have been searching for women who could testify about experiences with Clinton that might prove a pattern of behavior.

Their research has led them to several women who have testified about sexual encounters with Clinton and ultimately to Lewinsky. In a deposition Saturday, Clinton was asked by Jones's lawyers about a number of women with whom he has been linked, according to a source.

The affidavit Lewinsky gave is sealed in federal court in Little Rock. In it, she is named only as a "Jane Doe" and says she should not have to testify in the Jones case because she had no relevant information, according to a source familiar with the document. Lewinsky said she never had a sexual relationship with Clinton, that he never asked for one and that she never benefited or suffered on the job as a result of any sexual overtures, the source said.

James Moody, a lawyer for Tripp, said last night that "Linda has been subpoenaed for the Paula Jones case and beyond that I cannot comment."

Tripp formerly worked in an administrative position in the Bush White House and then in the White House counsel's office during the first years of the Clinton administration. She joined the Pentagon press office in August 1994.

Last summer, Tripp was quoted in a *Newsweek* story about seeing a woman emerge from the Oval Office after she allegedly had a romantic encounter with Clinton. Tripp said Kathleen Willey, another White House aide, appeared in the hallway with her makeup smeared and clothing askew, Tripp said, and told Tripp she had just had an encounter with Clinton.

Willey was subpoenaed by Jones's lawyers and tried to resist testifying but ultimately was forced to tell her story under oath earlier this month. According to a source familiar with her account, she said she went to Clinton seeking a better job and he grabbed her, started kissing and groping her and said, "I've always wanted to do that."

Bennett, Clinton's lawyer, has denied that Clinton engaged in any improper behavior. After the *Newsweek* story ran, Bennett publicly questioned Tripp's credibility. Some time after that, Tripp began recording her conversations with Lewinsky, who coincidentally was working in the same Pentagon press office.

Lewinsky started at the White House as an unpaid intern in the office of then–Chief of Staff Leon E. Panetta in the summer of 1995 and impressed colleagues there with her dedication, according to a source familiar with her job history. During the government shutdowns several months later, she volunteered to come into work and manned phones left unattended, earning gratitude among White House officials, according to the source.

Lewinsky was hired in December 1995 as a staff assistant in the Office of Legislative Affairs, where she worked in the correspondence section opening and handling letters from members of Congress. At times, according to the source, she would be responsible for delivering correspondence to the Oval Office, usually leaving it with the president's confidential assistants, Nancy Hernreich or Betty Currie, and she sometimes ran into Clinton during these duties.

"She's like 10,000 other kids who come to the White House," said a colleague. "They're all star-struck and they all want to see him. . . . Did I notice that? Yeah. But I didn't see anything beyond that." She left the Pentagon several months ago to move to New York, associates said.

A Justice Department official said there was no question about approving Starr's request.

"Starr made it clear that he needed this," the Justice source said. "We did not want to look like we were slowing down the process." As a result, Reno made her decision "right away."

The source said that Justice officials were shocked by the allegations. "It was really a situation where people were floored," the source said.

Staff writer Dana Priest contributed to this report.

Starr Examines Clinton Link to Female Intern

DAVID WILLMAN and RONALD J. OSTROW, staff writers

A panel of federal judges has authorized the Whitewater independent counsel to examine whether President Clinton encouraged a woman to testify falsely regarding the nature of their relationship, people familiar with the matter said Tuesday.

An attorney representing the woman, who served as a White House intern until spring 1996, said he and his client conferred over the last several days in Washington with the staff of independent counsel Kenneth W. Starr, who was appointed in August 1994 to probe the Whitewater case.

The significant broadening of Starr's mandate vaults the independent counsel's inquiry beyond allegations of financial irregularities in Arkansas. It brings the power of a criminal investigation to allegations related to Clinton's sexual behavior.

The woman apparently at the center of Starr's new area of inquiry, Monica S. Lewinsky, 23, is a former White House intern. She has recently signed a sworn dec-

Los Angeles Times, January 21, 1998, page A1. Copyright © 1998 Times Mirror Company.

laration in the Paula Corbin Jones suit, stating in part that she has not had a sexual relationship with the president.

According to people familiar with the matter, among the allegations Starr is now investigating is whether Clinton deployed his friend and trusted adviser, Vernon Jordan, to discuss with Lewinsky her testimony or to otherwise shape her account in the Jones case. Jordan did not return messages left for him Tuesday night.

On the basis of a tip from an associate of Lewinsky's who was familiar with her tenure at the White House, Starr's office began investigating and sought the broadened mandate, sources said.

Sources told the *Washington Post* that the associate provided Starr with audiotapes of more than 10 conversations she had with Lewinsky over recent months in which Lewinsky graphically recounted details of a 1½-year affair she said she had with Clinton.

Lewinsky's attorney, William H. Ginsburg of Los Angeles, said he does not know whether his client has had an intimate relationship with Clinton.

In an interview, Ginsburg said the declaration was signed before he began representing Lewinsky. Her original attorney, Francis Carter, ceased representing her as of Monday and declined to explain why when reached for comment.

"I can't tell you what's true and what's not true," Ginsburg said. "She signed the declaration and stands on it at this time. . . . But I'm smart enough after 30 years as a trial lawyer to know that there's always a surprise around the corner. If he, Clinton, did have a sexual relationship with a 23-year-old intern, I question his judgment. If he didn't, then I think Ken Starr and his crew have ravaged the life of a youngster."

White House Special Counsel Lanny J. Davis referred questions regarding the new allegations to a private lawyer, Robert S. Bennett, who is representing Clinton in the sexual-harassment case brought by Jones. Bennett could not be reached for comment Tuesday night.

On Saturday, the president was questioned under oath for several hours at Bennett's office by lawyers representing Jones.

Her suit is scheduled to go to trial in May, in Little Rock, Ark. The federal judge presiding over the case has ordered parties in the matter not to comment publicly; it was not known Tuesday whether Clinton was asked about Lewinsky on Saturday.

Ginsburg and an official at the Pentagon, where Lewinsky worked as a public-affairs assistant from April 1996 until about three weeks ago, described her as diligent and hard-working. They said Lewinsky has remained in Washington since leaving the Pentagon job and was expected to assume a new position, in corporate public affairs in New York, next month.

"I've known her since she was a little girl," Ginsburg said. "She always has been a very well-behaved, bright kid, now a young lady."

Lewinsky grew up in Beverly Hills and attended Lewis and Clark College in Oregon before joining the White House as an intern, Ginsburg said.

A spokeswoman for Starr, Deborah Gershman, could not be reached for comment Tuesday night. But, according to people familiar with the independent counsel's investigation, prosecutors have focused heavily on the allegations related to Lewinsky for at least a week. One lawyer aware of the matter said Starr "is not investigating the president's sex life. They are investigating people being encouraged to lie."

To win the expanded investigative authority, Starr first submitted his request, last week, to the Justice Department. Officials said the department then forwarded Starr's request to a special three-judge panel in Washington appointed by Chief Justice William H. Rehnquist to oversee the independent counsel.

This is not the first time that Starr's staff has delved into allegations of Clinton's infidelity. In June 1997, reports surfaced that prosecutors had questioned present and former Arkansas state troopers regarding Clinton's personal practices as governor.

Those inquiries elicited strong criticism of Starr from the White House and other supporters of the president, who complained that the independent counsel had strayed far from his mandate of probing the underlying financial transactions at the root of Whitewater.

The new questions, which prompted Starr to seek an expansion of his jurisdiction, are but the latest of a personal nature to visit Clinton since he first sought the presidency in 1992. It was during his campaign for the Democratic nomination that year that Clinton, joined by his wife, said in a nationally broadcast interview that he had caused pain in their marriage.

"I'm not prepared tonight to say that any married couple should ever discuss that with anyone other than themselves," he said when asked about extramarital affairs during an interview on CBS-TV's *60 Minutes* on Jan. 26, 1992. When the interviewer, CBS correspondent Steve Kroft, noted that "that's not a denial," Clinton responded:

"Of course it's not. . . . I have acknowledged wrongdoing. I have acknowledged causing pain in my marriage. I think most Americans who are watching this interview tonight, they'll know what we're saying. They'll get it."

Coming on the heels of allegations by Gennifer Flowers, a former Arkansas state employee and cabaret singer, that she and Clinton had a 12-year affair, the candidate's comment was interpreted as an acknowledgment of infidelity. Then, less than a year into his presidency, the *American Spectator* magazine and the *Times* reported comments from Arkansas state troopers who said that they at times had assisted the governor's extramarital exploits.

Through it all, voters have not been dissuaded. Clinton overcame Flowers' allegations to win the pivotal New York primary in 1992 and defeated President Bush that fall. Last November, with Jones' allegations still unresolved, Clinton overwhelmingly won reelection.

Times research librarian Janet Lundblad contributed to this story.

Witness Says He Saw Clinton and Lewinsky Alone in Study

BRIAN DUFFY and GLENN SIMPSON, staff reporters of the *Wall Street Journal*

A longtime White House steward told a federal grand jury that he saw President Clinton and Monica Lewinsky alone together in a study adjacent to the Oval Office, according to two individuals familiar with his testimony.

Bayani Nelvis, 50 years old, was among the first witnesses summoned before the grand jury by Independent Counsel Kenneth Starr after he received court approval to expand his investigation of Mr. Clinton to include allegations involving Ms. Lewinsky. Mr. Nelvis, who is assigned to a small kitchen-pantry that has access to the Oval Office and adjacent study, provided additional testimony to the grand jury on Wednesday.

Mr. Nelvis approached Secret Service personnel and described having seen Mr. Clinton with Ms. Lewinsky in the Oval Office, according to one person familiar with the event. This person would not characterize Mr. Nelvis's description of exactly what he saw or when. Mr. Nelvis is particularly valuable to Mr. Starr because unlike Secret Service agents, who are responsible for the security of the president, there is no bar to his testimony.

Mr. Nelvis's testimony could be significant if it can be corroborated. Among the questions Mr. Starr and his staff are attempting to answer is whether Mr. Clinton testified falsely in a deposition or whether he discussed a plan in which Ms. Lewinsky would provide false testimony in a lawsuit. Should Mr. Starr develop sufficient evidence that that occurred, he could bring criminal charges of perjury or obstruction of justice.

During a deposition Mr. Clinton gave last month in the sexual harassment lawsuit filed against him by Paula Jones, Mr. Clinton was asked whether he had ever met alone with Ms. Lewinsky. According to a person familiar with Mr. Clinton's testimony, the president responded that Ms. Lewinsky had met with Betty Currie, his personal secretary.

The two individuals familiar with Mr. Nelvis's testimony said that he reported recovering tissues with lipstick and other stains on them after the alleged meeting between Mr. Clinton and Ms. Lewinsky and that he disposed of them in the kitchen-pantry. The individuals said Mr. Nelvis, who has served in the White House for more than 15 years, informed the Secret Service of the meeting between Mr. Clinton and Ms. Lewinsky because he "was personally offended" by it.

The fact that Mr. Nelvis has testified to the grand jury was first reported by ABC News last night.

Mr. Nelvis did not respond to several calls to his residence Wednesday, and his attorney did not reply to messages left at his office by a reporter.

Individuals familiar with Mr. Starr's inquiry said his staff attorneys have spent hours this week and last questioning several current and former White House aides in an effort to determine whether Mr. Nelvis would have had the access he described in his testimony and could have witnessed a meeting between Mr. Clinton and Ms. Lewinsky. In his testimony before the grand jury on Tuesday, former White House aide George Stephanopoulos said, he was questioned by Mr. Starr's attorneys for nearly an hour "about a floor plan of the first floor of the West Wing" of the White House, where the Oval Office, the study and the kitchen-pantry are located.

An individual familiar with Mr. Stephanopoulos's testimony said he confirmed that Mr. Nelvis did have the access to the Oval Office and the adjacent study that he described to the grand jury. Ms. Currie was similarly questioned about Mr. Nelvis's testimony during her grand jury appearance last week, and an individual familiar with the matter said she confirmed the White House steward had access to the Oval Office and study.

Secret Service Agent Saw Encounter, Source Says; Witness Said Ready to Testify

DAVID JACKSON, the *Dallas Morning News*

Independent counsel Kenneth Starr's staff has spoken with a Secret Service agent who is prepared to testify that he saw President Clinton and Monica Lewinsky in a compromising situation, sources said Monday.

As an emotional Mr. Clinton denied again Monday that he had "sexual relations" with the former White House intern, a lawyer familiar with the negotiations said Mr. Starr's staff expects cooperation from this new witness.

"Starr has this person in his hand," said the lawyer. "This person is now represented by the independent counsel. This person is now a government witness."

Mr. Clinton's fiery, finger-shaking rebuttal to the allegations of sexual impropriety were his first public remarks about the case in four days.

"I'm going to say this again," said Mr. Clinton, standing with first lady Hillary Rodham Clinton at a White House event, his eyes visibly moistening. "I did not have sexual relations with that woman, Miss Lewinsky. I never told anybody to lie. Not a single time. Never. These allegations are false, and I need to go back to work for the American people."

Late Monday, William Ginsburg, Ms. Lewinsky's attorney, said he has given Mr. Starr a complete proposal for his client's possible grand jury testimony.

"We are now in a position where the ball is totally in Judge Starr's court, and Judge Starr has to tell us what he wants to do," Mr. Ginsburg told reporters.

Ms. Lewinsky is scheduled to testify Tuesday, but attorneys warned that her appearance could be put off as Mr. Starr debates whether to give her immunity from perjury prosecution. Attorneys familiar with the probe also said that Mr. Starr is concerned about high-profile testimony on Tuesday night's State of the Union address.

Regarding reports of a witness to a Clinton-Lewinsky encounter, Mr. Ginsburg added: "I don't know anything about a witness."

"This person is real," said the lawyer familiar with Mr. Starr's investigation. Other attorneys familiar with the case declined to name the witness but said the witness has met with prosecutors.

Mr. Starr's office refused to comment.

White House press secretary Mike McCurry said he spent much of Sunday chasing press reports of a witness in the White House. He said those efforts were without result, but allowed that he had not been in touch with the Secret Service. He noted that the agency has its own press operation and "they can speak to that if they choose."

But Mr. McCurry denounced press leaks he claimed were coming from Mr. Starr's staff. "There's a grand jury empaneled, and they are taking testimony on this and we've got papers filled with stuff coming out of these proceedings," Mr. McCurry said. "That's, I think, against the law."

The Secret Service declined to comment.

The Secret Service witness is part of Mr. Starr's investigation into charges that Mr. Clinton and his advisers encouraged Ms. Lewinsky and other witnesses to lie in the sexual misconduct suit brought by Paula Corbin Jones, according to attorneys familiar with the case.

Some officials, speaking on the condition they not be named, questioned whether Secret Service agents would have been in a position to see any improprieties involving Mr. Clinton.

And they noted that in transcripts of conversations between Ms. Lewinsky and a friend, Linda Tripp, Ms. Lewinsky has reportedly said no one ever caught her and the president together.

"I don't believe there's a Secret Service agent," the official said.

The *Dallas Morning News* on Monday reported that a witness saw Mr. Clinton and Ms. Lewinsky in a "compromising position." ABC News reported someone seeing them in an "intimate encounter."

"Both reports are right," said the attorney familiar with the case.

In the meantime, Mr. Clinton's attorneys have asked a federal judge in Arkansas to expedite the Jones case, arguing that the publicity surrounding the Lewinsky situation was distracting him from his job.

Ms. Lewinsky, who is negotiating immunity from criminal perjury prosecution, has been subpoenaed before a federal grand jury scheduled to meet Tuesday. So has attorney Vernon Jordan, the Clinton friend who has helped Ms. Lewinsky find legal representation and a job.

Attorneys cautioned that the negotiations with Ms. Lewinsky are fluid and could delay her grand-jury appearance. They also noted that Mr. Clinton's State of the Union message may also influence who appears before the grand jury and who does not.

"Judge Starr is very mindful of the potential of embarrassment or distraction," said another source familiar with the investigation. "Judge Starr has directed that the staff take all steps to minimize embarrassments or distractions."

Mr. McCurry said the president had decided to make a direct and simple denial precisely because he did not want further distractions from his State of the Union message.

"Hopefully, they will have heard him say what he had to say today," the press secretary said. "And tomorrow night, if they choose to check in on the State of the Union speech . . . they will . . . be interested in what the president proposes for the future of the country."

Throughout the brief White House gathering, during which the president announced a $55 million grant from the Mott Foundation for his long-sought after-school programs, Mr. Clinton and his wife stood closer than their assigned placards taped to the floor.

Mr. Clinton's remarks received warm applause from the two dozen guests gathered. Among them was Sen. Christopher Dodd, D-Conn., who was general chairman of the Democratic National Committee during Mr. Clinton's last campaign. Mr. Dodd said the president "deserves the benefit of the doubt . . . until we know more."

The stakes surrounding Mr. Clinton's utterances are heavy. In recent days Mr. Clinton's credibility, as measured in several national polls, has slid precipitously.

And a congressional staffer, who asked not to be named, said aides on the House Judiciary Committee have begun basic research on the impeachment process, "but that doesn't mean it's being done gleefully."

Other potential legal problems loomed as well.

Any plan to use a Secret Service agent as a witness could set up another courtroom confrontation between Mr. Starr and the White House, if the latter argues that Secret Service observations are protected by executive privilege.

Though Mr. Starr is investigating possible charges of obstruction of justice, not adultery, attorneys say he must investigate Ms. Lewinsky's claims of an affair, if only to pressure her into testimony before a grand jury.

Ms. Lewinsky denied any sexual relationship in a sworn statement to Ms. Jones' lawyers dated Jan. 7. Mr. Clinton reportedly denied an affair in his Jan. 17 deposition with Ms. Jones' lawyers.

Mr. Starr's prosecutors are reviewing letters retrieved from Ms. Lewinsky's apartment, records of her White House visits, and gifts Mr. Clinton purportedly gave her, including a dress.

Ms. Lewinsky told her friend Ms. Tripp that she had a dress stained with evidence of a sexual encounter. Attorneys said that Mr. Starr's investigators have the dress she described and have submitted it for DNA analysis, but they do not know whether Ms. Lewinsky was telling the truth about the dress stain.

Administration officials have suggested that Ms. Lewinsky may have been fantasizing about an affair, noting her one taped comment that "I lie all the time."

Transcripts of tapes obtained by *Newsweek* indicate she uttered the line when discussing the possibility of lying about an affair.

"I was brought up with lies all the time," Ms. Lewinsky said. "That's how you got along . . . I have lied my entire life."

This phase of Mr. Starr's investigation stems largely from the Jones lawsuit, which was the subject of new legal maneuvering on Tuesday.

Because of the intense publicity, Robert Bennett, the attorney defending Mr. Clinton in the Jones trial, asked U.S. District Judge Susan Webber Wright to move up the trial currently scheduled for May 27.

Mr. Bennett's legal brief complained about unfair allegations in the news media, saying "the virtually unregulated processes of civil discovery have become a vehicle for parties allied in an attempt to destroy the president."

"More significantly [*sic*], however, is the fact that the Office of Independent Counsel [Mr. Starr], intentionally or unintentionally, directly or indirectly, has joined forces with Paula Jones," Mr. Bennett wrote.

Attorneys for Mrs. Jones indicated they would oppose the change.

The Rutherford Institute, a conservative Virginia think tank that is assisting the Jones lawsuit, criticized Mr. Bennett's comments.

"This is simply an attempt to distract the public from Kenneth Starr's criminal investigation," said institute President John Whitehead.

Mr. Clinton must contest the Jones lawsuit because the Supreme Court last year rejected his argument that presidents should be immune from civil litigation until they retire from office.

"The events of the last few days have shown that the higher courts' confidence that this case should proceed without undue distraction to the nation's business was unfounded," Mr. Bennett said.

Staff writers Catalina Camia, Allen Pusey and G. Robert Hillman contributed to this report.

The President Under Fire: In the Media; Retracting a Retraction, Self-defense and Revelation

JANNY SCOTT

The *Dallas Morning News,* the newspaper that made news by becoming the first news-gathering organization to officially retract a front-page story on the White House sex scandal, went itself one better yesterday and retracted the retraction. Sort of.

New York Times, January 29, 1998, page A18. Copyright © 1998 the *New York Times* Company.

The original retraction involved an article that the *Morning News* had posted on its Web site late Monday. It said that the independent counsel's staff had spoken with a Secret Service agent who was prepared to testify that he had seen President Clinton and Monica S. Lewinsky in "a compromising situation."

Early Tuesday, after the article appeared on the front page of an early edition of the paper, the editors pulled it and posted a five-paragraph retraction on the Web site saying that the source for the article, a longtime Washington lawyer familiar with the case, had said the story was wrong.

Yesterday, the story was reincarnated.

This time, it said one or more "current or former Secret Service agents" had observed "an ambiguous incident" involving Mr. Clinton and Ms. Lewinsky. An intermediary had talked with the independent counsel's office about possible cooperation in the office's investigation, the paper said.

Carl P. Leubsdorf, the paper's Washington bureau chief, said the paper never thought there was a problem with the first story. But it felt it had no choice but to retract it when the principal source got cold feet after seeing it on the Web site well before the paper's press run was complete.

"I think the story on the Web site had an impact on how this played out," he said. "It speeded up the news cycle. I don't know what would have happened if this were a few years ago and the story had appeared in all editions and the next morning the source had said, 'I was mistaken about a couple of things.'"

Darrell Christian, the managing editor for the Associated Press, said he received a call at home at about 1 A.M. on Tuesday telling him that the *News* was retracting the story, which the Associated Press had incorporated into one of its own stories and put out on the news wire three or four hours before.

In the interest of speed, the agency killed its entire story, later substituting another, rather than simply killing the paragraphs from the Dallas story. It was probably too late for many papers that had picked up the AP story, Mr. Christian said; the AP story was already in print.

The talk of the talk shows and instant darling of the tabloids yesterday was Andrew Bleiler, the pony-tailed former drama teacher from Oregon who placed himself in press custody Tuesday evening on his lawn in Portland shortly before Mr. Clinton launched into his State of the Union Message.

Mr. Bleiler, a husband and father of two who says he had a five-year, extramarital affair with Ms. Lewinsky, had taken a leave from his job and gone into hiding when Ms. Lewinsky's name hit the news last week. But reporters camped on his lawn and besieged the Vancouver, Wash., school district where he works as a theater technician.

Louis A. Brancaccio, the managing editor of the *Columbian,* the daily newspaper in Vancouver on the Columbia River, said yesterday that his paper was the first to identify Mr. Bleiler by name. Within hours of the publication early Tuesday afternoon, Mr. Bleiler had been rousted. He emerged with his wife and his lawyer.

So there he was, yesterday morning, on the cover of the *Daily News* and the *New York Post*. His lawyer, Terry Giles, was on the NBC television program *Today* and elsewhere describing Ms. Lewinsky as a liar obsessed with sex who used to say she was going to the White House "to get my presidential kneepads."

By mid-afternoon, Michael Reagan, the radio talk show host and Ronald Reagan's son, was on another talk show host's show on CNN, saying Mr. Bleiler's wife "did not look like a happy camper." She should file for divorce, he suggested helpfully. "I'll pay. That guy is an idiot!"

As for Mr. Brancaccio, no regrets.

"We felt comfortable that the earlier relationships that Lewinsky may have had were important in the overall context of the story, because if Clinton does have to defend himself against her claims, her character will come into question. So this is a story that basically built on Lewinsky's character."

And the Bleilers?

"Sometimes private lives get caught up in big-picture stories," he said. "That's what we've got here."

—3—

Columbine School Shooting: Live Television Coverage

‣‧‧‧‧◦‧‧‧‧◂

Alicia C. Shepard

EDITORS' NOTE

On the morning of April 20, 1999, two students at Columbine High School in Little-ton, Colorado, opened fire on their classmates. As local television stations struggled to provide live coverage and timely information of the unfolding events, the rest of the nation quickly tuned in. The shooting was the third most closely followed news story of the 1990s, according to a study of six hundred stories of the decade by the Pew Research Center for the People and the Press.[1]

Alicia Shepard, a senior writer for the *American Journalism Review* and an experienced observer of the press, details the minute-by-minute decisions at each of the three local stations.

Knowing that families and friends of Columbine students were relying on their coverage, television personnel had to decide what pictures should be shown live and what, if anything, should be withheld until the outcome was known. In addition, there were cell phone calls from inside the school and conversations with trauma-tized eyewitnesses, almost all of whom were juveniles. How should those live inter-views be handled?

Journalism is often a balancing act between providing information and remain-ing sensitive to the community's needs and the ongoing investigation. It becomes all the more difficult when that balancing act is performed live.

The dynamic of the coverage changed when the national media entered the pic-ture. Shepard's narrative also explores the implications of their sending so many reporters and anchors to the scene.

Tuesday, April 20, 1999. News director Patti Dennis walks in late to the 8:30 A.M. meeting. The room is full. Her executive producer at NBC affiliate KUSA-TV fills her in. Looks like a slow news day. For no particular reason, Dennis glances around the room and unwittingly gives her staff a heads-up. "I don't know why," she says, wriggling her hands, "but, oooh, I feel spot news com-ing in my fingers."

Her instincts are prescient. At around 11:20 A.M., something odd crackles over the newsroom police scanner. Dennis is in her office when she hears an assignment editor yell: "There's a kid at a school with a gun!" Probably no big deal, she thinks. Teen brings gun to school, adult wrestles teen to ground, gun is confiscated. Nonetheless, a KUSA reporter calls the Jefferson County Sheriff's Department.

"You already know more than I do," the media spokesman says, explaining that officers are dashing out to Columbine High School, a suburban school with two thousand students about a half hour south of Denver.

Suddenly telephones erupt in the newsroom. Callers want to know what's going on.

Quickly, it becomes apparent to Dennis that this is not some kid brandishing a gun to impress friends. This is real. KUSA has limited information, but Dennis still feels a responsibility to go on air.

At 11:35 A.M., KUSA breaks into *Leeza,* a daytime talk show, alerting viewers of a "possible shooting" at Columbine High School. "Grenades may be involved," says an anchor voice over a map of the school's location. There are no pictures. It is too soon. Within four minutes, they switch back to *Leeza.*

At Denver's other network-affiliate television stations, CBS's KCNC-TV and ABC's KMGH-TV, reporters get the same news from police scanners. By 11:45 A.M. every newsroom in Denver is lurching into Big Story mode. Adrenaline pumping, assignment editors order crews to the school, to local hospitals, to nearby neighborhoods. Reporters grab notebooks and maps; photographers reach for gear. They run to their cars. Assignment editors page all crews in the field, telling them to get to Columbine High. Fast.

At 11:55 A.M., KUSA officials push *Leeza* off the air for good. They will stay live for the next ten hours. Their competitors follow: KCNC at noon, then KMGH. "Breaking News" flashes across the screen on all channels.

Telephones continue ringing. It's the same in every Denver newsroom. *Ring.* "We don't know anything yet." Hang up. *Ring.* The constant ringing only heightens the confusion. "What's happening?" frantic callers demand. "Are children dead?" "Where's Columbine High School?"

Dennis is stunned. In twenty years at KUSA, she has never had a story generate so many calls so quickly. At about noon she and her executive producer, David Kaplar, head for the control room to monitor the live feeds that soon start coming in from the field.

KUSA's business reporter, Gregg Moss, is first on the scene and begins reporting via cell phone. At 12:07 P.M., he interviews a girl who had been inside the school. "I heard they had guns and grenades," she says. "We thought it was a fight."

Twenty minutes later, KUSA's microwave satellite truck is in place, and live video of Moss is beaming to viewers. The first time Dennis sees feeds of children on stretchers, she reacts as a parent might. She wouldn't want to see her daughter on a stretcher on television. She tells field crews: "No tight shots. Parents don't know. I don't want to see any faces. It's not appropriate. Too many parents are wondering what's happening. I don't think it's right to show anyone injured seriously. That compromises their privacy."

Police and ambulances arrive at Columbine High from all over the Denver area. Ambulances, earsplitting sirens blaring, race down Main Street in Littleton, the closest town to the school. The noise alerts the weekly paper. Several reporters rush to the scene. Denver radio, print, and television reporters descend on Columbine High. Police are now closing one street after another, making it impossible to drive near the school. Reporters abandon their cars and run toward the modern, 250,000-square-foot school. Hundreds of people—parents, neighbors, friends, the curious—rush toward Columbine, only to be halted by police tying yellow tape to trees to mark off the scene.

Chaos prevails. Photographers arrive ready to capture live a potential hostage situation. Reporters stand outside the yellow police tape screaming questions at police. Are the killers alive? Are they holding hostages? Inside the school, fire alarms clang, tripped by detonated bombs. Water gushes from sprinkler systems.

Shortly after 1:00 P.M., students begin escaping from the high school. Some are wounded and bleeding. Many are crying. Students give police and reporters wildly varying accounts of the shooting spree inside the cafeteria and library. Some are eyewitnesses; others report information heard from friends. Police share nothing with the expanding crowd.

The afternoon wears on. 1:00 P.M. 2:00 P.M. 3:00 P.M. Still no word on the gunmen. Still no announcements from the sheriff's department. Television is filled with live footage from the scene but no answers. Heart-ripping footage is captured of police dragging a limp body across the schoolyard. Police offer no explanation. Calls continue to pour into KUSA. But most information collected over the phone or from the field is merely speculation.

At 4:04 P.M., almost five hours after the first shots, Jefferson County Sheriff's Department spokesman Steve Davis holds a press conference with sheriff John Stone. "We do have some fatalities," says Davis. "The number isn't known.

It's not known whether they are teachers or students. We think the suspects have been found inside the building and are dead."

Stone confuses the situation by giving numbers. He tells reporters twenty are wounded and "as many as twenty-five people are dead." He concludes, "It appears to be a suicide mission."

A BIG STORY

This is the kind of day for which journalists spend careers training. It is authentically a Big Story: one that changes a community, and how people feel about being journalists. As it is happening, however, there will be no time for thoughtful discussion among colleagues about journalistic ethics. Instead, instinct and judgment honed by years in the profession will guide the snap decisions television journalists make in covering one of the worst school shootings in history while the country watches live.

The story stays strong for at least ten days. But the first day is unquestionably the most intense. Covering Columbine for television challenged every resource each station had. Yet no aspect of journalistic training would be tested more than the ability to make decisions about what to air that first day, under enormous emotional and psychological pressure.

This case looks, in particular, at two of the complex decisions each newsroom faced:

- Under what circumstances should you withhold information or pictures once you have them, and what issues should be factored into that decision? Which news value should take priority: providing full, timely, accurate news coverage to viewers or attempting to minimize harm?
- How does a newsroom handle interviewing live eyewitnesses on television or cell phones—especially juveniles—who may spontaneously say something wrong or put others, including themselves, in danger?

AT KUSA-TV, THE NBC AFFILIATE

The first curve ball comes at KUSA shortly after noon. Columbine student Jonathan Ladd calls. He's transferred to executive producer Kaplar in the control room. Kaplar invokes KUSA's normal procedure for dealing with kids: "What's your name? How old are you? Where are you? What have you seen? Would you be willing to tell us live on TV?"

Dennis is a little edgy about putting a student no one has met or spoken to at length on the air. But they need new information. The locator map is getting old, and co-anchors Kyle Dyer and Gary Shapiro are repeating the same stuff. They decide to go with the kid.

Ladd is switched over to the anchors. He tells them he heard an explosion but didn't see anything. Dyer, an anchorwoman who had joined KUSA four years ago, is winging it. She and Shapiro were getting ready for the noon report when the news broke. "We ran out to the set with the plan to go on right away and say what we heard and how we had crews on the way to the school," says Dyer. "We had no idea that it was that big of a deal."

Dyer, 31, had graduated from journalism school less than ten years earlier, in December 1989. Her first job was as a field producer and assignment editor at a television station in Washington, D.C. She went on to report for an Indiana television station and then was an anchor in Louisville, Kentucky. With seven nieces and nephews, she is particularly upset by any story in which a child is hurt. She's about to experience the worst day of her career.

At 12:15 P.M. KUSA puts another student on air live via telephone after Kaplar quickly screens him. His name is Bob Sapin and he says he's calling from his hiding place at school. He talks for three minutes. He's breathing hard; he sounds scared.

"They were all in black. They had submachine guns. I'm hiding behind the school in the bushes," he tells anchors Dyer and Shapiro. "I'm praying to the Lord that they don't come out the back door." Dyer reassures him police are at the school.

Co-anchor Shapiro, 45, a native Nebraskan and a seventeen-year veteran at KUSA, calmly urges Sapin to get to the police. By 12:38 P.M. KUSA's helicopter arrives, piloted by weatherman Tony Lamonica, who broadcasts the pandemonium of the school scene.

At 12:45 P.M. Sapin, the student hiding in bushes, calls back. "I saw two killers," he tells viewers. "They had black masks and black trench coats. Needless to say, I was scared."

Sapin says he was in Mr. Connor's math class when the shooting began. "My math class ran," he says. "They got away. My curiosity got the best of me. I wanted to see if I could help in any way. But when I saw the men from outside where I was hiding in the bushes, I was afraid. I chickened out."

"No, you didn't, Bob," reassures Dyer, who, although not a parent, feels protective of Sapin. She has never covered a story of this magnitude.

By 1:00 P.M. another student inside the school, James, is on air live via a cell phone. His last name is never mentioned. "I'm in a classroom with locked doors," James says. "It's really noisy outside. I hear a lot of screaming. I'm all by myself." He didn't hear any gunshots, he admits, just a "bunch of threats."

Dyer steps in. "You need to get off the phone right now and call 911 immediately," she instructs.

At 1:09 P.M., James calls again, saying telephone lines are jammed. He can't get through to police. "People are running up and down the hall yelling, 'They're inside the cafeteria,'" he says. "I'm just staying underneath the desk. I just hope they don't know where I am."

Dyer promises to get James help. "Don't tell us where you are," she orders.

At 1:23 P.M., student Jonathan Ladd is again live via telephone. "I've calmed down some," Ladd says. "One of my friends called his mother [from the school]. She said he's hiding in the choir room."

CONFUSION AT THE TRIAGE SITE

Out in the field, KUSA cameraman Brad Houston and reporter Ginger Delgado team up at the makeshift triage site in a residential cul-de-sac. Delgado and other television reporters initially speak live via telephones to anchors, describing the confusion.

When Delgado, 34, arrives, she's overwhelmed. In ten years as a reporter, she's never seen anything like what was unfolding. "Kids were crying. Bleeding. Screaming. They were in complete shock," says Delgado, who had joined KUSA three years before. "The majority had blood spattered on their clothing."

She's frazzled. She barely knows where to begin. She turns to Houston and asks: "What do you shoot first?" They wonder how best to interview kids and how to shoot the bloody scene before them with as much tact as possible.

"Cruisers would pull up with bloody kids spilling out," says Delgado. "I needed to talk to some kids to see what they saw or heard. But you didn't know how to approach them. I tried to be really sensitive and understanding. I meticulously approached the kids, asking nicely: 'Do you mind if I ask you some questions?' Surprisingly, most of them agreed. Most of the kids were willing to go on camera and say what had happened. Most of the kids at the triage site had been close to the scene."

Interviewing juveniles is tricky. They are often emotional and less circumspect than their elders in what they might say on the air. So television reporters customarily pre-interview kids before putting them on camera. "It's one way of weeding out kids that might say something that you will regret letting get on the air," says Delgado.

But things are happening too fast for pre-interviews. Delgado starts speaking to students while Houston shoots the scene and transmits video back to KUSA's control room, where Dennis will decide what to air.

Houston comes up with a way to give Dennis an option: he shoots scenes two different ways. Since neither Houston or Delgado knows exactly what has happened or whether anyone is dead, Houston shoots so that viewers cannot see faces well enough to identify specific teens.

"When we pulled up, I saw kids lying on the grass; I saw blood on the driveway," recalls Houston. "I went to the truck, pulled out my tripod, and knew that I had to stay back from the people. I stayed away from the families and victims. What was important to me as a member of the community was to stay away from becoming a part of the story and just capture what was happening—as opposed to putting my camera on my shoulder and walking into it."

But he also shoots tight footage of kids' faces. If it isn't aired then, it might work later, when emotions are not as raw.

But it turns out that the gory footage airs almost immediately. KUSA has a partnership with CNN under which the station and the cable network swap video regularly. Houston's footage is fed back to the station raw, which means that CNN has access to it. When it is fed raw, KUSA loses all control. The only way the "bloody stuff" will not be aired nationally is if KUSA does not send it. Or if Houston edits out the blood before sending. But they have decided there's no time for that.

Once tape gets outside the newsroom, it is extremely difficult to pull it back in. Days later, KUSA sends out a photo that causes it endless trouble. The station runs a yearbook photo of gunman Eric Harris. Only it isn't Harris. It is a fellow student named Ryan Snyder. His family is not amused. The station quickly apologizes. But it is too late to prevent others from using it. NBC, KUSA's parent network, runs the incorrect photo on *Dateline* on Friday, April 23. The photo also appears on KUSA's own Web site. "Journalists from all over the globe wanted to partner with us and use our tapes," said Dennis. "Tapes were duplicated and the mistake was sent around the world."

Despite internal memos and a picture of the "wrong" Harris posted around the newsroom with a bold sign, "DO NOT USE THIS PHOTOGRAPH," KUSA rebroadcasts the "Snyder as Harris" photo again over the weekend. The station runs eight corrections. "Using a yearbook put together by students as a reference can be dangerous," says Dennis. "Our photographer used the photo based on the reference in the back of the book. It was wrong. We spent the entire weekend calling, making sure we blocked out the wrong photo. We did a lot of work to try to mitigate one image that didn't belong on a very sensitive story."

The First Day at KCNC, the CBS Affiliate

KCNC's news director Angie Kucharski is in her office when she starts hearing a buzz in the newsroom. She walks out, she hears the news, and her adrenaline level takes off. She joined the CBS affiliate only two weeks ago. She's held a total of one staff meeting and still checks the newsroom photo board to match names with faces. Kucharski doesn't even know where Littleton is. But she knows a random shooting inside a high school is a huge story.

"At some very basic level, spot news is spot news," says Kucharski, who came to KCNC from WBNS-TV in Columbus, Ohio.

She can't do much to help the assignment desk. Instead, she acts more as a coach than a hands-on manager. She reasons that she has a room full of veterans. "When I started realizing their talent, their compassion and ability, I decided to leave it to them," says Kucharski, who has ten years' experience managing newsrooms. "I don't know everything, but sometimes being a good leader is knowing when to get out of the way."

KCNC general manager Marv Rockford is an eighteen-year veteran whose career included a stint as news director. He comes to the newsroom to help. Kucharski knows he's a valuable resource, so both head for the control room after crews are dispatched. Kucharski says she tries to weigh every decision in terms of "safety issues, sensitivity to parents and families, and informing the public." She repeatedly asks editors, "Are the pictures and sound compatible with community values?" Kucharski knows viewers do not expect to see dead bodies on their screens.

KCNC, too, gets calls from kids. At 12:03 P.M., they put a student on the air that one anchor calls "Jenine." She is crying hysterically and her words are difficult to decipher.

"They started shooting people," Jenine gasps during a three-minute call. "At first, I didn't think it was real. Then we saw blood. We saw these two kids. They were white. Eric Harris and we didn't know the other one's name. But they had black trench coats on. They were shooting people and throwing grenades. We saw three people get shot. They were just shooting. They didn't care who they were shooting."

KCNC then reports that the school is being evacuated, according to its police radio.

Blanket coverage is just beginning, and KCNC has already named an alleged murderer—Eric Harris—on the air, without any confirmation from law enforcement or other sources.

As the day continues, details leak out—often from overwrought students and parents. Reporters try to prevent students from speculating or repeating third-hand information. But it's tough. KCNC reporter Mike Fierberg is live at 12:25 P.M. with two teenage girls. Before they can say a word, Fierberg spits out: "We don't want you to tell us rumors or conjectures. I just want to know what you saw. Not what you heard." It is one way local television reporters try to control what is said over the air. Despite his protestations to viewers about trying to be responsible, at 12:53 P.M., Fierberg volunteers the kind of detail that drives police and FBI agents crazy. He tells viewers that a SWAT group has entered the school. "They were fired at," reports Fierberg, "and the SWAT team did indeed return the fire."

Soon after local stations report SWAT team maneuvers live, the Jefferson County Sheriff's Department asks for help: "Please don't show live helicopter coverage or tell what the SWAT team is doing. It could tip off the gunmen." At 1:00 P.M., police still don't know if the gunmen—later positively identified as Eric Harris and Dylan Klebold—are dead.

"We did talk to one parent who has been in contact with his kid who called on a cell phone," reports Fierberg. "A student and others locked themselves in one of the rooms. We won't tell you which room."

KCNC anchor Katie Kiefer also explains at one point: "We don't want to give away too much in case the gunmen are watching."

Overall, the three stations try to respect the sheriff's request. By 2 P.M. television journalists are taking care to speculate less and avoid disclosing details that might endanger police or students still trapped inside Columbine High. Journalists still do not know if there are dead children.

At 2:00 P.M., KCNC gives them a hint. The station airs a live interview with Bree Pasquale, a hysterical, sobbing student in blood-soaked clothing. "Every one around me got shot," says Pasquale, gulping for air. "I pleaded for him not to shoot me. So he shot another girl. It was all because people were mean to him last year. There are at least ten people dead."

Almost an hour later, KCNC, albeit inadvertently, confirms by video a death. At 2:51 P.M., a KCNC camera catches and airs a shot of police dragging an obviously dead body from the school. Within seconds, the station cuts away, prompting reporter Paul Day to say: "I'm very reluctant to characterize what that was."

Anchor Amy Spolar is stunned and blurts out: "We need to go back to that picture." But the station never does. Kucharski makes sure of that.

"I think for the most part, we all put the competitive part behind," Kucharski will agree later. "We were genuinely concerned that we wanted this to turn out okay."

DAY ONE AT KMGH-TV, THE ABC AFFILIATE

On the morning of April 20, news director Diane Mulligan and planning director Gail O'Brien are driving to Boulder, Colorado. There, the grand jury investigating the death of 6-year-old beauty pageant contestant JonBenét Ramsey will soon announce which, if any, arrests will be made. The public has a morbid fascination with JonBenét, who turned up dead on Christmas morning 1997. Mulligan and O'Brien are checking out the logistics for covering the outcome.

KMGH is Denver's third-ranked station, and has been for twenty years. Mulligan is its eighth news director in ten years. Not surprisingly, the station has a chip on its shoulder. Six months ago, KMGH revamped its format and began trying to rebuild its reputation. Since this is Mulligan's first job as a news director after working as a network assignment editor, she is determined that her station excel on the Ramsey story.

Halfway there, O'Brien's pager goes off. She calls in to hear vague details about a school shooting. Since O'Brien handles daily coverage, Mulligan drives fifteen minutes back to Denver and drops O'Brien off. Once again she heads for Boulder, flipping on her car radio. She hears that bombs are exploding at a local high school. Again, she turns around and races back to the station. On the way, she calls the assignment desk and orders an "All Page." Rarely used, this directive means that all staffers must call or come to the newsroom.

"I'm an assignment editor by trade," confesses Mulligan, "and I really wanted to be on the desk. But Gail is really good at moving people, and after we got most people out, I had to begin dealing with the networks. It was just nuts. Every station wanted our video."

At noon, the sheriff's command post asks KMGH's helicopter, flying overhead, to land in Clement Park and pick up a sheriff's deputy to get an aerial view of the school. The station agrees.

Meanwhile KMGH runs into trouble on the ground. Its microwave truck gets to the scene almost as quickly as police. But by the time the first crew arrives, they cannot reach their truck. Police have secured the scene and refuse to let the KMGH crews past the yellow tape.

"We did a lot of reporter cell phone calls and helicopter video until we could get other microwave trucks there," says Mulligan. "We were last from the ground, but first from the air." In addition, Mulligan's station received many cell phone calls from students inside the school. But, unlike the other stations, Mulligan decided against using them because they could not be sure of the callers' identities. "We're clean," she says later.

As the day progresses, KMGH explains its coverage decisions to the public. At about 2:30 P.M. anchor Bertha Lynn tells viewers that the footage the station is about to show of students fleeing the school was shot earlier. The station is airing it now that it knows the students are safe.

"You may on occasion see video of people being given cover by SWAT teams holding up weapons," says Lynn. "One of those will show about a dozen students running for cover with SWAT team members. This happened about two hours after the initial shooting."

By 2 P.M. KMGH knows kids are dead. It even knows some names. Students who were in the cafeteria or library tell reporters the names of others killed before their eyes. But KMGH is reluctant to broadcast any names. What if, by some chance, they are wrong? The station's competitors, too, know names, but they do not air a single dead child's name.

"We knew kids were dead at about 2 P.M.," recalls Mulligan. "But we didn't know if the shooters were dead or how many more students were inside. So we didn't report it. If you report people are dead and there are hostage negotiations going on, that may be something police don't want out there. We wanted the police to report any deaths. We could take no chances on being wrong about kids dying."

Taping the drama and showing it later is an approach each network station uses to varying degrees. The approach satisfies law enforcement officials, who generally want television to tape-delay coverage during a crisis situation. But such delay tends to run up against journalistic instinct. What about the public's right to know? How do you ensure that police and other officials are responsible? Mulligan answers that, although delaying tape may put the station at a competitive disadvantage, she cared more about being sensitive to the community than being first.

Since arriving at the station in March 1998, Mulligan has been trying to establish the "ethical line" she wants her staff not to cross. She watches 90 percent of the main shows and then discusses them afterward and posts her concerns. "This absolutely made a difference," she said later. "Your newsroom has to know where the ethical line and the sensitive line are before something like this happens or else you have terrible problems."

At 2:38 P.M. KMGH's helicopter zooms in on the school library with riveting live video of a student. "Look, you can see a bloody student in the window," gasps anchor Lynn.

The camera catches an armored vehicle creeping toward the library window. SWAT team members, crouching behind it, inch toward the school. The vehicle stops under a second-story window. A dazed Patrick Ireland, 16, his left arm dangling unnaturally, appears ready to jump. "That poor person," says Lynn.

Minutes before, Mulligan was sitting in her office talking with the general manager. She had spent the first hours in the control room, but eventually her continued presence there seemed unnecessary. She reflexively looks up at a television in her office and hears Lynn talking about the bloody student. Mulligan dashes back to the control room.

She's thinking: "I don't know if he's dead. Who is watching? I don't want to see the body hit the truck. It would have been just too much."

Officers reach up and pull Ireland down. Just as he's about to slam into the truck, Mulligan orders her producer to cut away. The outcome is not shown. Is Ireland dead? Is he critically injured?

"You have to decide what's appropriate for viewers at that time," says Mulligan. "You know friends and family are watching and that they are getting their information as it happens."

No explanation of what happened to Ireland is given within the next half hour by KMGH. Later the country will learn that three bullets in Ireland's head paralyzed his right side.

Competitor KCNC also captures the Ireland drama. But it holds the video until 5:26 P.M., after the school siege is over and Ireland is safe. KCNC shows Ireland crashing onto the truck, and viewers then watch him trying feebly to sit up.

It was a coup for KCNC and KMGH to get the shots. KUSA did not. Earlier KCNC reporter Paul Day and photojournalist Bill Masure had talked their way into a home with a third-floor vantage point. There they capture Ireland's climactic rescue. They use an old rattan hammock as a blind to keep police from spotting them. But they can't go live. They aren't close enough to their microwave truck.

The Ireland video is shown over and over—locally and nationally—until it is seared into the public's collective memory of Columbine. At one point, ABC's *20/20* replays the Ireland footage four times within twenty minutes.

That night, Mulligan sleeps in her office. An aide drives to her house for clean clothes. "I have never had a story that impacted me like this," she says.

"We were all crying at some point in the newsroom. It was so unbelievable. The magnitude of it just went on and on. It lasted for 10 days."

THE ONSLAUGHT OF THE NATIONAL MEDIA

By day two, the national media had descended. Network crews began arriving on Tuesday afternoon. Every satellite truck within an eight- to twelve-hour drive from Denver was rented. Overnight, the number of television crews on the scene increased from about 20 to between 100 and 150. Whatever excesses the local television stations had been responsible for, things were about to get worse. One reason was the sheer size of the press horde that was now swarming over the story.

"For the national electronic media, coverage of the ongoing story at Columbine High School is just beginning," warned *Rocky Mountain News* television columnist Dusty Saunders. "Get used to it, Colorado."

On Wednesday morning Denver awoke to NBC *Today* show host Katie Couric broadcasting live from the school. CNN, Fox News, ABC, CBS, and NBC each flew in scores of people. So did such major newspapers as the *Washington Post,* the *New York Times* and the *Los Angeles Times.* Journalists arrived from Japan, England, and France to capture the horrendous tragedy.

Smaller newspapers—the *New Orleans Times-Picayune,* the *Philadelphia Daily News,* and the *Cleveland Plain Dealer*—also sent reporters. The scene quickly became a sea of wall-to-wall media.

"I went to Clement Park [where students were gathering] and felt sickened and upset," says KUSA photojournalist Eric Kehe. "When I turned on my camera, suddenly about twenty cameras showed up behind me. If I swung another direction and started taking pictures, everyone would see what I was doing and swarm those people."

KUSA's Brad Houston found the out-of-town media scene equally disturbing. "From the moment we realized how big a story this was and the magnitude of it," adds Houston, "we started thinking how to cover the story sensitively without intruding on people's grief. If somebody doesn't want to talk, somebody else will. We didn't have to badger people. But not everybody took that tack."

At first, it appeared that those connected to Columbine warmed to the attention. But that didn't last. As desperate outside journalists heckled families, police, neighbors, and camera-shy students for interviews, the community grew angry and began resenting the media intrusion. "Some members of the national media were chasing food workers at the school down to their cars," recalls Gail O'Brien. "A lot of times, our guys said it was the national media stalking people, and so they told them: 'Hey, we have to live here. Cut it out.'"

The onslaught was hard on local journalists who tried to be sensitive to their community. They felt that they paid a price for the aggressive insensitivity displayed by some national colleagues. Months later, when local television crews were covering any story related to Columbine, they found high school students and others still angry at the media. One time, Kehe drove to the high school to cover a class reunion. When he returned to his KUSA-marked car, "Media Sucks" and a skull and crossbones had been painted on it.

"The scary thing is this is our community," says Kehe. "Our neighbors. Our friends. We pray at the same church. Our kids go to the same schools. We are going to be very sensitive to how we approach people. When [journalists] are flying in from 1,000 miles away, they are there just to get the stories. They don't have to consider how they treat people. We are left to mend fences."

Denver journalists agree that regaining the community's trust will take a long time.

EPILOGUE

What motivated the killers in the Columbine case, Eric Harris and Dylan Klebold, may never be fully understood. A self-made videotape released eight months after the shooting reveals the boys' level of self-loathing and hate for popular, athletic, or minority classmates. But there had to be more. Psychologists, educators, and historians will study the worst school bloodbath in history for years.

By the close of day one, reporters, photographers, managers, and assistants involved in Columbine coverage left work emotionally and physically wasted. KUSA's Ginger Delgado put in sixteen hours, returning to her apartment at 1:00 A.M. Many others worked just as long, going home to catch a few hours' sleep, only to return early the next morning.

"I literally walked in my apartment, slammed the door, and started crying and couldn't stop," says Delgado. "It was the images that were haunting me and the people I talked to. The somberness. You couldn't help but feel the pain and sorrow even though I didn't even know anyone involved."

An adrenaline rush kept journalists going the first few days. But by days three and four, some begged to be taken off the story. It was too painful, day after day, covering grieving families, funerals, and distraught teens, and witnessing an endless river of tears. Psychologists came to newsrooms to counsel staffers.

"We didn't have tears the first few days," recalls KCNC's Kucharski. "They came after three days, a week. Don't underestimate how horribly shaken people are to see bloody bodies and crying parents."

Taking care of the staff with food, warm jackets, heaters in station tents (on day two it snowed), and even hugs, became a critical assignment for the three news directors.

"Something I was not prepared for at all," admits Mulligan, "was the impact on the newsroom. You have to take care of the people in the field. My general manager and I went to Starbucks to get thermoses of coffee and cookies for my people in the field and gave people hugs."

In October 1999, six months after the shooting, CBS News broadcast a chilling surveillance video obtained by its Albuquerque affiliate, KRQE-TV. The ninety-second segment shows a grainy, black-and-white image of Klebold and Harris shooting at a homemade propane-tank bomb in the cafeteria, students running for cover under tables, and the bomb exploding.

Worried that such graphic images might victimize survivors and their families all over again and declaring that the video did not advance the story, the three Denver stations—including CBS affiliate KCNC—opted to not show it. In their defense, CBS and KRQE-TV claimed that the tape's news value outweighed any negative impact. The video was widely shown around the rest of the country.

The Columbine school massacre took a toll on everyone involved, peripherally or directly. The whole metropolitan Denver area went into mourning. Few were left unscathed by the ruthless, random slaughtering of twelve students and a teacher. Later KCNC anchor Bill Stuart would publicly admit to being treated for depression after covering the massacre.

Columbine High School reopened on time for the 1999–2000 academic year. A year later, Denver citizens passed the anniversary without any significant trauma. But the story will remain with the community for a long time. Again and again, as with any major, heartbreaking story, the tragedy returns to the national spotlight in connection with other events: Columbine football championships, graduations, an injured student's first steps, a mother's book about her daughter's death, a mother's suicide. And there are the anniversaries. The first. The fifth. The tenth. And so on. Each time, Denver television stations face anew the question of how to report the news and minimize harm to those victimized by two highly troubled teenage boys.

DISCUSSION QUESTIONS

1. Under what circumstances should you withhold information or pictures? What issues should be weighed in making such a decision?

2. What is the proper way of handling live eyewitness interviews on television or over cell phones? Should juveniles be treated any differently?

SOURCES

The information in this case study is based on videotape of the day's coverage as well as conversations with individuals at the three network-affiliate television stations. Chief among them were the three news directors: Patti Dennis of KUSA, Angie Kucharski of KCNC, and Diane Mulligan of KMGH. Various cameramen and reporters were also interviewed, including Eric Blumer of KCNC and Ginger Delgado, Eric Kehe, and Manny Sotelo of KUSA. Outside the newsroom, the author interviewed Gary Noesner, FBI Chief Negotiator, and Bob Steele, an ethicist at the Poynter Institute.

NOTE

1. Pew Research Center for the People and the Press, "Record News Interest in Littleton Shooting," April 26, 1999.

Columbine School Shooting Timeline
APRIL 20, 1999

11:10 A.M. —Eric Harris arrives alone at the student parking lot at Columbine High School and parks his 1986 gray Honda Civic. Dylan Klebold arrives minutes later, parking his 1982 black BMW.

11:14 A.M. —Harris and Klebold walk into the school cafeteria with duffel bags carrying two twenty-pound propane tanks timed to go off at 11:17 A.M. This is the time the two believe the cafeteria will be most packed. They go back to their cars to wait for the explosion.

11:19 A.M. —The first 911 call comes in from a citizen who heard an explosion three miles southwest of the school. Harris and Klebold had planted pipe bombs there to divert law enforcement. At the same time, the first gunshots are fired by Harris and Klebold, who have gone back into the school and are standing at the top of the west steps (the highest vantage point) wearing black trench coats. Students are shot randomly. Some, like Daniel Rohrbough, are killed instantly at close range.

11:22 A.M. —A school custodian hits the record button on the VCR in the cafeteria and calls the police resource officer assigned to the school, who is out for lunch.

11:23 A.M. — The first 911 call from a Columbine student is received, reporting a girl possibly paralyzed by a gunshot in the south parking lot.

11:25 A.M. — The Jefferson County Sheriff's Department sends out a dispatch over the police radio: "Attention south units. Possible shots fired at Columbine High School, 6201 South Pierce, possibly in the south lower lot towards the east end. One female is down." This dispatch is heard over several newsroom scanners.

11:27 A.M. — Deputy Neil Gardner, the resource officer assigned to Columbine, arrives with lights flashing and exchanges gunfire with Harris. Gardner is wounded and radios for help. More officers arrive. The sheriff's department dispatcher says that hand grenades may have been detonated.

11:29 to 11:36 A.M. — Harris and Klebold have moved to the library and are shooting at students inside as well as out the window at law enforcement officers and fleeing students. Within seven minutes, ten people are killed and twelve more are injured; thirty-four escape injury.

11:36 to 11:44 A.M. — The two go into the hallway toward the science area. They shoot into empty rooms. A report made a year after the tragedy says that at this time "Witnesses say the gunmen do not appear to be overly intent on gaining access to any of the rooms. The gunmen easily could have shot the locks on the doors or through the windows into the classrooms, but they do not. Their behavior now seems directionless."

11:46 A.M. — The video shows that the gunmen are in the cafeteria for about two minutes.

11:47 A.M. — Denver's KMGH-TV announces confirmed gunshots fired at Columbine High School during its late-morning news program.

11:56 A.M. — Klebold and Harris, after shooting into the school office, at the ceiling, and at art in the hallway, move back to the cafeteria. Klebold is holding a TEC-9 semiautomatic pistol. Shots are fired, and the video shows the pair surveying the damage in the cafeteria.

12:06 P.M. — The first SWAT team, hiding behind a fire truck, approaches the school. Television news coverage broadcasts the team's movements.

12:08 P.M. — After firing a last shot at police from the library window, Harris and Klebold use their 9mm semiautomatic weapons to kill themselves.

12:20 P.M. —A student interviewed on television says that the gunmen shot his friend. He says he recognizes the shooters as Columbine students but does not know their names.

12:28 P.M. —Local television and radio stations broadcast a hotline number for parents of Columbine students.

12:41 P.M. —News broadcasts ask students who have escaped from the school to call the sheriff's office or 911. The phones at the sheriff's department are instantly jammed.

1:22 P.M. —SWAT teams continue their search and rescue operation inside the building.

1:44 P.M. —Three males dressed in black clothing are detained by police in a field near the school. Television cameras catch the encounter live, but no one knows what is happening. The images raise questions about whether the three are involved. Later it is learned they are not.

2:19 P.M. —A parent waiting tensely at a nearby elementary school, which has been set up for reunions, is taken to a hospital complaining of chest pains.

2:33 P.M. —President Bill Clinton talks to the country on national television about the Columbine shootings.

2:30 to 3:00 P.M. —Police learn that the two gunmen are dead, according to spokesman Steve Davis of the Jefferson County Sheriff's Department. But they do not tell the press or the public.

2:38 P.M. —Student Patrick Ireland, standing in the library window, is slipping in and out of consciousness owing to bullet wounds. Police rescue him.

2:47 P.M. —A SWAT team rescues about sixty students from the science area. KUSA videotapes the event.

3:12 to 3:17 P.M. —Fifty more students are evacuated.

4:04 P.M. —Steve Davis of the sheriff's department holds a press conference with sheriff John Stone. They announce fatalities but give no names. Stone says, "As many as twenty-five are dead." He is wrong.

4:45 P.M. —SWAT teams finish searching the 250,000-square-foot school. The deceased inside the school are pronounced dead by a doctor.

Appendix

Guidelines for Interviewing Juveniles

AL TOMPKINS, the Poynter Institute for Media Studies, St. Petersburg, Florida

Understanding how young people see the world around them often demands that we hear what they have to say. Adults aren't the only ones with worthy views of news. But interviewing young people raises some of the most challenging questions faced by journalists.

Especially in breaking news situations, juveniles may not be able to recognize the ramifications of what they say to themselves or to others. Journalists should be especially careful in interviewing juveniles LIVE because such live coverage is more difficult to control and edit. Juveniles should be given greater privacy protection than adults.

The journalist must weigh the journalistic duty of "seeking truths and reporting them as fully as possible" against the need to minimize any harm that might come to a juvenile in the collection of information.

When interviewing juveniles, journalists should consider:

Journalistic Purpose and Quality of Information

- What is my journalistic purpose in interviewing this juvenile?
- In what light will this person be shown? What is his/her understanding or ability to understand how viewers or listeners might perceive the interview? How mature is this juvenile? How aware is he/she of the ramifications of his/her comments?
- What motivations does the juvenile have in cooperating with this interview?
- How do you know that what this young person says is true? How much of what this young person says does he/she know firsthand? How able are they to put what they know into context? Do others, adults, know the same information? How can you corroborate the juvenile's information?
- How clearly have you identified yourself to the juvenile? Do they know they are talking to a reporter?

Minimize Harm

- What harm can you cause by asking questions or taking pictures of the juvenile even if the journalist never includes the interview or pictures in a story?

From participants in a seminar on "Children, Families, and Social Issues," held May 1–6, 1998, at the Poynter Institute for Media Studies. Later published in Al Tompkins, *Aim for the Heart.* Chicago: Bonus Books, 2002, p. 76.

- How would you react if you were the parent of this child? What would your concerns be, and how would you want to be included in the decision about whether the child is included in a news story?
- How can you include a parent or guardian in the decision to interview a juvenile? What effort has the journalist made to secure parental permission for the child to be included in a news story? Is it possible to have the parent/guardian present during the course of the interview? What are the parents' motivations for allowing the child to be interviewed? Are there legal issues you should consider, such as the legal age of consent of your state?

If you conclude that parental consent is not required, at least give the child your business card so the parents can contact you if they have an objection to the interview being used.

EXPLORE ALTERNATIVES

- What alternatives can you use instead of interviewing a child on camera?
- What are the potential consequences of this person's comments, short-term and long-term?
- What rules or guidelines does your news organization have about interviewing juveniles? Do those guidelines change if the juvenile is a suspect in a crime and not a victim? What protocols should your newsroom consider for live coverage that could involve juveniles?
- How would you justify your decision to include this juvenile in your story to your newsroom, to viewers or listeners, to the juvenile's parents?

THE GOLDEN RULE FOR INTERVIEWING CHILDREN

"Do unto other people's kids as you would have them do unto your kids."

Phoner Guidelines for KUSA-TV, Denver, Created after the Columbine Shooting

When using a caller on the air, it is imperative that KUSA-TV determine the person's relationship to the story, and we must establish confidence that the caller is in a position to offer legitimate eyewitness or insider information about the news event.

It is our policy to use the following guidelines before we put a telephone call on the air:

1. Eyewitnesses are more reliable if the station initiates the call. In breaking news, use the Internet, Pro Phone or the Criss Cross [address- rather than name-based

phone directories] to find people in the area of the news event who might have an eyewitness account of what is happening.

2. If a telephone caller contacts 9News with breaking news information, the staff person must try to establish the motives of the telephone source and take those motives into account when evaluating the integrity of the call.

3. If you receive a telephone call from someone who claims to have urgent information, ask for a telephone number so that you can return the call in an attempt to verify the information.

4. Be skeptical of a caller who contacts the station and is asking or willing to "go live." Most callers are actually searching for more information when they call the station in a breaking news event.

5. Ask questions that will verify the telephone caller's proximity to the breaking news and investigate if the telephone caller can identify individuals who might be involved the news event.

6. Remind all callers not to use names of individuals on the air and not to implicate anyone as a suspect or victim during the course of the telephone call.

7. Do not let telephone callers make inflammatory statements on the air. If they do, challenge the accuracy of the statements.

8. When in doubt, DON'T! If you are not sure about the authenticity of the caller, get the information and a return telephone number. Pass the pertinent information along to the control booth. Find someone in the newsroom that can further research the validity of the telephone call.

9. Evaluate whether the caller is putting himself or others in jeopardy by talking on the telephone or by going on live television with information.

10. Do not let the pressure to "get on the air" affect the decisionmaking or -validating process. Accuracy is everything!

Lessons from Littleton, RTNDF99: Guidelines for Covering Bomb Threats in Schools

AL TOMPKINS, the Poynter Institute for Media Studies, St. Petersburg, Florida

AFTER LITTLETON: COVERING WHAT COMES NEXT

A serious and perhaps defining debate occurred in newsrooms after the Littleton, Colorado, school shootings: "How do we responsibly cover the after-effects of Littleton?"

These guidelines are included in the Radio and Television News Directors Foundation (RTNDF) workbook for electronic news managers, reporters, and producers. The workbook contains television and radio case studies, guidelines for difficult decisions, and sample codes of ethics. The workbook, video, and audio tape are distributed at RTNDF's "Newsroom Ethics: Decision-Making for Quality Coverage" workshops. The guidelines are also available in a slightly edited version at www.rtnda.org/ethics/bomb.shtml. Copyright © 1999.

In the wake of the shootings, school systems across America dismissed classes and sent kids home while bomb squads and bomb-sniffing dogs searched lockers and school classrooms.

Newsrooms were confronted with their own long-standing policies against covering bomb threats. Often these well-intentioned policies were established because of concerns that reporting such threats would breed others. The question facing journalists after Littleton was: "Do we stick by the 'don't-report' rule even as suspects are arrested and in some cases schools are closed?"

Checklist for Covering Bomb Threats

- You should ask yourself the following questions: What is my journalistic duty in reporting this story? What do our viewers need to know? What is the threat to life or property? What are the consequences of the event itself? How significant is the evacuation and the interruption of normal life in your community? What is the impact this event has on law enforcement or emergency crews' ability to respond to other calls? What else is this story about? What is the story behind the story? (In some cases, racial slurs and threats have been sprayed on school walls.)

- Think about the possible consequences of your actions and decisions. Reporting a false threat could lead to copycat threats. Reporting arrests might discourage such threats by showing the consequences for threatening others. However, reporting a bomb threat may raise the public's level of insecurity even when it is not warranted. Repeated broadcasting of bomb hoaxes can have the effect of "crying wolf," with the public becoming less responsive when actual danger arises. However, reporting on the volume and range of threats could inform our viewers and listeners about the pressures our police and schools [sic] officials are under. It could be important for the public to understand why officials react as they do.

- Be careful about the tone of your coverage. Avoid words like "chaos," "terror," and "mayhem"; they are subjective words. Play it straight. Tone down your teases, leads and graphics. The tone of what you report should not contradict the careful reporting of facts you include in your stories.

- Think carefully before "going live" in covering these stories. You have less editorial control in live situations. The emphasis on "live" may warp the attention these stories deserve.

- Think carefully about the placement of the story in your newscast. A lead story carries different weight from a story that is deeper in the newscast. How can you justify the positioning of your coverage?

- Cover the process more than the events. What thought are you giving to the bigger issues involved in this story? How easy is it for schools, the phone company, or cops to track down a threatening caller? How seriously are violators treated? Have you ever followed one of these cases through the legal system to find out what happens? How many bomb threats did police handle last year? How many resulted in prosecution? How many of those prosecuted went to jail or were actually punished? What was the extent of the punishment? Do your schools have caller ID systems in place? Do they or should they record incoming phone calls?

- Minimize harm—we sometimes cause harm in the process of performing our journalistic duty, but it should only be harm we can justify. Special care should be given when covering juveniles. You should carefully consider whether placing a prank phone call warrants naming a juvenile. In one instance, a TV station could not talk with the juvenile suspected of placing the prank phone call, so the station interviewed the suspect's teenage brother. What harm do we cause by sending a news photographer to a school that has been threatened by a caller?

- How do you explain your decisions to your staff? How much discussion have you had in your newsroom about your coverage before and after an event? What experts or persons outside your newsroom could you contact for their perspectives about how you should treat this story? Thoughtful stations hold these conversations about coverage before they are faced with a crisis. Front-end decision-making that includes many voices in the conversation results in fuller and more thoughtful coverage.

- Do you explain your decisions to your viewers? Do you justify the position of the story in the newscast? If you decide to name minors do you tell your audience why? Do you explain your decision to run certain information or why you choose to leave information out?

Lessons from Littleton, RTNDF99: Guidelines for Covering Hostage-Taking Crises, Police Raids, Prison Uprisings, Terrorist Actions

BOB STEELE, the Poynter Institute for Media Studies, St. Petersburg, Florida

In covering an ongoing crisis situation, journalists are advised to:

- Always assume that the hostage taker, gunman or terrorist has access to the reporting.

Bob Steele, "Guidelines for Covering Hostage-Taking Crises, Police Raids, Prison Uprisings, Terorist Actions," Lessons from Littleton, RTNDF99, 1999. These guidelines are included in the Radio and Television News Directors Foundation (RTNDF) workbook for electronic news managers, reporters, and producers. The workbook contains television and radio case studies, guidelines for difficult decisions, and sample codes of ethics. The workbook, video, and audio tape are distributed at RTNDF's "Newsroom Ethics: Decision-Making for Quality Coverage" workshops. The guidelines are also available in a slightly edited version at www.rtnda.org/ethics/crisis.shtml. Copyright © 1999.

- Avoid describing with words or showing with still photography and video any information that could divulge the tactics or positions of SWAT team members.

- Fight the urge to become a player in any standoff, hostage situation, or terrorist incident. Journalists should become personally involved only as a last resort and with the explicit approval of top news management and the consultation of trained hostage negotiators on the scene.

- Be forthright with viewers, listeners, or readers about why certain information is being withheld if security reasons are involved.

- Seriously weigh the benefits to the public of what information might be given out versus what potential harm that information might cause. This is especially important in live reporting of an ongoing situation.

- Strongly resist the temptation to telephone a gunman or hostage taker. Journalists generally are not trained in negotiation techniques and one wrong question or inappropriate word could jeopardize someone's life. Furthermore, just calling in could tie up telephone lines or otherwise complicate communication efforts of the negotiators.

- Notify authorities immediately if a hostage taker or terrorist calls the newsroom. Also, have a plan ready for how to respond.

- Challenge any gut reaction to "go live" from the scene of a hostage-taking crisis, unless there are strong journalistic reasons for a live, on-the-scene report. Things can go wrong very quickly in a live report, endangering lives or damaging negotiations. Furthermore, ask if the value of a live, on-the-scene report is really justifiable compared to the harm that could occur.

- Give no information, factual or speculative, about a hostage taker's mental condition, state of mind, or reasons for actions while a standoff is in progress. The value of such information to the audience is limited, and the possibility of such characterizations exacerbating an already dangerous situation are [sic] quite real.

- Give no analysis or comments on a hostage taker's or terrorist's demands. As bizarre or ridiculous (or even legitimate) as such demands may be, it is important that negotiators take all demands seriously.

- Keep news helicopters out of the area where the standoff is happening, as their noise can create communication problems for negotiators and their presence could scare a gunman to deadly action.

- Do not report information obtained from police scanners. If law enforcement personnel and negotiators are compromised in their communications, their attempts to resolve a crisis are greatly complicated.

- Be very cautious in any reporting on the medical condition of hostages until after a crisis is concluded. Also, be cautious when interviewing hostages or released hostages while a crisis continues.

- Exercise care when interviewing family members or friends of those involved in standoff situations. Make sure the interview legitimately advances the story for the public and is not simply conducted for the shock value of the emotions conveyed or as a conduit for the interviewee to transmit messages to specific individuals.

- Go beyond the basic story of the hostage-taking or standoff to report on the larger issues behind the story. Examine the how and why of what happened, report on the preparation and [actions] of the SWAT team, or the issues related to the incident.

In covering a pending raid or law enforcement action, journalists are advised to:

- Be extremely cautious to not compromise the secrecy of officials' planning and execution. If staking out a location where a raid will occur or if accompanying officers, your reporters and photographers should demonstrate great caution in how they act, where they go, and what clues they might inadvertently give that might compromise the execution of the raid. They should check and double-check planning efforts.

Minnesota Basketball Cheating Case

⊱┄⟡┄⟢┄⟡┄⟨⟢

Geneva Overholser

EDITORS' NOTE

On the eve of the 1999 NCAA basketball tournament, the *St. Paul Pioneer Press* uncovered a cheating scandal in the University of Minnesota's basketball program that turned out to be, in the words of the university's president, "one of the most serious cases of academic fraud ever reported to the NCAA."

The story broke on March 10, one day before the team was to play in the NCAA tournament, and resulted in the suspension of five players. In a year when the team was considered by some better than it had ever been, loyal Minnesotans widely condemned the paper for ill intentions and bad timing.

Geneva Overholser, professor at the Missouri School of Journalism and former editor of the *Des Moines Register,* ombudsman at the *Washington Post,* syndicated columnist, and *New York Times* editorial page writer, reports this case.

The narrative focuses in particular on questions of timing, on when a story is considered ready to go, and on the public's right to know.

Among other things, the right to know implies that journalists represent the public in much the same way as elected government officials. Journalists are privileged to go places and to learn things that the public simply cannot. A further implication holds that the public should know those things journalists know, for freedom of the press is justified by the fact that the information is considered public, not private, property.

In this case, the *St. Paul Pioneer Press* knew that a scandal was brewing in the Minnesota basketball program and that the university had self-reported to the NCAA and was conducting an investigation and compliance review. The paper withheld this information from the public for months. Only the reporter, sports editor, and executive editor knew that the story was in the works. It was not even mentioned to other staffers or to the publisher. Was the paper justified in its timing? What does it mean in reporting to "have the whole story?"

George Dohrmann got a tip.

Dohrmann, a genial 26-year-old, is an energetic fellow to whom "sports is everything," as one of his Notre Dame professors remembers. A reporter with the St. Paul *Pioneer Press,* Dohrmann would normally have been covering Minnesota's professional basketball team, the Timberwolves, once football season ended. But a long and dreary NBA lockout meant that the Twin Cities' Target Center was seeing no action in the final months of 1998. He found himself with time to pursue something a source had told him. The source said that a woman named Jan Gangelhoff might be able to tell Dohrmann a few things about "the climate of working" at the University of Minnesota's athletic department—a subject of interest to Dohrmann, who had been vaguely following several leads about the university's basketball team, the Gophers.

Gangelhoff had left the university earlier in the year and was now working at a casino in the small town of Danbury, Wisconsin. When Dohrmann contacted her, Gangelhoff confirmed that she did have something interesting to share with him. She had recently received a letter from the director of men's athletics at the university, stating that, as the result of an NCAA compliance review, it was necessary to "disassociate" Gangelhoff from the basketball program.

Dohrmann drove to Danbury, where Gangelhoff showed him the letter. It seemed an odd thing for the director to have sent. Gangelhoff had already left the university, and she was not sure what to make of the letter.

It was clear that the university had reported some violation to the NCAA. But Gangelhoff, who had tutored many basketball players over a long period of time, did not know exactly what the violation was. And Dohrmann, of course, had no idea how serious it might be.

Back at the newsroom, Dohrmann took the matter up with Emilio Garcia-Ruiz, the paper's sports editor. Both men had come to St. Paul within the past couple of years—the reporter following the editor—from the *Los Angeles Times.* At the *Times,* they had worked together on a story about UCLA's basketball team that had taught them a number of lessons about pursuing an investigative college sports story. One of those lessons was that a university that sees trouble will quickly look for "a viable explanation they can basically sell" to the NCAA, as Garcia-Ruiz puts it.

The letter to Gangelhoff, the two thought, signified that the University of Minnesota had self-reported something. But what was it? And was there more going on than had been reported? Was it worth investigating even if whatever they found might turn out to be a non-story? The university might already have reported whatever the paper found. And, if it had not yet done so, once it got wind of the paper's nosing around it might rush in a report—just as UCLA had done with Dohrmann's and Garcia-Ruiz's work in Los Angeles.

They also had to consider the other local daily, the *Minneapolis Star Tribune*. Competition between the two papers is hot, and neither has much of a taste for getting beaten on a story.

Knowing all this, the two considered going with a story right then. There had been some sort of NCAA violation; that was clear from the letter. Perhaps there was enough here to report to their readers, and they should go to the university and ask what exactly had been reported.

The other alternative was to try to find out on their own exactly what was afoot. The UCLA experience had rankled the two journalists. The team got off the hook because the university came up with documentation that satisfied NCAA investigators even though it seemed incredible to Dohrmann and Garcia-Ruiz. They felt it was essential to get into the paper what was actually going on—not simply that there had been a violation—without alerting the university until it was absolutely essential.

Dohrmann's own view was "If it is not in the newspaper, then the NCAA will not recognize it. We have to get it in the paper." They decided to try to get to the bottom of the matter.

But so far they didn't have much to go on. There was the letter, yes. Beyond that, there was only Gangelhoff—a 50-ish, disgruntled, former employee working for a casino, as Garcia-Ruiz puts it.

There was a lot of work to be done.

THE REPORTER AND EDITOR AND THEIR ENVIRONMENT

Along with their UCLA experience, the relatively recent arrival in St. Paul of the two principals at work on this story affected their decisions about how to handle it. Indeed, Garcia-Ruiz wonders if the scandal would ever have broken if the only sports staffers around had been the old-timers who dominated both papers' sports staffs.

These veterans worked within a broader culture, one unusually unsuspecting about any kind of wrongdoing. The Twin Cities are filled with settled, comfortable Midwesterners—people with deep roots and a powerful pride of place. "Minnesota nice" is the prevailing tone, and not just in radio host Garrison Keillor's mind. Minnesotans toe the line and behave decently—at least that's the behavior they presume will prevail, among themselves and others.

The dynamic and bustling Twin Cities—Minneapolis and St. Paul—dominate Minnesota economically, politically, culturally and intellectually. Minneapolis is the state's largest city by far, St. Paul its capital. In the heart of the Twin Cities area, astride both banks of the Mississippi River, sits the huge

University of Minnesota campus. The university plays a powerful role in the life of the state. Minnesotans in overwhelming numbers send their children to be educated in its classrooms and their sick to be tended in its hospitals. In a far-flung and otherwise largely rural state, the University of Minnesota is a great unifier. Loyalties to it are fierce and strong. In no arena is this more true than in athletics. The university has the state's only big-time college teams, and Minnesotans are proud and fanatic supporters of them.

You could say that, in such a setting, a sports story is never just a sports story. The price of error in reporting on the object of such fierce loyalty is high—from public anger to professional ostracism, perhaps even to the loss of a job. And in such an environment the competition thinks nothing of jumping on an error even before the offended source does. This is especially true because sports reporters in college towns tend to grow unusually close to the athletic departments and teams they cover, traveling together with the players and coaches. Even if they are not always "hometowners," they at least desperately want the teams to succeed.

The last thing most of these sports journalists want to do is to hurt the team.

The Twin Cities' sports journalism community was particularly close to Clem Haskins, the beloved coach of the Gophers. When the *Pioneer Press* did in the end go to Haskins for a comment on the story, this was his response: "I've been here 13 years, don't you know me, what I stand for as a man, as a person? I haven't changed. All I'm trying to do is win a game. All I'm worrying about is beating Gonzaga. It's all I'm concentrating on. All I'll say is, I will talk when the tournament is over."

But Dohrmann and Garcia-Ruiz had never gotten close to Haskins. And neither was hampered by the locally prevailing notion that "It couldn't be happening here." Even after they had uncovered a level of fraud that no one would have imagined, Garcia-Ruiz declared, "I don't think George and I have been surprised by any of it. The thing is, we never had that doubt about the institution—that it just couldn't be corrupt."

Still, Dohrmann and his editor knew that the closeness of the sports writing community meant that others would be quite ready to turn on them if their work fingered some of the Twin Cities' most beloved figures. There would be an unusually high level of scrutiny. They would have to pass a test that they came to refer to, between themselves, as "making the story Sid-proof"—after a columnist in the *Star Tribune* named Sid Hartman.

Accordingly, whenever Dohrmann would come back from talking with Gangelhoff, Garcia-Ruiz would press him about how much he knew, how much he could prove, and how he could prove it. They decided that certain standards of proof would have to be met: They would report only things the NCAA could prove. They wanted everything on the record. And they were always working with the notion that the story could turn out to be a dead end. "I told [executive editor] Walker [Lundy] the Friday before the story ran that it could be nothing," says Garcia-Ruiz. "They could have self-reported it all."

But for now, so determined were they to get more, to keep the bar of proof high before they counted on anything, that they didn't even raise the issue with Lundy, or with managing editor Vicki Gowler. It was too early.

CULTIVATING THE SOURCE

After that first visit, when Dohrmann had driven over to meet her and to see the letter, Jan Gangelhoff was uncertain what might come of contact with the press. She was struggling with how much she ought to reveal. At one point, she tried to contact someone at the university to let them know what was going on. But no one called back.

Dohrmann, meanwhile, had decided that, since Gangelhoff had been close to the basketball program, "she would at least be an amazing source of background information. I needed to get her to trust me." He placed regular phone calls, took her to lunch when she came to Minneapolis, drove to Danbury now and then to see her.

Meanwhile, Garcia-Ruiz was telling him that he needed someone else—in addition to the source who had originally put him onto Jan—off whom to bounce information. Dohrmann thought Elayne Donahue, the retired head of the university's academic counseling unit, might fill that role. He contacted her. Donahue said that she would not offer up anything, but, yes, she would be willing to respond if George asked her about what he was finding out elsewhere.

Now, as Dohrmann describes it, "I would have a triangle of people I could confirm things with. And then I could sit down with Emilio and ask, 'What does this mean?'" He was sitting down with Emilio more and more frequently, and the copy desk was noticing the conversations. "They started asking what we were doing," the sports editor recalls.

But still the two weren't talking.

Gradually, Gangelhoff began to reveal a few things. "She said she went on trips with the team," he said. "I figured she was doing more than tutoring." When she said she had accompanied the team to Hawaii, he was more confident than ever that Gangelhoff had played a pivotal role in the players' lives.

"But I had to convince her to have enough trust in me so she'd talk," he said.

". . . and so she'd talk on the record," added his editor.

Garcia-Ruiz was not interested in anonymous sources. Indeed he felt that even on-the-record comments from Gangelhoff would not be enough. He would need collaboration. "We weren't going to allow it to be a 'he said, she said' story."

The reporter would come back and recount what Gangelhoff said she had done, remembers Garcia-Ruiz. "And I'd say, 'That's nice, but you don't have the story,'" He could just imagine the critics poking fun at the *Pioneer Press,* resting their big exposé on the claims of an embittered former university staffer. He wanted the story Sid-proof.

And Dohrmann was game to keep trying. When he works with a source long-term, he says, "I don't just want to convince them I care about their lives. I want them to care about *my* life." In addition to keeping up with the latest in Gangelhoff's life, he would tell her what was going on in his. He would keep her posted on his reporting on other stories, on what he and his fiancée were doing.

And, one day in January, the time and effort began to pay off.

"I called her, and she said, 'I was just thinking about you. I kind of have decided that you can ask me things, and I'll tell you the truth.'"

Dohrmann lost no time in taking Gangelhoff up on her offer. "Did you do papers for the players?" he asked her. "Yes," she replied. He told her he would be coming over tomorrow to talk.

Dohrmann drove to Danbury and sat down with his source and a tape recorder. Gangelhoff, he says, "is a reporter's dream. She writes stuff down. She has a great memory."

The story poured out. The size and shape of the NCAA infractions began to grow clearer to Dohrmann.

THE QUESTION OF TIMING

Back in St. Paul, despite Gangelhoff's forthrightness, Garcia-Ruiz remained dissatisfied. "I didn't think we'd get proof," he says. "What was she gonna have to show us?" Something concrete—a paper Gangelhoff had written for a player, a taped phone conversation—was what Garcia-Ruiz felt was needed, and it didn't seem to be forthcoming. Meanwhile, the strike was over, and the NBA season had started. Dohrmann was needed to cover the games. "We didn't have anybody else," recalls his editor.

Over the days that followed, as their story was held, Garcia-Ruiz and Dohrmann would check the *Star Tribune* every day to see if the competition had the story. After all, as Dohrmann points out, the letter that the university had sent Gangelhoff was out there. "We always had to think about it."

Still, the time lag made sense to Dohrmann, "I really felt I needed to give Gangelhoff room to breathe." Though she had professed her willingness to talk, she was clearly worried about what the effect would be. She talked with her sister about it, she told Dohrmann. She was really struggling.

Besides, Elayne Donahue, the former academic counselor for the university who was his confirming source, was out of the country until March 1.

Finally, at the beginning of March, he called Gangelhoff. "Let me come up," he asked. She agreed. They met at the Chippewa Corners Cafe in Danbury. He sat down at the table and she told him, right off the bat: "I can give you proof."

Gangelhoff had kept innumerable computer files of the work she had done. Unfortunately, she told Dohrmann, she was not sure exactly what she had, and it was all mixed in with everything else she'd done on her computer over the years. The two went back to her apartment and started going through her hard drive. They came up with 450 files—papers she said she had done for players, intermingled with personal letters and other work. And all of it was riddled with viruses.

Dohrmann took the stuff, on disks, back to his office and printed it out. Then he put everything into two huge legal boxes and carted them over to Garcia-Ruiz's house.

By now, Garcia-Ruiz had let Lundy know how hot the story was getting, although "even then, I told him that I thought it was going to be hard to prove," the sports editor remembers. Still, Lundy had begun to expect something big. He definitely wanted to go with the story, as soon as they could nail it down. But he understood that the timing was going to be controversial.

He had a chat with his managing editor, Gowler. "This story is gonna hit somewhere as the team is going into this tournament," Lundy said. He added later, "I thought some would say, 'Hey, wait a minute—did you time this?'"

Gowler, as it turned out, had been thinking quite a bit about timing, thanks to a prior experience in which timing had made a big difference. When she was executive editor at a paper in Duluth, Minnesota, Gowler had presided over a package of interviews with candidates emphasizing their comments on education funding issues. The package came out in September, just as school started, and the teachers felt that it was exceedingly prejudicial.

They felt its tone was anti-teacher, and the paper caught hell for the decision to run the package when it did.

"Since then, I've tried to think about timing," says Gowler. "Not just, 'Is the story fair?' but 'Is the timing fair?' We could do everything right, [yet still] feel that the story coming out now could mean something would happen that wasn't right."

Nonetheless, after raising this fear—and talking with Lundy about the story and their options—Gowler concluded that the piece should run whenever it was completed. "We knew the timing would be unpopular, but we knew it would be worse to wait. It came down to a rock and a hard place. It seemed like the right thing to do was to run the story when it was ready."

For his part, Lundy says he never doubted that having the story's readiness determine the timing was the thing to do. "You have to have a reason to hold it. Is there a reason to hold it? I couldn't think of one that didn't have something to do with rooting for the home team."

Putting the Story Together

Garcia-Ruiz and Dohrmann spent hours in the sports editor's basement sifting through Gangelhoff's papers, reading them, comparing them. Soon they began to make telling discoveries: The same paper, turned in by two different players, years apart. Papers with exactly the same mistakes in them, turned in by one player and then another. It was clear that Gangelhoff's claims were solid. And they had the proof.

"That night, about 1 A.M., we knew we were good to go," said Garcia-Ruiz.

The paper hurriedly relieved Dohrmann of coverage of the basketball games, replacing him with a high school sports writer hired from the *St. Petersburg Times* a few days before.

"We told her, you're on basketball," says Lundy with evident pride. "Now she's our NBA writer."

Dohrmann hopped on a flight to Grand Rapids to talk to the first of the players implicated by the papers. Then he flew to Indianapolis to talk to a second player. Both confirmed Gangelhoff's description of the work she had done for them and others.

They confirmed, too, that the coaches had known about it.

At the beginning of the next week, Garcia-Ruiz put other staffers on the job of calling the nineteen other players. "We decided first thing Monday morning that we had to try to talk to all of them," he said. Meanwhile, Dohr-

mann had written a rough draft of the story, without university or player comment, and Garcia-Ruiz gave it to Lundy to read. But he was still downplaying
it to his boss: "We knew we had what Gangelhoff had done. But we didn't
know what Minnesota had told the NCAA." The nagging thought persisted
that perhaps the university had already reported all of the incidents they were
so laboriously discovering.

But it was soon to be banished. The Monday phone calls to players had
alerted Haskins and other university officials, one of whom angrily called
Gangelhoff to ask her what in the world she had done. Clearly, they did not
have the ease of conscience, the sense of security, they would have had if
everything had already been reported.

Garcia-Ruiz now shed his doubts. They had a big one. And it was Sid-
proof.

Still, there was a lot of last-minute work to do. Garcia-Ruiz called the
sports information office (SIO) at the university and said he needed to talk
to the athletic director and to the basketball coach. The SIO promised that
the officials would call him back. Meanwhile, said the editor, "George was
going nuts. They could fire up a quick letter and do all the reporting now,
we figured." Still, there would be no story until they had the university's
comments.

When the next morning passed without the promised phone calls, Garcia-
Ruiz called the SIO again, pressing to talk to the coach. The team was already
in the air, came the answer. They were headed for Seattle, the site of the
Gophers' game with Gonzaga.

The *Pioneer Press* worked its way up the ladder. An education reporter
called the university president, who was out of town. Yes, the president
agreed, he would definitely make sure that the athletic department got back
to Garcia-Ruiz. The call worked. Finally, at 6:00 P.M. the vice president for student development and athletics, McKinley Boston, returned Garcia-Ruiz's call.
Boston questioned the credibility of Gangelhoff's allegations, claiming they
were inconsistent with statements she had made in the past. Shortly afterward, a *Pioneer Press* columnist, in Seattle to cover the tournament, knocked
on Clem Haskins's door. Haskins delivered his speech about how they *knew*
who he was—that he wouldn't do something like that. He was just concentrating on beating Gonzaga. He'd talk to them after the tournament.

Okay, said Walker, we're going with the story tomorrow.

But they still had to reach the four players on the team who were implicated in the scandal, the editor thought. "If we're gonna name 'em, we gotta
talk to 'em. If we couldn't find a player, we couldn't say he was a cheater."

"I was real concerned that we be fair to the people this was landing on," he says. "Frankly, I didn't feel responsible for the reputation of the university. I figured others were responsible for that."

Pioneer Press staffers at the tournament drummed up players for interviews, but university officials had already gotten to them. They refused to comment.

Back at the paper, editors decided they had done all they could. They were ready to go. "At least 20 men's basketball players at the University of Minnesota had research papers, take-home exams or other course work done for them during a five-year period, according to a former office manager in the academic counseling unit who said she did the work," said the lead of the story on the March 10 front page. The Gophers' first tournament game was set for March 11.

That evening was a great time for Lundy. "The 10:00 news had no record of [the story]. The *Star Tribune's* Web site, startribune.com, had nothing on it. The presses were running. I thought, 'Now I know what the Japanese forces felt like when they came over the mountains, and there were the battleships waiting in the harbor.'"

THE STORY IS PUBLISHED

Nancy Conner's phone was ringing off the hook, along with the phones at the main switchboard, those at the editorial desk, and many throughout the newsroom. Conner, the *Pioneer Press's* reader advocate, had heard of the story for the first time when Lundy read the lead at the 4:30 staff meeting the afternoon before. "I didn't know how concerned people would be about the timing," she said. "I just thought it was a damned good story."

Now she saw that there was a lot more to it than that. Readers were furious—in droves. "People were telling us we weren't public-minded, that we were ruining lives. We had destroyed something that the players had fairly earned—an opportunity to play this game." The e-mail messages were even worse than the phone calls—unsigned screeds, laced with vitriol, bristling with obscenity.

Then Governor Jesse Ventura entered the fray. At a press conference he called the *Pioneer Press's* actions "despicable." He accused the paper of rigging the timing so the story would come out right before the game, all for the sake of "sensationalism journalism."

Lundy says, "I just wish he'd found time to say that academic cheating is not a very good thing either."

The governor's tirade triggered even more calls and letters. The tone was consistent: The paper's timing showed malice aforethought, and its actions were inexcusable. "Cheating happens throughout college, and not just with athletes," wrote Jon Schmoll of St. Paul. "The fact that you used these students, at this exact time, one day before the tournament started, is totally inexcusable."

Brian Deal of Lake Crystal wrote: "You should be more than ashamed of yourself. It's time the media stopped being the self-appointed watchdog of society. We are all tired of it. Thanks for crushing the hopes of a state that has endured the Vikings' loss, the Twins' debacle and the NBA strike. I hope the editor feels he has served some grand purpose, whatever that may be."

"We *are* one of society's . . . watchdogs," said Walker Lundy later. "In fact, that's our job," a role that is set forth and protected in the Constitution. "We had very solid evidence that the University of Minnesota was fielding an unacceptable basketball team. They had corrupted the basic reason a university exists, which is to educate people."

The university's response, meanwhile, was swift and powerful. It suspended the four players named among the cheaters. Two of them were starters.

Sure enough, Gonzaga beat the Gophers.

"We expected them to suspend the players, but then appeal. People had told me that it was likely they could get a waiver, so that the players could play," said Lundy. "When we put the stories in the paper, I didn't know the university would be obligated to suspend them."

The fans were heartsick. "We don't have a long and storied athletic history here," Lundy points out. "And Clem Haskins had taken a pretty average team and gotten them to play better than anyone would have thought, and gotten them into the tournament: a bunch of underachievers who really played well together. The community had rallied around them. It was great. Clem Haskins was the man."

To make matters even more dramatic, the behavior that the *Pioneer Press* was bringing to light was not the kind of thing Minnesotans thought went on in their midst. "Minnesotans are proud of the fact that we don't have that kind of stuff," acknowledges Lundy. "So, in the middle of this celebration, comes the *Pioneer Press* to piss all over everything, presenting this revered coach as a cheater and the players they loved as cheaters."

Worse yet, he said, "We really have only this one university, and the *Pioneer Press* was saying its academic mission is corrupt. It's a terribly rude thing to say."

For her part, Conner decided that the readers were asking a good question when they wondered whether the paper could not have run the story sooner. "I decided to interview people here to find out if I was comfortable with what we had done."

She ultimately did satisfy herself. "I ended up being an advocate for the paper," she said. "I told people that I understood why they were upset, but that I thought we did the right thing. I asked readers, 'Should a paper hide information? You wouldn't want us to do this about anything else [other than sports]. What if we had found this out about Gonzaga?' Would they have wanted us to hide it then?"

A COLUMN FAILS TO SATISFY

With so many readers so unhappy, Lundy decided he should write something for the next day's paper about the timing question. "Because we hadn't answered the question the first day, lots of people thought we had timed it. It's hard, in 750 words, to explain the process." But he thought he'd better try to explain what he saw as the value of the work, and what he felt was the inevitability of its timing.

The column didn't have exactly the effect he had hoped. "Silly me. I thought once I wrote the column . . . people would say, 'Oh, okay, I get this.' Instead people wrote and said, 'I don't believe you.'"

A week after the story ran, Conner—counting phone calls from around the building and adding them to e-mail and letters—had tallied about a thousand responses.

Many of the calls were going to Lundy, and quite a few of them were calling him a liar. The number of people who compared him to President Clinton, then in the midst of his nationwide deception in the Monica Lewinsky affair, was, he noticed, particularly striking.

What might have happened if the paper had run a note of explanation on the day the story ran? "I dunno," says Lundy. "I don't think it would've made any difference. You look like you're feeling like you have to defend something."

But some of the others involved think that being more forthcoming with readers on the day the story ran could have made a difference.

Managing editor Gowler is among them: "I think that's the one thing I would have done differently—trying to explain to readers" what the editors' thinking was.

Garcia-Ruiz, too, says that "had we been able to anticipate" the response, an editor's note might have been in order. "But it just floored me completely" how big the response was. "We never even dreamed that [the story] would be forty-five minutes of the one-hour news report the next day."

Another vote for a same-day explanation comes from Conner: "I wish that we had gone ahead for once and written an editor's note that explained some of the background, showed the fairness and the depth of the reporting that went into it—and done it on the first day."

She's glad Walker did write such a piece the second day, she adds, but doing it afterward "was in more of a defense mode."

Still, Conner notes that after the column—and following the initial deluge of complaints—"the supporters came out of the woodwork."

"The thing is, people didn't see immediately how this could serve students better in the future." It's her hope that it will help force universities to "come to grips with playing college athletics and being a scholar" and how the two can be balanced. "This hurt some players but, in the end, future athletes are going to have a better situation."

As for Jan Gangelhoff, Dohrmann says that she "has heard enough people say she did the right thing to now really, really believe that she did. She realizes that what she did was wrong. So now she's really happy she did this thing to correct it—so it doesn't happen to kids in the future."

And how did Lundy end up feeling about it all? "I'm sorry anybody lost a job," he says. "But when I get my gold watch, I'm going to talk about this as one of the best things I've ever seen happen."

The Impact of Competition

Star Tribune editor Tim McGuire agreed that the *Pioneer Press* had done a fine piece of work. As he told the *American Journalism Review,* which ran a piece on the Gopher stories, "I wasn't thrilled. I was disappointed" to see the competition break such a big story. But McGuire did not seek to undercut the work in any way.

"The *Star Tribune* people were very professional in their response," says Lundy. "They gave us full credit for the story, and threw nine people at it the next day. But when you're that far behind and you didn't have Jan Gangelhoff, it was very hard to catch up."

McGuire sees this differently. "I think this newsroom reacted very well," he says, in following up with reporting that broke other parts of the story.

Minnesota's former governor, Arne Carlson, thinks the competition that fuels such remarks played a role in the reporting and play of this story. In the wake of the cheating scandal, Carlson pronounced the university a victim of the newspaper war.

Garcia-Ruiz understands the analogy. "The war between the *Dallas Morning News* and the *Dallas Times Herald* killed the Southwest Conference," in his view. "That could've happened here, but I don't think it did."

Indeed, Garcia-Ruiz argues, the competition made the paper more responsible, not less: "I'll tell you what it did to us. It actually made us more cautious. We dotted our *i*s and crossed our *t*s more carefully" because we figured that the other paper would be watching.

Lundy acknowledges that the situation is "hotly competitive." Not for nothing is "hell-raising" one of the goals on the flip chart when his staff sits down at 9 A.M. each day to assess how that morning's paper looks in retrospect. And not for nothing is the *Trib*'s front page pasted up there right alongside the hometown sheet.

Still, Lundy maintains, "On this one, [the competition] played no role."

Epilogue

In all, 548 *Pioneer Press* readers canceled their subscriptions over the Gophers story. (The paper sold an extra eight thousand copies the day the story ran.)

Editors usually expect that most of those subscribers who cancel in anger will return to the fold before long. As Lundy says, "If you're the only game in town, they have to." But not in this case. "Here they have an alternative." And in fact most of the cancellations have stuck. Six months after the story broke, the circulation director calculated the net loss at 433.

Another financial hit came in advertising. The university's athletic department had its advertising reps call to explain that, thanks to the story, "the mood was so bad" that they could no longer advertise with the paper. They canceled their contracts, which had been worth about $30,000 a year.

A piece of journalistic fallout was the football team's initial reluctance to speak to *Pioneer Press* reporters, demanding that the paper issue a formal apology for the effects of its work on the basketball scandal.

As for what the newspaper's publisher thought of his staff's work, and all the developments that followed, Lundy notes, "I had put him in the loop toward the end. You know, publishers aren't too keen on surprises. He was thrilled with the story."

Eight months after the story was published, the university released a report, prepared for it by a law firm, concluding that Clem Haskins had lied to investigators about "widespread academic misconduct" and had also told his players to lie. It criticized the athletic department, academic counseling supervisors, and faculty members for allowing the cheating to occur. Hours before the release of the report, two other top athletic officials—McKinley Boston, the vice president for student development and athletics, and the men's athletic director—resigned. Haskins, who had resigned under pressure in June and taken a $1.5 million buyout, denied any knowledge of Gangelhoff's activities and said he had told no one to lie.

Said the university's president, Mark Yudof: "I am angry. I felt I was lied to my face . . . the problem was much deeper, and . . . this program was corrupt in almost any way one can think about it."

The report was forwarded to the NCAA, which, after its own investigation, punished the Gophers with four years of probation and placed restrictions on their recruiting. A little over a year after the story broke, it brought George Dohrmann the 1999 Pulitzer Prize for beat reporting. Several weeks later, Dohrmann announced he was leaving the *Pioneer Press* staff to take an investigative reporting position with *Sports Illustrated.*

DISCUSSION QUESTIONS

1. Was the *Pioneer Press*'s decision to run the story when it did the best decision? How well did it serve the public interest? Did the public have a right to this information earlier? If so, did the paper serve a higher purpose by withholding it? Should it have withheld it until after the NCAA tournament?

2. Who made the decisions about the handling of the story, and what principles guided them? Were the decisions professionally and ethically sound?

3. Should the paper have anticipated the public response? Would fuller explanations from the paper have made a difference in the response? Does the degree of public unhappiness mean that the paper did the wrong thing?

SOURCES

The information for this case study is based on a thorough reading of relevant news articles and letters to the editor in the St. Paul *Pioneer Press,* an article on the coverage in the *American Journalism Review,* a piece by David Brauer in the city magazine, and numerous interviews.

Unless indicated otherwise in the text, all quotes come from interviews conducted in person on September 29–October 1, 1999, with George Dohrmann, Emilio Garcia-Ruiz, Vicki Growler, and Walker Lundy, and with a staffer at the *Minneapolis Star Tribune* who asked to remain anonymous, or from follow-up interviews via telephone, e-mail, or fax.

Brauer, David. "Before the Fall: Was the *Pioneer Press*'s Gopher Cheating Scoop Carelessly Timed?" *MPLS.ST.PAUL* (May 1999): 28–30.

Robertson, Lori. "Body Slam," *American Journalism Review* **21** (May 1999): 52.

Appendix

U Basketball Program Accused of Academic Fraud

GEORGE DOHRMANN, staff writer

At least 20 men's basketball players at the University of Minnesota had research papers, take-home exams or other course work done for them during a five-year period, according to a former office manager in the academic counseling unit who said she did the work.

Four former players, Courtney James, Russ Archambault, Kevin Loge and Darrell Whaley, confirmed that work was prepared for them in possible violation of the student code of conduct and NCAA regulations. Another former player, Trevor Winter, said he was aware of the practice.

James, Archambault and the office manager, Jan Gangelhoff, said knowledge of the academic fraud was widespread.

"These are serious allegations," University of Minnesota President Mark Yudof said Tuesday. "We've called in legal counsel. I want to look into this promptly. But they are just allegations at this point."

Gangelhoff, 50, said that from 1993 to 1998 she estimates she did more than 400 pieces of course work for players, including some starters on the 1996–97 Final Four team.

"They bring in these high-risk kids, and they know that everything they did in high school was done for them," Gangelhoff said. "It's got to stop somewhere."

Gangelhoff said she "struggled for a long time" whether to disclose the allegations. When asked to prove them, Gangelhoff provided the *Pioneer Press* with computer files containing more than 225 examples of course work for 19 players, dating to 1994, that she says she wrote and players turned in. Gangelhoff said she kept only about half her files.

Gangelhoff also provided printed copies of five pieces of course work that she said had been turned in by students. Some of the papers had grades and instructor's comments written on them. All five pieces also appeared in Gangelhoff's computer files.

Elayne Donahue, the retired head of the academic counseling unit, said she was unaware of the fraud but warned athletic department administrators that the office manager was tutoring players in violation of department policy and was ignored.

Coach Clem Haskins, interviewed briefly at his hotel in Seattle where the Gophers play Gonzaga in the first round of the NCAA tournament on Thursday, said the allegations were "news to me."

"I've been here 13 years, don't you know me, what I stand for as a man, as a person? I haven't changed," Haskins said. "All I'm trying to do is win a game. All I'm worrying about is beating Gonzaga. It's all I'm concentrating on. All I'll say is I will talk when the tournament is over."

Haskins referred all further comment to McKinley Boston, the vice president of student development and athletics, who questioned the credibility of Gangelhoff's allegations.

"Some of her current allegations seem to be inconsistent with statements she made in the past," he said. "We've had similar allegations made by others [about Gangelhoff], but this is new stuff."

Two former players denied Gangelhoff's allegation that she did work for them. Jermaine Stanford and Ryan Wolf said they completed all their own assignments. Three former players, Micah Watkins, Voshon Lenard and Hosea Crittenden, refused comment. Bobby Jackson said he and Gangelhoff did the work on the papers, with Gangelhoff typing them.

Gangelhoff said she did work for four players on this year's team: Kevin Clark, Miles Tarver, Antoine Broxsie and Jason Stanford. Clark and Tarver refused comment at their Seattle hotel Thursday night. Broxsie and Stanford were not made available for comment by school officials.

Normally, under the team's media policy, all inquiries for player interviews must be directed through school officials.

Five other former players could not be reached for comment.

When asked how he knew players were getting papers done, Winter, who graduated with a degree in business, attended the Carlson School of Management and now plays for the Timberwolves, said it was "common knowledge. It was just one of those things. It was unfortunate.

"If you know your teammate's getting help, if you know that somebody's helping with papers, you just [have the attitude that] 'I don't want to get involved in it.' It's like if you have a friend that's a convicted felon. You don't go around telling everybody he's a convicted felon. You just kind of let it go. It's him. It's his life. It's his choices. It's not me."

The *Pioneer Press* investigation also found these allegations:

- Gangelhoff said she was caught doing a take-home exam with Loge in November 1996 but was allowed to continue to work with players. Loge, who left the program because he wanted to play for a smaller school, confirmed the incident.

- Gangelhoff and two players, Archambault and James, said an assistant coach drove the players to Gangelhoff's Minneapolis home for tutoring sessions, a possible violation of NCAA rules. Archambault was dismissed from the team in February 1998 for rules violations, and James chose to turn pro instead of serving a season-long suspension after being convicted of fifth-degree assault in August 1997.

- Gangelhoff said she often had different players turn in the same paper for different classes, or she used excerpts from one paper in another. An analysis of the documents provided to the *Pioneer Press* revealed seven instances of duplication, including one paper that Gangelhoff said was turned in by three different players for three different classes.

- Donahue, the academic counseling chief, denied a request to allow Gangelhoff to tutor Broxsie last spring after she had been approved to tutor him during the winter quarter. But Gangelhoff said that Haskins paid her $3,000 in cash to continue tutoring the player.

    "Clem Haskins absolutely denies any payment to Jan Gangelhoff for this purpose, or any other," Yudof said. "I think the world of Clem Haskins."

    Gangelhoff said Haskins paid her in cash and that after spending $1,000 to pay bills, she deposited the rest. When asked by the *Pioneer Press* for proof, she provided a bank statement showing she deposited $2,000 on June 29. But the statement did not indicate whether the amount had been deposited in cash.

- Gangelhoff said she never was asked by a member of the coaching staff to do course work for players but said she considered it compensation when she was taken on trips to two road games, including accompanying the team when it played at the Big Island Invitational in Hawaii in the 1995–96 season. "Why else do you think I got to go to some of the places I did?" said Gangelhoff, who said she also attended team banquets and parties for the selection of the NCAA tournament field.

    Boston said he was unaware Gangelhoff had gone to Hawaii.

    "That's a new one on me," he said. "You will have to ask Haskins why he invited her along."

    A request Monday to interview athletic director Mark Dienhart; Alonzo Newby, the team's academic counselor; and Chris Schoemann, the school's NCAA compliance director, was ignored by the school's sports information staff. And phone messages left for Newby and Schoemann were not returned.

- Gangelhoff said some of the first papers she wrote were edited by Newby and former assistant coach Milton Barnes, now the head coach at Eastern Michigan University. Barnes, reached by telephone, denies the allegation.

    "Coach Barnes would read them and say things like: 'Now, is this something so and so would say?' And if it wasn't, I would go back and rewrite it to make it sound more like something the player would write," Gangelhoff said.

    Barnes said: "I don't know anything about it. I don't recall anything like that. She may have me confused with somebody else, that's all I can say."

Boston said the school has self-reported one potential NCAA violation involving Gangelhoff.

On Oct. 26, Dienhart sent Gangelhoff a letter disassociating her from the program even though she had left the school the previous summer.

In the letter, obtained by the *Pioneer Press,* Dienhart wrote that the school had "recently reviewed activities in the men's basketball academic counseling unit." It said the action against her had been "reviewed and approved" by the NCAA.

Gangelhoff said after she received the letter, "I came to the conclusion that something has to change" and she decided to make the allegations public.

An NCAA official denied comment about the letter.

"There was reason to question her based on one incident that came to our attention," said Boston, who refused to give further details about the incident. "Our NCAA compliance officer [Schoemann] investigated her and basically determined that in one particular instance there was an allegation that was valid. We self-reported that one violation to the NCAA. But beyond what was determined in that one particular investigation, everything she is alleging is new information."

Gangelhoff said Schoemann questioned her twice about possible violations, but otherwise her actions went unchecked. Her first meeting with Schoemann came after Gangelhoff was caught helping Loge look up answers for a take-home exam during study table in the Bierman Athletic Building.

Loge, now attending Fergus Falls Community College, confirmed that Gangelhoff helped him look up the answers and admitted as much to Schoemann. Gangelhoff told Schoemann she helped Loge but claimed that she was unaware it was a take-home exam and that she couldn't help him. Gangelhoff said she was never reprimanded or questioned further about the incident. Loge said he was not disciplined for the incident. Gangelhoff said Schoemann confronted her again a few months later and asked whether she was tutoring basketball players.

"I lied," Gangelhoff said. "And those were the only two times I was questioned."

Archambault said he never was questioned by Schoemann, and James said he was questioned once but lied to Schoemann.

"He asked if Jan did papers. Of course, I said no," James said. "At that time, I didn't want to get Jan in trouble. And, at the same time, I didn't want to get coach Haskins in trouble."

Gangelhoff said when she left the university she never intended to reveal that she did course work for players. But the letter of disassociation angered her, she says, because she never was asked to give her side of the story.

"You look at other programs that are successful that have strong academics, and why can't [Minnesota] have that?" she said. "What are we doing wrong that we can't get these kids to learn? . . . Something has to change or [Minnesota] will continue to bring kids in and then throw them away."

Gangelhoff said she did the course work to help academically at-risk athletes she thought were unprepared for college. Academic services' policy forbids front-office personnel from working with student-athletes. But Gangelhoff, an American Indian, said she felt a particular bond with African-American student-athletes.

"The big thing was that they trusted me. I was like a mother figure to them," Gangelhoff said. "My sisters and I, we treated them like family. We had dinners for them. We exchanged Christmas and birthday presents. And I always praised them."

As office manager, Gangelhoff worked for Donahue. But she said Newby was aware of her tutoring activities.

Gangelhoff said Newby arranged players' schedules so that they took courses with her or courses that she had already completed. Gangelhoff took classes from 1993 to '95 while employed full time as office manager. She received her degree in 1995 in InterCollege Program, a self-designed degree program offered by University College.

Gangelhoff was in the same 1994 class with players Winter, Lenard, Crittenden and Jayson Walton.

"We were in the same class, and, miraculously, we were in the same work group," Gangelhoff said. "I wrote the research paper [on alcoholism among American Indian youth]."

Winter said: "It was a group thing, a group project. She's American Indian. She had a lot more input than the rest of us did. She was a member of the group. It was all above board. . . . That was four years ago. Who knows [the truth] if I say I did 95 percent of the work and she just proofed it. . . . She may have proofed it. She may have written the whole thing. I honestly can't tell you what everyone's contribution was. . . . In groups, somebody does do most of the work."

James and Archambault said members of the coaching staff were aware that Gangelhoff was doing course work for players.

"The coaches knew. Everybody [in the basketball program] knew," Archambault said. "We used to make jokes about it. . . . I would go over there some night and get like four papers done. The coaches would be laughing about it."

James said, "Everybody knew we were going to see Jan."

Although Archambault said Haskins was aware of the practice, Winter said the coach may not have known.

"Clem is the basketball coach," Winter said. "When it comes to academics, there are coaches he puts in charge. If something is against the rules, he honestly, from me to you, has nothing to do with it. If there's things going on, he doesn't want to know about it. So, he has that buffer."

The buffers, he said, were assistant coaches and academic advisers.

Instead of the common practice of tutoring players at the Bierman Athletic Building, Gangelhoff said, she did most of her work at home. She said she drove players to her house or assistant coaches did. Archambault and James confirmed they got rides from an assistant coach, a possible NCAA violation. Under the NCAA's extra-benefits rule, athletes are not allowed services unavailable to other students.

Donahue said she heard from one of her employees that a coach was driving two players to Gangelhoff's home in the spring quarter of 1998, when she was no longer approved to tutor. She said she passed that information on to Dienhart and Schoemann but said that to the best of her knowledge, no investigation took place. Gangelhoff said she never was questioned during that period or since she stopped tutoring last June.

Once in the home, Gangelhoff said the players would either sit next to her as she typed the course work or be in an adjacent room.

"It depended on what we needed to do," Gangelhoff said. "If it was a [homework] assignment and they had been to class, we would talk about what happened in class and what they heard and what they thought about the assignment. And then, they would grab the remote and go watch TV, and I would type [the assignment] up.

"On the research papers, we would rarely meet. They would just give me the assignment and I would do it and then they would pick it up. Sometimes I would read the papers to them and explain them to them just in case they got asked in class about them."

Archambault said: "I thought I was going to actually learn how to write a paper. I never learned in high school. But then I sat down and she just started typing."

Bobby Jackson said Gangelhoff's primary role for him was as a typist, which is also a possible violation of the NCAA extra-benefits rule. Gangelhoff's files turned over to the *Pioneer Press* show 28 papers under Jackson's name.

"She definitely helped me out," said Jackson, who also plays for the Timberwolves. "She didn't totally do all the papers for me. . . . When we were on the road, of course we needed help. She did the typing. Once we got everything arranged, she did the typing. I'm not going to say she sat down and totally wrote the paper by herself. No. I was doing my papers myself, with the research and everything. At some point in time, she was finding books for us and stuff. Never a point in time she wrote my paper for me."

Winter said he understands why Gangelhoff's work became so prolific.

"I think it was more of a fact of laziness than it was of people really needing the help or really cheating to get by," he said. "During the season it really gets to be a wear. Not to sound like a pampered athlete—and I did the work—some people lose concentration. They miss a class here and there when on the road and get behind a little bit.

"It's easier to say, 'Will you help me do this class?' or 'Will you help me get this paper done?' than actually putting in the work. I would say the help the players got was more due to laziness than it was due to the fact they couldn't actually do the work."

Donahue said she was not surprised to learn from the *Pioneer Press* last week of Gangelhoff's allegations that she did course work for players.

"I believe anything is possible with Clem," she said. "But I am surprised by how widespread [the allegations are]."

Donahue said she suspected Gangelhoff was working with basketball players in violation of department policy but did not know she was doing course work.

"I believed she was tutoring, but because I didn't know where she was doing this, I had no proof," Donahue said.

Donahue described her relationship with Haskins as "strained" and said the two often disagreed on Newby's roles and whether Newby should have reported to her. While still at the university, Donahue said she was hesitant to make accusations against Newby and Haskins for that reason.

"There was a difference of philosophies. . . . I believed that [basketball players] should do their homework," Donahue said. "I believe they are in college to become educated. And I worked toward supporting students so they could earn a degree. My understanding of [the basketball program] was that you enabled students to become irresponsible. 'It's OK to have someone else do the work.'"

By the spring quarter, Gangelhoff had moved back in with family in Wisconsin. But she continued to do course work, often driving from Wisconsin weekly to meet with players at her sister's home in Minneapolis. But she stopped tutoring because Newby never asked her to continue working with players during the summer, and she began a new job in August.

"It just sort of fizzled out," she said.

Gangelhoff substantiated her claim of writing the papers by pointing out that she often duplicated work or had different players turn in the same paper for different classes.

Gangelhoff said that one of the papers she produced, a 2,000-word essay comparing Martin Luther King Jr. to Malcolm X, was turned in by three players.

"I did that all the time," Gangelhoff said. "Different courses meant different professors so they wouldn't know. I would turn in papers I had written for my classes or take parts of one paper that I used for one player and put in a paper for another player."

In the papers supplied to the *Pioneer Press,* Gangelhoff at times wrote first-person essays for players. Gangelhoff said she tired of writing papers by the end of her tenure and wrote primarily about topics that interested her.

Among the 1998 work Gangelhoff turned over to the *Pioneer Press* were papers she said players turned in on the menstrual cycle, women's gains in the workplace and eating disorders. Two papers referred to the plight of the same woman, a one-time employee at US West, and in one of those she identifies the woman as her sister, Jeanne Payer.

Payer also tutored Archambault, Walton and Wolf, Gangelhoff said. Payer was approved to tutor by Donahue, who said she was unaware at the time of her hiring that Payer was Gangelhoff's sister. Payer could not be reached for comment, but Gangelhoff said Payer also did course work for the athletes in violation of NCAA rules during the 1997–98 school year.

Gangelhoff asked that Payer, who is ill, not be contacted.

"Alonzo [Newby] needed help. I needed help, and Jeanne was unemployed at the time," Gangelhoff said. "I said to Alonzo, 'Hire Jeanne,' and he thought that was an excellent idea."

Archambault said: "In the two years I was there, I never did a thing. Either Jan or Jeanne did everything."

Staff writers Judith Yates Borger, Kris Pope, Bob Sansevere and Jeff Seidel contributed to this report.

We Ran Story When It Was Ready

WALKER LUNDY, editor

Good morning.

I'm writing this mid-week column in response to a number of readers who called or e-mailed us Wednesday to complain about the timing of The Story.

The simple truth is we ran the story when it was ready to run. With my hand on the Bible, it's not any more complicated than that.

We didn't run it in order to "take the pleasure of these young people, who have worked so hard to get to that tournament," as Gov. Jesse Ventura snapped to the Capitol press corps. Heck, he doesn't even know me. How could he know if I was that despicable?

Nor did we run it so the Gophers would lose their first-round game, as another reader suggested. Basketball is my sport. I LOVE the game. When the Gophers made their Final Four run, I lived and died in front of my television, rooting for the Gophers. My wife makes jokes when I yell at the TV set. I'll be keeping one eye on the TV in my office when they take the court against Gonzaga this afternoon. Personally, I want them to win. But when I swap my fan's hat for my editor's hat, I can't be a homer.

The third accusation was that we ran the story to sell papers. Well, we do like to sell papers, but if we had wanted to maximize sales, we would have held the story until Sunday when our circulation—and price—is the highest.

The simple truth is we ran the story when it was ready to run. Here's the background:

In December, a source of sportswriter George Dohrmann's introduced him to Jan Gangelhoff, a former office manager at the University of Minnesota's academic counseling center. She gave him a copy of a confidential letter from Mark Dienhart, director of men's athletics at the university, that said the university was "disassociating" itself from her. It offered no further explanation.

Sports Editor Emilio Garcia-Ruiz's curiosity was piqued. He instructed Dohrmann to pursue the matter. Three months later, after more than two dozen interviews with Ms. Gangelhoff, Dohrmann didn't have a story yet. He wanted proof of her allegations.

Finally, a week ago Saturday, she produced a handful of computer disks with copies of hundreds of term papers she said she wrote for Gophers basketball players. She also had some original papers marked with grades and instructor's comments that matched papers on the computer disks. But Dohrmann still didn't have a story.

Another key interview had to be with Elayne Donahue, a retired counseling director at the university. She was out of the country until last Wednesday.

Dohrmann interviewed her when she returned. By week's end, we were ready to start trying to contact the 20 former and current players who were implicated and to get the university's side of the story.

That process began Monday. Garcia-Ruiz asked an athletic department spokesman to arrange interviews with top officials from the department. The spokesman called back to say no one would be available until Tuesday morning.

The officials were still unavailable Tuesday morning. Around midday, they flew to Seattle with the team for today's game. By late Tuesday, we had reached every player we could find. Some confirmed Ms. Gangelhoff's allegations, some denied them, others declined comment, and we couldn't find a few. Having given the athletic department officials two days to respond, we made the decision Tuesday afternoon to go with the story. Later that day we did get comment from university President Mark Yudof, Vice President for Athletics and Student Development McKinley Boston and finally basketball coach Clem Haskins.

For Dohrmann, they were the last pieces of a complex reporting puzzle involving multiple interviews with more than 10 sources and examinations of hundreds of term papers, take-home exams and other course work. After multiple edits and rewrites and a read by our attorney, Paul Hannah, the story was finally ready. As I have said a hundred times since Wednesday morning:

The simple truth is we ran the story when it was ready to run. Should we have taken the advice of Ventura, who declared us "despicable" for publishing the story Wednesday?

We had three other options:

1. Run the story a few weeks earlier before Dohrmann had done the lengthy, meticulous reporting job. Any votes for that one?

2. Simply kill the story outright, as at least two readers I talked to suggested. If you like this option, you'd probably be happier reading a different kind of newspaper than the *Pioneer Press.*

3. Hold the story until the Gophers lost, thus not hurting their chances to bring honor and glory to the state's most prestigious university with a big-time college basketball victory.

Of the three options, this was the most popular among those readers, like the governor, who questioned our motives. The problem with this solution is that it would be unethical. You may argue that the story may affect the outcome of today's game. But holding the story to help the home team also may affect the outcome of the game. That's unfair to the other team, which would be playing a team that may have ineligible players. We would also hear from another segment of readers who would say we sat on the story because we were homers. And they would be right.

I know my argument won't fly with some Gophers fans who have blinders on. They just want the home team to win no matter what. They may have forgotten the real purpose of a university.

The simple truth is we ran the story when it was ready to run.

One final point: I didn't mind being called despicable by a man who doesn't know anything about me, but I would have felt better if the governor of Minnesota had also managed to squeeze in a comment or two about how academic fraud isn't a good idea, either.

Of course, he's also the governor who, on his first day in office, had this advice for an overflow student crowd on the University of Minnesota campus:

"Win if you can.

"Lose if you must.

"But always cheat."

Readers Respond in Droves to U Story

NANCY CONNER, reader advocate

"It's great that you published the story, but not at that time—that's why the Gophers lost," Jed Otteson said Thursday.

He was among hundreds of readers reacting to allegations published Wednesday and Thursday in the *Pioneer Press* about academic fraud in the University of Minnesota men's basketball program. Although many made it clear they wouldn't condone cheating, the majority of callers protested the timing of the breaking news, one day before the team played its first game in the NCAA tournament.

"After what you guys did to the Gophers and the timing of that article—which did not have to come out this week—it will be an 80-degree day in January before I read your paper again unless you make a public apology on the front page," said a nurse named Julie, who added that most patients at her hospital agreed with her.

The newspaper's circulation department reported late Thursday afternoon that 197 readers canceled their subscriptions over the two days in protest.

More than 220 readers called the newsroom to discuss the stories. Editor Walker Lundy also received 250 e-mail messages, and another 185 readers sent e-mail messages to the reader advocate address.

"This story could have been broken after the season without any problem," Denny Smith of St. Cloud, Minn., said. "It's not a fair thing to do to kids who have worked hard all their life to play in the NCAA tournament."

Others voiced support, including this e-mail Wednesday:

"Your piece on today's front page deserves the attention it is about to receive. Good reporting, good writing—a solid news story about something that is important to the community. Kudos to George Dohrmann and his bosses for printing news."

St. Paul Pioneer Press, March 12, 1999, page 6A. Copyright © 1999 PioneerPlanet/St. Paul (Minnesota) *Pioneer Press*. All rights reserved.

Because of the unusually high volume of messages, it will take several days to respond to each person who wants to discuss the newspaper's decision and the stories.

Readers can join an online discussion about the allegations by clicking on the PioneerPlanet's Water Cooler on www.pioneerplanet.com.

If you would like your comments to reach a wider audience, you can submit a letter to the editor to be considered for publication on the *Pioneer Press* Opinion Pages.

Can't Anybody Around Here Take a Joke?

GARY GILSON, executive director, Minnesota News Council

Based on complaints the News Council has received in recent months, some people can't, and won't. They say that jokes are usually made at someone's expense, and they don't want to pay the freight with their hurt feelings.

Based on your personal standard, would you publish or not publish the following cartoons?

Example: *Pioneer Press* editorial cartoonist Kirk Anderson's comment on the University of Minnesota basketball team's academic-cheating scandal. It showed black ballplayers on the court, with white men in the stands saying, "Of course, we don't let them learn to read or write!"

THE PLANTATION

A lot of black people took offense, saying that plenty of blacks, including athletes, read and write very well, and that the cartoon perpetuated a stereotype. The City of St. Paul's human rights commissioner even asked for a review board to screen cartoons for racial sensitivity before publication.

Others said they saw Anderson's cartoon (as he intended it to be seen) as indicting whites who exploit black athletes by taking so much of their time for sports that they have little or no time to study.

Example: A *Minnesota Daily* "Humor Issue" article fabricated a story of an assault on a foreign teaching assistant by a frustrated student. An angry reader said it was "reprehensible to suggest that violent anger is the proper response to someone's difficulties in speaking English."

Others saw humor in the spoof story because they recognized a truth: the frustration of many students whose education depends upon T.A.'s who may be academically gifted, but cannot speak English very well and thus can't communicate.

Example: An outstate weekly newspaper regularly ran a freelance column that included Ole and Lena jokes, making Scandinavians the butt of stories about ethnically based stupidity. A subscriber, whose ancestors were Norwegian, complained.

Others we spoke with, mostly people of Scandinavian extraction, liked the jokes and wanted more.

That seems to be crucial, according to a seasoned professional in the hurt-feelings business. Mort Ryweck, retired director of the Jewish Community Relations Council (JCRC), says acceptable use of ethnic humor depends upon the setting, the intent, the teller, the listener and the current climate. Is it hostile? Friendly?

Ryweck's successor, Jay Tcath, recently resigned from JCRC and starting a similar job in Chicago, asks: Are there rules, or guidelines—for example, "Don't make fun of people based on their ethnic, religious or physical description"—to which there may be exceptions? Has the group being targeted been historically and brutally victimized?

If the teller is a newspaper columnist, such as the late Chicagoan Mike Royko, who took tongue-in-cheek pokes at Poles, drunks and Chicago politicians and newspapermen, Tcath says, "Give him a pass."

If we don't give some jokes a little leeway, says Tcath, "How can we have a culture that is engaging, humorous and self-critical, without homogenizing the society?"

That argument doesn't satisfy the complainant in the Ole and Lena case. He says those jokes put down Norwegians, and he sees no excuse for it. The columnist who wrote those jokes has now stopped, and the complainant is happy, but a lot of readers and the publisher are not. They liked to laugh, even at their own expense. Obviously, they didn't think the expense was too great.

I recently met an Indian woman who has one of the best dispositions of any human being I've ever known. I told her about a journalism class I once taught where a majority of the students were black. One day a few of them turned to the only Indian student in the class and said they'd never heard Indian humor. Would he give them an example? He did:

An Indian was dancing around a hole in the ice on Lake Superior, swigging whisky and chanting, "Ho-ho-ho-ho-ho, four," "Ho-ho-ho-ho-ho, four," and he spotted a Finlander watching him with great curiosity. The Indian waved to the Finlander to join him, and he kept passing the bottle back and forth as they danced around the hole in the ice.

"Ho-ho-ho-ho-ho, four," the Indian chanted, over and over, until the Finlander drank so much that he fell into the hole and disappeared forever under the ice. The Indian went on dancing, now chanting, "Ho-ho-ho-ho-ho, five!"

My new Indian friend howled at the joke. She howled because for a change the Indian, a representative of a historically brutalized group, came out on top.

Ah, but what about the Finns?

Years ago, when so-called Polish jokes flooded the United States, an enterprising researcher decided to ask residents of Poland what they thought of Polish jokes. The Poles were baffled; they said they had not heard of Polish jokes. So someone told them a few. "Aha!" said the Poles, "You mean the Czech jokes."

To paraphrase Gilda Radner, "It's always somebody."

If a joke teller exerts power over the butt of the joke, and uses the joke to maintain his power, the joke teller is out of line and should be confronted. Nat Hentoff, the journalist and civil libertarian, says the best antidote to bad speech is not censorship, but more speech. I agree. How about you?

——5——

The Massacre in El Mozote

STANLEY MEISLER

EDITORS' NOTE

In 1981 the *Washington Post* and the *New York Times* both reported a massacre in the village of El Mozote, El Salvador, by the Salvadoran army, which had been trained in antiguerrilla warfare by the U.S. military. Both stories were based on one-sided information and were largely disputed by the U.S government.

Veteran foreign correspondent and author Stanley Meisler reported internationally for the *Los Angeles Times* from 1967 to 1998, during which time he covered Africa, Madrid, Mexico City, much of Latin America, Toronto, Paris, and the United Nations. Currently he contributes to various magazines, including *Smithsonian* and *Foreign Affairs*.

Meisler writes this case from the perspective of the reporters and the editors who wrote the El Mozote massacre stories. The narrative examines the journalistic responsibilities of information gathering and verification involved in reporting the story when you have access to only one side.

In particular, the case explores whether the reporters took the right steps to acquire the most accurate information. And how would you as an editor verify the story before running it and then deliver it to your readers?

These issues of one-sided information arise not only in covering tense foreign affairs like El Mozote but also in covering all kinds of sensitive stories, especially those in which one side is at fault or refuses to provide any information.

In 1981, at the height of the cold war, the new Reagan Administration rushed arms and funds to the army of El Salvador in a determined campaign to prevent the country from falling to leftist rebels the way Nicaragua had fallen during the Carter Administration. Sensing the whiff of a possible new Vietnam, editors assigned correspondents and stringers there to find out what was going on. Watching the rebels in action was an obvious story, and American reporters repeatedly asked leftist contacts in the capital of San Salvador and elsewhere to arrange for them to travel with the revolutionary guerrillas. "As I remember it," says Ray Bonner of the *New York Times*, "I wanted to go in with the guerrillas. I think every reporter down there wanted to go in with the guerrillas. How could you not want to go in with the guerrillas?"

Both Bonner and Alma Guillermoprieto, a stringer for the *Washington Post*, had received separate invitations from the guerrillas in December 1981 to enter Morazán, a province in northeastern El Salvador largely under rebel control. But the rebels called off the visits before the two reporters arrived. The Salvadoran army was mounting a massive offensive against the guerrillas in Morazán. This was not the time for the guerrillas to entertain foreign correspondents.

Soon after New Year's Day 1982, Bonner, back in New York, received word from the rebels that they were extending the invitation once more. He and free-lance photographer Susan Meiselas, who had won international acclaim for her photographs of the Nicaraguan civil war, prepared to fly to Honduras to enter Morazán together.

New York Times and *Washington Post* reporters regard themselves as competitors. But dangerous assignments like coverage of the wars in Central America foster camaraderie among foreign correspondents. Just before departing New York, Bonner phoned Guillermoprieto in Mexico City.

"Ray said he would hate himself for telling me," she recalls, "but he finally said he was going in."

Guillermoprieto was shocked. No one had reached her to reinstate her invitation. "I got beserk," she says. She sought help from Mexican journalists who had contacts with the guerrillas in Morazán. Those contacts had helped her set up the aborted trip in December. "I picked up all the threads," she says. Three days after Bonner had telephoned, she received word from the guerrillas that they would allow her, too, into their territory. Guillermoprieto flew to Honduras, relieved yet fretful about Bonner's head start.

Neither correspondent had had much news experience in those days. Bonner, then 39, was a former Marine officer, San Francisco lawyer, assistant district attorney, Nader's Raider and law instructor who had decided a few years earlier to seek a career in journalism. He had set out for Latin America and, as he puts it, "started bumming around." As a free lance he attracted attention at the *New York Times* with some dispatches from Bolivia. The *Times* soon found itself shorthanded in Central America because its veteran Mexico City correspondent, Alan Riding, had received death threats from right-wing extremists in both El Salvador and Guatemala. Bonner, having asked to string in those two countries, arrived in San Salvador just before Salvadoran national guardsmen, acting under orders from above, executed four American nuns near the airport in early December 1981.

"I got there on Sunday, the nuns were killed on Tuesday," he says, "and the rest is history." Within a month, the *Times* hired him as a reporter. He was assigned to the metro staff in New York but spent most of the year on loan to the foreign desk, heading in and out of Central America.

Guillermoprieto, then 32, was not yet a staff reporter for any publication. During the last two and a half years, she had worked as a stringer for a London newsletter, for the *Guardian,* and, since mid-1981, for the *Washington Post.* Operating out of Mexico City, where she had been born and raised, Guillermoprieto was able to speak and write both English and Spanish fluently.

The editors had no hesitation about approving the trips into rebel territory. Bonner says he received "the usual caution: 'We don't want you to do this if you don't think it's safe. Be careful, etcetera, etcetera.'" But Bonner had no intention of canceling his trip out of fear. Bonner, in fact, had long ago shrugged off the fears of working in the city of San Salvador. Despite the obvious hatred of him by right-wing extremists, he would jog by himself every morning. "I used to say they would never kill a *New York Times* reporter," he recalls. "Then I'd think, 'Wait a minute. They killed four nuns. Why do I say that?'"

Like Alan Riding of the *Times,* Guillermoprieto no longer traveled to San Salvador because of right-wing death threats. But she does not recall discussing safety when she talked about the impending trip to guerrilla territory with Jim Hoagland, the assistant managing editor for foreign news, and Karen De Young, the foreign editor. In Guillermoprieto's mind, there was simply no question that the story was worth the risks involved. Though she might find herself in extreme danger, she understood that these were the rules of the game. She does recall asking whether the *Post* would pay for her gear as well as her airfare. "I was a stringer," she said. "Stringers get treated like dirt." The *Post* agreed to pay for her gear.

ON THE SCENE

Reports of a massacre by the Salvadoran army were spreading before Bonner and Guillermoprieto entered Morazán. The Rev. William L. Wipfler, the director of the human rights office of the National Council of Churches in New York, telegraphed U.S. Ambassador Deane Hinton for "confirmation or otherwise" of the reports of a massacre. He also left a message for Bonner in the

Mexico City office of the *New York Times*. The message never reached Bonner. Radio Venceremos, the voice of the rebels, which had shut down during the government offensive, resumed broadcasting in late December and issued its first massacre account—a highly emotional one—on Christmas Eve. Salvadoran President José Napoléon Duarte, in a national broadcast a week later, denounced the massacre story as "a guerrilla trick."[1]

Despite these public accusations and counteraccusations, Bonner and Guillermoprieto, outside El Salvador at the time, were so preoccupied with making arrangements to enter Morazán that neither recalls knowing anything about the massacre before meeting the guerrillas. Bonner and Meiselas checked into the Maya Hotel in Tegucigalpa, Honduras. Their instructions were to go to a designated coffee shop and look for a contact carrying a copy of *Time* magazine. They found him not in the coffee shop but wandering on the road nearby. The contact led them by car on January 3 to a mountainous area near the border of El Salvador. "We removed our trousers, then held our shoes above our heads while crossing a wide river," Bonner would write a few years later. "I was scared. I flashed back so many years earlier, to when I had been in Vietnam and how patrols were ambushed at night. Our Salvadoran escorts were so poorly armed . . . that I knew they would be no match for an army patrol."[2] There would be three night marches before they reached rebel-controlled territory.

Guillermoprieto checked in at the Maya Hotel a few days later. While waiting two days for an escort, she walked up and down the hills of Tegucigalpa in what she now calls "a desperate attempt to get into shape." She later followed the same arduous and dangerous route as Bonner and Meiselas, with escorts resentful that they had to endanger themselves by guiding a third journalist. Fording the wide river in her bikini underwear bottom, she slipped, ruining her camera and damaging her pack.[3] After three nights of walking, she came to a rebel camp where Bonner and Meiselas were waiting to take the route back to Honduras.

"They were going out as I was coming in," she says. "I was jealous and envious and enraged about being scooped. But I didn't realize they had the story." After talking with Bonner, in fact, she felt better, for he seemed excited about seeing the guerrillas in combat. "I was interested in seeing how their society was organized," she says. "I wasn't that interested in combat."

On her first day in rebel territory, the guerrillas led her to El Mozote and nearby villages. Guillermoprieto came upon awful sights that had shocked Bonner and Meiselas a few days earlier. The "sickly sweet smell of decomposing bodies"[4] permeated the air.

BODIES IN THE RUBBLE

The two American journalists and the American photographer saw dozens of bodies beneath the rubble of the village and lying in nearby fields. They found little bodies in dresses rotting in the charred ruins of adobe houses. The village church was in ruins. An array of bones lay in the burned sacristy. Skulls, rib cages, femurs, a spinal column, and countless other pieces of bone poked out of rubble. They found charred bones in two of the burned houses of the village. These scenes, photographed by Meiselas, would appear in the *Washington Post* and the Sunday magazine of the *New York Times*. "By the end of the day," says Guillermoprieto, "I realized that something untoward and unspeakable had taken place."

In a nearby refugee camp, Guillermoprieto, like Bonner, interviewed Rufina Amaya, the sole survivor of the El Mozote massacre. Guillermoprieto also interviewed two survivors from attacks on other villages. Aside from these eyewitnesses, she interviewed a dozen other civilians, who told her that their relatives had been killed by the Salvadoran soldiers. In all, Bonner said, he interviewed thirteen peasants who told him that Salvadoran soldiers had killed their relatives. Both Bonner and Guillermoprieto were allowed to interview the civilians without the presence of guerrillas. The rebel soldiers also gave the reporters their version of events, and Guillermoprieto said that an American working in the area described what he believed had taken place. Bonner said that he too had met an American, whom he identified as Joe David Sanderson. According to Bonner, Sanderson was killed in combat a few months later.[5] Bonner also received a list from some villagers with the names of 733 peasants killed by the Salvadoran army. Bonner was told that the survivors had compiled the list.

From their separate interviews and observations, Bonner and Guillermoprieto, who did not consult each other afterward, put together more or less the same basic account of what had happened.[6]

In mid-December, a few weeks before the American reporters entered Morazán, the Atlacatl Battalion of the Salvadoran army had destroyed the village of El Mozote, killing almost everyone there. The Atlacatl was an elite, thousand-man battalion trained in counterinsurgency and rapid deployment by U.S. Special Forces military advisers. The Atlacatl, commanded by Lt. Col. Domingo Monterrosa, was taking part in a Salvadoran army search-and-destroy offensive in northern Morazán, an area largely in the hands of the rebels.

The Atlacatl soldiers marched into the village in the late afternoon of December 11. The village had fifteen to twenty mud brick homes around a square, with a church and a small building that served as a kind of sacristy. The villagers did not regard themselves as rebel supporters, and some government soldiers had assured a local businessman that no villager would be harmed if all remained in their homes.

The Atlacatl soldiers, however, pounded on the homes and forced everyone to come out and lie down on the square in the darkness. After an hour and a half, the villagers were allowed to go back into their homes. "We were happy then," Rufina Amaya told Guillermoprieto. "'The repression is over,' we said."[7]

But before dawn the next day, the soldiers forced everyone back into the square. After a few hours of standing, the soldiers separated the men from the women and children and herded the men into the church. The women and children were put into a single home.

The soldiers beat and interrogated the men and then led them blindfolded from the church in small groups. At noon, the soldiers pulled young girls and women out of the house and took them to the hills outside the village, where they raped and killed them. The soldiers returned for the older women, marching them in small groups to another house where soldiers waited to shoot them. Some soldiers hesitated about killing children. But their officers berated them. Amaya told Bonner that she had heard her nine-year-old son scream, "Mama, they're killing me. They've killed my sister. They're going to kill me."[8]

After the carnage, the Atlacatl Battalion burned down the buildings of El Mozote and moved on. Rufina Amaya, who had heard the screams of her husband and other children as they were murdered, managed to slip away. Both before and after the massacre, the soldiers killed civilians in other villages. But no other village suffered a slaughter as massive and as complete as El Mozote. Hundreds of civilians had died.

GUILLERMOPRIETO'S REPORT

Guillermoprieto felt that she had to get her story out right away. It was not so much the fear of being scooped. But she was sure that, if Bonner's story appeared on the front page of the *New York Times* and hers reached the *Post* more than a day later, the editors would cut it and place it inside. "I was desperate," she says. "I was going to lose this story. It was going to be on page 17, four paragraphs." What had happened, she believed, was a monstrosity, and she wanted everyone in Washington to take notice.

After gathering more detail from villagers and guerrillas on the second day, she sat down and wrote the story in closely packed script on seven pages of her notebook. She rolled the pages into a plastic film canister and persuaded a young rebel courier to take it to Tegucigalpa. Her plan to get the copy to the *Post* involved several simple but crucial steps. "Miraculously, it worked," she says. Following her instructions, the courier phoned an American radio journalist in Tegucigalpa. He picked up the canister and, heeding the plea on the handwritten copy, dictated the story to the *Post*.

Guillermoprieto's visit was cut short a few days later when the guerrilla commander informed her that he could no longer guarantee her safety. It was probably time to go anyway. She had banged a leg on a rock, and it was swelling. "When I got back to the Maya Hotel in Tegucigalpa," she says, "I was a nightmare. I had this enormous purple leg. I called the *Post* and asked, 'When did the story run?' And Karen [foreign editor De Young] said we were waiting to talk with you."

This upset Guillermoprieto. She said she felt they didn't believe the story. "Both Jim [assistant managing editor Hoagland] and Karen thought I was overwrought and got too emotional and was too sympathetic to the guerrillas. What happened was so unbelievable that they didn't believe it." There was only one consolation. She had not been scooped by Bonner. No story of his on the massacre had yet run in the *Times*.

The delay in publishing Guillermoprieto's story was less an issue of disbelieving it than of cautious editorial practice. Since De Young had covered the Nicaraguan civil war and other Central American stories as a highly regarded correspondent, she and other *Post* editors were sensitive to the need in Washington to produce full evidence in any story exposing the brutality of the armies of anticommunist dictatorships in the region. Without such evidence, the stories would be dismissed as left-wing propaganda.

Hoagland took the phone to talk with Guillermoprieto. "Jim spent an hour grilling me," she says. "God bless him; he was convinced." As Hoagland recalls the hour-long conversation, "We wanted to go over the details that had to be explained. . . . It was not an unbelievable story to me. But we had to ask the basic question that all editors ask—'How do we know that?'" After the talk, he says, "I was satisfied that we had shown the scope of what we knew." Even though there was a possibility the *Post* would be scooped by Bonner, Hoagland says he had no intention of running the story until he had talked with Guillermoprieto and satisfied himself about the evidence.

The story was heavily edited by De Young. Guillermoprieto, who now writes for the *New Yorker*, says she tends to write at length and take time before getting to the heart of a story. She believes that the first half of her story was incoherent and that De Young used mostly the second half. After conferring with her, De Young and Hoagland inserted a key paragraph. It stated that the rebels had invited her to the province two weeks after their radio station had broadcast reports of the massacre. "It was clear that the guerrillas' purpose was not only to demonstrate their control of the region," the paragraph read, "but also to provide what they said was evidence of the alleged massacre in December." Hoagland says readers need to know "when you are in a situation where you are dependent on your hosts for food and lodging and, in fact, your life."

After her talks with Hoagland and De Young, Guillermoprieto slept for a day. She felt feverish but wrote quickly, finishing her series on life behind guerrilla lines. The story already in the hands of her editors was published in the *Post* on Wednesday, January 27, 1982, with the headline: "Salvadoran Peasants Describe Mass Killing: Woman Tells of Children's Death."

Datelined Mozote, the story began as follows:

> Several hundred civilians, including women and children, were taken from their homes in and around this village and killed by Salvadoran army troops during a December offensive against leftist guerrillas, according to three survivors who say they witnessed the alleged massacres.
>
> Reporters taken to tour the region and speak to survivors by guerrilla soldiers, who control large areas of Morazán Province, were shown the rubble of scores of adobe houses they and the survivors said were destroyed by the troops in the now deserted village community. Dozens of decomposing bodies still were seen beneath the rubble and lying in nearby fields, despite the month that has passed since the incident.
>
> In Washington, Salvadoran Ambassador Ernesto Rivas Gallont said, "I reject emphatically that the Army of El Salvador" was engaged in "killing women and children. It is not within the armed institutions' philosophy to act like that." He acknowledged that the "armed forces have been active in that part of the country," particularly during a December offensive against the guerrillas, but said that their actions had "definitely not been against the civilian populations."
>
> The survivors, including a woman who said her husband and four of her six children were killed, maintained that no battle was under way during the second week in December when the alleged massacre took place.

BONNER'S REPORT

Although the *Times* had already published the start of the Bonner series, his first article did not discuss the massacre. There was nothing by Bonner to match the Guillermoprieto story in the first edition of the *Times* for that day.

Bonner flew to Mexico City to write his series on life behind guerrilla lines. He did not rush out a story on the massacre but included it as the second piece in his series. He sent it to the *New York Times* as one in a batch of three articles. His fourth would follow. "I was so green and naïve in journalism that I didn't know what I had," he says. "I didn't know what impact it would have."

Craig Whitney, then deputy foreign editor of the *Times,* edited the series. After the first piece was published, he worked on the massacre story and then, much like Hoagland and De Young at the *Post,* set it aside, assuming he could talk with Bonner about it the next day. "The reporting was there," he recalls. "The next step was making sure by asking the obvious questions. How do you know it happened? What is the evidence? How do we know how many people were killed?" But Whitney received a call at home that evening informing him that Guillermoprieto's story had appeared on the front page of the first edition of the *Post.* "I said run the story," says Whitney. "I edited it and talked with Ray on the phone, and it ran. It ran on page one. There was never any doubt that he had the basic facts." Bonner says, "The story probably had a fair amount of editing because it probably needed it. I wasn't an experienced writer at that time."

The story appeared on the front page of the final edition of the *Times* on Wednesday, January 27, the same day that the Guillermoprieto story appeared on the *Post*'s front page. The headline read "Massacre of Hundreds Reported in Salvador Village."

Also datelined Mozote, the *Times* story began as follows:

> From interviews with people who live in this small mountain village and surrounding hamlets, it is clear that a massacre of major proportions occurred here last month.
>
> In some 20 mud brick huts here, this reporter saw the charred skulls and bones of dozens of bodies buried under burned-out roofs, beams and shattered tiles. There were more along the trail leading through the hills into the village, and at the edge of a nearby cornfield were the remains of 14 young men, women and children.
>
> In separate interviews during a two-week period in the rebel-controlled northern part of Morazán Province, 13 peasants said that all these, their relatives and friends, had been killed by Government soldiers of the Atlacatl Battalion in a sweep in December.
>
> *733 Victims Listed*
>
> The villagers have compiled a list of the names, ages and villages of 733 peasants, mostly children, women and old people, who they say were mur-

dered by the Government soldiers. The Human Rights Commission of El Salvador, which works with the Roman Catholic Church, puts the number at 926.

Bonner's story did not have a paragraph like the one in the *Post* story stating that the guerrillas had invited him in so that he could look at the massacre site. But, though almost all the evidence in his story implicated the Salvadoran army as the perpetrators of the massacres, the Bonner story did say, "It is not possible for an observer who was not present at the time of the massacre to determine independently how many people died or who killed them."

Although Bonner was too inexperienced to realize the impact that his story would have in Washington, he now feels that his inexperience was probably an advantage. "I was not journalistically trained," he says. "I wasn't trained in the culture of the *New York Times,* and I wasn't trained even in the culture of journalism. If I did a good job, . . . I sometimes wonder how much of that was because I did not have journalistic training. I think I'd be much more cautious in what I wrote today, and I'm not sure it would be better. . . . I had no idea what the impact of the *New York Times* was. . . . Maybe that was good because I just wrote what I saw."

Guillermoprieto expected the stories to have more of an impact than they did. "I was surprised at the lack of world outrage," she says. "By my standards, what I had hoped for, there was no impact. I felt as if I were in a nightmare when you try to scream and have no voice."

REACTIONS BACK HOME

The stories on the front pages of the two most influential newspapers in the country upset and embarrassed the Reagan Administration. They appeared a day before President Reagan sent Congress his certification that El Salvador was "making a concerted and significant effort to comply with internationally recognized human rights."[9] The certification—required by law as a condition for continued military aid—was ludicrous if the stories were true.

In San Salvador, Ambassador Deane Hinton, who had already assured the National Council of Churches that he had no reason to believe that reports of a massacre were true, sent Todd Greentree, a political officer, and Maj. John McKay, a military attaché, to investigate. Greentree and McKay flew over El Mozote but, since it was in rebel territory, never set foot in it. On the ground, where they were joined by deputy chief of mission Kenneth Bleakley, they interviewed refugees but mainly in the presence of Salvadoran soldiers. The conclusions of the embassy officers, sent to the State Department in a cable over Hinton's signature, were cautiously worded.

"Although it is not possible to prove or disprove excesses of violence against the civilian population of El Mozote," the cable said, "it is certain that the guerrilla forces . . . did nothing to remove them from the path of battle . . . nor is there any evidence that those who remained attempted to leave. Civilians did die during Operation Rescate, but no evidence could be found to confirm that government forces systematically massacred civilians in the operation zone." There was a good deal of ambiguity in the cable, but it clearly blamed the rebels for leaving civilians "in the path of battle."[10] This implied, of course, that they were killed by chance in battle and not by the deliberate actions of bloodthirsty, abusive soldiers.

Citing the investigation by the two embassy officers and repeating the words of the cable, Assistant Secretary of State Thomas O. Enders told both a Senate Foreign Affairs Subcommittee and a House Appropriations Subcommittee a week after publication of the stories that "there is no evidence to confirm that government forces systematically massacred civilians in the operations zone." Enders also said that the number of dead civilians could not possibly have reached Guillermoprieto's estimate of several hundred or Bonner's of five to seven hundred since government records list the population of El Mozote as only three hundred.[11] This ignored the fact that both correspondents had reported that the massacres occurred in more villages than just El Mozote.

The administration's belittling of the news accounts soon led to a right-wing campaign against the reporters, especially Bonner. In an editorial, the *Wall Street Journal*, citing as evidence the paragraph that the *Post* editors had inserted in Guillermoprieto's story, said that Bonner had clearly taken part in "a propaganda exercise" and "there is such a thing as being overly credulous." The presence of the "propaganda" paragraph in the *Post* story deflected the attack from Guillermoprieto, and the *Journal* did not criticize her directly. But that did not mean it believed her account. Much of the American press in El Salvador, according to the *Journal*, was following a Vietnam War style of reporting "in which Communist sources were given greater credence than either the U.S. government or the government it was supporting." But Bonner seemed the main culprit. The editorial accused *Times* editors and reporters who had defended Bonner of "[closing] ranks behind a reporter out on a limb."[12]

The attacks intensified. George Melloan, who had contributed to the editorial, went on the televised *McNeil-Lehrer Report* to say that "obviously Ray

Bonner has a political orientation."[13] The conservative newsletter *Accuracy in Media* castigated Bonner for carrying on "a propaganda war favoring the Marxist guerrillas in El Salvador." Ambassador Hinton, in a breakfast with Washington reporters in June, dismissed Bonner as an "advocate journalist."[14]

The attacks were too furious to be ignored in the *Times* newsroom. "There were all kinds of aspersions on Ray as a person and as a reporter," recalls Craig Whitney, soon promoted to foreign editor. . . . "They [the administration] and their friends were really vicious about Ray and quite unfair. We probably applied more rigorous standards to his stories after then. But criticism makes me contrary and more determined than ever to get the story into the paper."

In August, seven months after the El Mozote stories were published, executive editor A. M. Rosenthal withdrew Bonner from Central America and assigned him to the business section in New York. Rosenthal insisted at the time and continues to maintain today that the relatively inexperienced Bonner needed more training as a journalist and more understanding of the way the *Times* works. The reassignment, however, was interpreted in some journalistic circles as a repudiation of Bonner and a surrender to pressures from the Reagan Administration.

This interpretation infuriates Rosenthal. Citing the *Times'* history of defying Washington—especially its publication of the Pentagon Papers during the Nixon Administration—he retorts, "The *Times* has a pretty good record. Why in God's name should we become whores for Ray Bonner?" He says any suggestion that he punished Bonner for writing the El Mozote story "is a lie."

But Rosenthal, who covered communist Poland as a young foreign correspondent and had a reputation as a tough cold warrior, acknowledges that he may have been worried about Bonner's attitudes toward the Salvadoran government and toward the Salvadoran rebels. "As a matter of fact," he says, "I had doubts about a large part of the press corps." It was no accident that he hired Shirley Christian of the *Miami Herald* as a *Times* correspondent after she wrote an article in the *Columbia Journalism Review* denouncing American reporters for favoring the leftist Sandinista rebels during the Nicaraguan civil war. While the need for training was the primary motive for reassigning Bonner, Rosenthal continues, "I'm not saying we were not worried about his articles. He's a good reporter, but he's not Jesus Christ Almighty."

Bonner agrees that he was not reassigned because of State Department pressure over the El Mozote story. A colleague informed him that Rosenthal told several *Times* editors and reporters at a private meeting, "If I have to choose between Bonner and the State Department, I'll take Bonner." But Bon-

ner believes that Rosenthal regarded communism as a far greater threat to
Central America than brutal, repressive regimes and was troubled by correspondents who spent what Rosenthal regarded as too much time exposing the
tactics of these regimes. Rosenthal, according to Bonner, was probably more
upset by Bonner's favorable view of the Sandinista regime in Nicaragua than
by the El Mozote story. Bonner says that three of his Nicaragua stories were
never published.

The reassignment, however, may have chilled coverage of El Salvador.
Reporters, according to Michael Massing of the *Columbia Journalism Review,*
became "wary of provoking the embassy." "If they can kick out the *Times* correspondent," said one foreign correspondent in San Salvador, "you've got to
be careful."[15] A *New York Times* correspondent heading off to Latin America
told Bonner, "I'm not going to get caught in the same trap that you did." The
whole episode, said another *Times* foreign correspondent, "had an intimidat-
ing effect on the foreign desk."

Bonner took a leave of absence to write a book on El Salvador and then
resigned from the *Times* in 1984. He became a free-lance writer, working
mainly for the *New Yorker.* In the 1990s, after Rosenthal retired as executive editor and began writing a column, Bonner returned to the *Times,* first as a contract writer and then as a staff correspondent assigned to Washington in 1999.

The *Post* rewarded Guillermoprieto by promoting her to a full-time job in
Washington as a reporter. But the promotion did not work out well. "The
whole thing was hexed from the beginning," she says. Her mother took ill and
died within two years. After the excitement of covering Central America, she
had to cover suburban Maryland for the metro desk. Instead of reporting
wars, she had to report on fires breaking out in middle-class American homes.
She felt a kind of culture shock. "It was a complete mismatch," she says.

She also felt "there was a ring of mistrust around me" because of her Salvador stories and the attacks on her by the Reagan Administration. The *Post*
in those days was subject to a continual barrage of criticism from the White
House. "There was tremendous pressure on us during the Reagan Administration," says De Young, the foreign editor. "People in the White House would
complain to high executives at the *Post* about the correspondents covering
Central America. That led to an air of mistrust. You know, if you call someone a leftist often enough, some of it sticks. But, having said that, I cannot
think of a single time that a story was changed or dropped because of pressure from the White House."

In a similar description of the atmosphere, Hoagland, the assistant managing editor, says it was not unusual for some editors to feel suspicious about

the reporting of a correspondent in the field. "It was sort of like what happened in newsrooms during the Vietnam War," he says. "There is a difference between the Washington view, based on what editors hear from officials, and the view of reporters in the field who see the problems and failures of U.S. policy." But Hoagland believes that he defended Guillermoprieto against the doubts of some editors and that he had a duty to defend her. "I defended someone who had risked her life for us and given us a scoop," he says.

After two years, Guillermoprieto won an Alicia Patterson Fellowship for travel in Europe and then accepted a job with *Newsweek* as its Latin American correspondent. She left *Newsweek* in 1987 to write a book and then became a staff writer for the *New Yorker.*

EPILOGUE

Guillermoprieto and Bonner were vindicated eleven years after the publication of their dispatches on the massacres.

As part of the accords that ended the Salvadoran civil war on December 31, 1991, the United Nations Secretary-General appointed a Commission on Truth to record the violations of human rights during the war and identify those responsible. The commission's members were former Colombian president Belisario Betancur as chairman, former Venezuelan foreign minister Reinaldo Figueredo Planchart, and Thomas Buergenthal, an American law professor who had once headed the Inter-American Court for Human Rights.

The commission issued its report in March 1993. In the section on El Mozote, the commissioners concluded that "more than 500 identified victims perished at El Mozote and in the other villages."[16] They added that "many other victims have not been identified" but gave no estimate of their number.

There was "full proof," the commissioners said, that units of the United States–trained Atlacatl Battalion "deliberately and systematically killed . . . the entire civilian population that they had found there." The commission added that there was "sufficient evidence" that the soldiers "massacred the noncombatant civilian population" in several nearby villages both before and after the El Mozote slaughter.

The commission's conclusions were based heavily on the findings of forensic experts. A team of four Argentine forensic anthropologists dug up and examined the bones in El Mozote and then passed the material on to a team of four American doctors in San Salvador for a forensic examination.

The most damning evidence was exhumed in the sacristy. The Argentines found the skeletal remains of 143 bodies there. Of these, 131 were of children under the age of 12. The evidence showed that many of the victims were lying on the ground when shot from above by the killers standing in the door and by the windows. The bullets uncovered were U.S. government ammunition for U.S. military M-16 rifles. The forensic experts concluded that the evidence "confirms the allegations of a mass murder." "There is no evidence to support the contention," the experts went on, "that these victims, almost all young children, were involved in combat or were caught in the crossfire of combat forces." The Commission on Truth condemned the El Mozote massacre as "a serious violation of international humanitarian law and international human rights law."

In all, the Commission on Truth received 22,000 complaints of human rights abuses during the war. In contrast to what the Reagan Administration had insisted about rebel exaggerations and rebel killings, the commissioners said that the victims attributed 85 percent of the abuses to the army and other agents of the state, paramilitary groups allied to the government, and right-wing death squads.

After the Commission on Truth published its report, Secretary of State Warren Christopher appointed a panel—made up of I. M. Destler, a professor at the University of Maryland, and two distinguished former foreign service officers, George S. Vest and Richard W. Murphy—to examine "the activities and conduct" of the State Department during the war.

The panel was generally kind to the State Department. It concluded that "within the parameters of overall U.S. policy, the Department and Foreign Service personnel performed creditably—and on occasion with personal bravery—in advancing human rights in El Salvador." But it did find a few exceptions, and El Mozote was the main one.[17]

The panel criticized Assistant Secretary of State Enders for failing to make clear to Congress that the two U.S. embassy officers had not set foot in El Mozote during their investigation. The department was chastised for going even further than Enders in trying to discredit the Bonner and Guillermo-prieto stories in its correspondence with members of Congress. Although Ambassador Hinton had cabled Washington in February with his suspicion that "something happened that should not have happened and that it is quite possible Salvadoran military did commit excesses," the State Department still insisted in July that it had "no evidence to support allegations of large-scale massacres." That statement went even further than the testimony of Enders that they had no evidence "to confirm" the massacres.

The panel found that the reports of the massacre had clearly called for "an extraordinary effort" by the State Department to investigate what had happened. But none was mounted. "The Embassy does not seem to have been inclined to press," the panel said, "and Washington preferred to avoid the issue and protect its policy then under siege." The panel concluded that U.S. statements on the case were wrong and "undermined the Department's credibility with its critics—and probably with the Salvadorans—in a serious way that has not healed."

DISCUSSION QUESTIONS

1. Did Ray Bonner and Alma Guillermoprieto do an adequate job of covering this story? Were their news accounts fair? Or did they, as the critics insisted, fall under the sway of the rebels and accept their version of events? Would you have written the story differently?

2. Were the editors wise to hold up the stories until the issues could be discussed with the reporters? Did the "disclaimers" that the editors inserted make sense? Would you as an editor have gone further to make the stories more "objective"? What would you have done?

3. Did the editors do an adequate job of defending their reporters? Was A. M. Rosenthal wise to recall Bonner from Central America? Should an editor like Rosenthal—a powerful figure in American journalism—need to consider the impact on other news organizations before making a decision like recalling Bonner?

SOURCES

The information in this case study is based on books, news articles, and personal interviews. The books and articles are cited in the notes. All other quotations are from interviews carried out in October 1999 with Raymond Bonner, Karen De Young, and Jim Hoagland in person and with Alma Guillermoprieto, Susan Meiselas, A. M. Rosenthal, and Craig Whitney by phone.

NOTES

1. Mark Danner, *The Massacre at El Mozote.* New York: Vintage, 1994, pp. 86–89.
2. Raymond Bonner, *Weakness and Deceit: U.S. Policy and El Salvador.* New York: Times Books, 1984, p. 110.
3. Danner, p. 98.
4. Alma Guillermoprieto, "Salvadoran Peasants Describe Mass Killing; Woman Tells of Children's Death," *Washington Post,* January 27, 1982, p. A01.
5. Bonner, *Weakness and Deceit,* pp. 132–33.
6. Guillermoprieto; Raymond Bonner, "Massacre of Hundreds Reported In Salvador Village," *New York Times,* January 27, 1982, p. A1.
7. Guillermoprieto.
8. Bonner, "Massacre of Hundreds."

9. Danner, p. 208.

10. Ibid., pp. 194–201.

11. Barbara Crossette, "U.S. Disputes Report of 926 Killed in El Salvador," *New York Times*, February 2, 1982, p. 1A.

12. Danner, pp. 229–33.

13. Ibid., p. 137.

14. Michael Massing, "About-Face on El Salvador," *Columbia Journalism Review* 22 (November/December 1983): 42–49 (quote on p. 44).

15. Ibid., p. 46.

16. The El Mozote case is covered in *From Madness to Hope: The 12-Year War in El Salvador,* Report of the Commission on Truth in El Salvador, United Nations Security Council Document S/25500, April 1, 1993, pp. 114–26.

17. Danner, pp. 272–78.

Appendix

Massacre of Hundreds Reported in Salvador Village

RAYMOND BONNER, special to the *New York Times*

From interviews with people who live in this small mountain village and surrounding hamlets, it is clear that a massacre of major proportions occurred here last month.

In some 20 mud brick huts here, this reporter saw the charred skulls and bones of dozens of bodies buried under burned-out roofs, beams and shattered tiles. There were more along the trail leading through the hills into the village, and at the edge of a nearby cornfield were the remains of 14 young men, women and children.

In separate interviews during a two-week period in the rebel-controlled northern part of Morazán Province, 13 peasants said that all these, their relatives and friends, had been killed by Government soldiers of the Atlacatl Battalion in a sweep in December.

733 Victims Listed

The villagers have compiled a list of the names, ages and villages of 733 peasants, mostly children, women and old people, who they say were murdered by the Government soldiers. The Human Rights Commission of El Salvador, which works with the Roman Catholic Church, puts the number at 926.

A spokesman for the Salvadoran armed forces, Col. Alfonso Cotto, called the reports about "hundreds of civilians" being killed by Government soldiers "totally false." Those reports were fabricated by "subversives," he said.

It is not possible for an observer who was not present at the time of the massacre to determine independently how many people died or who killed them. In the interviews, the peasants said uniformed soldiers, some swooping in by helicopter, did the shooting. The rebels in this zone are not known to wear uniforms or use helicopters.

"A Great Massacre"

"It was a great massacre," 38-year-old Rufina Amaya told a visitor who traveled through the area with those who are fighting against the junta that now rules El Salvador. "They left nothing."

Somewhere amid the carnage were Mrs. Amaya's husband, who was blind, her 9-year-old son and three daughters, ages 5 years, 3 years and 8 months.

New York Times, January 27, 1982, p. A1. Copyright © 1982 the New York Times Company.

Mrs. Amaya said she heard her son scream: "Mama, they're killing me. They've killed my sister. They're going to kill me." She said that when the soldiers began gathering the women into a group, she escaped and hid behind some trees in back of the houses.

From Dec. 8 to Dec. 21, according to Salvadoran newspapers, soldiers from the Atlacatl Batallion took part in a sweep through Mozote and the surrounding mountain villages as part of one of the largest search-and-destroy operations of the war against the leftist guerrillas who are fighting to overthrow the United States–supported junta. According to the villagers, no Americans accompanied the troops on the sweep.

Asked whether the Atlacatl Battalion had been involved in an operation in the northern mountainous region of Morazán in December, Col. Cotto said he could not provide specific details about military operations.

"We have been at war since 1979 against the subversives," he said. As part of that war, he said, air force and army units, including the Atlacatl Battalion, are continually conducting operations throughout the country.

280 CHILDREN REPORTED SLAIN

In Mozote, 280 of the 482 peasants killed, according to the list the villagers have prepared, were children under 14 years old. In Capilla, villagers say the soldiers murdered a father and his nine children, a mother and her five; in Cerro Pando, 87 adults and 62 children.

The Human Rights Commission has at other times also charged the army with killing large numbers of civilians during its operations. According to the commission, more than 100 were killed in the northern part of the province of Cabanas in November; 143, including 99 children under 16 years old, were said to have been killed in San Vicente in October, and about 300 in Usulutan in September.

Under banana trees at the edge of a cornfield near this village were 14 bodies. A child about 5 or 6 years old was among the heap. Spent M-16 cartridges littered the dirt about 15 to 20 feet from the bodies. The rebels do have some M-16 rifles captured from army units, and they are standard issue for the Atlacatl Battalion.

A few peasants, handkerchiefs or oranges pressed against their noses to help block the stench, poked among the rubble for anything salvageable.

Up the mountain trail a short distance, 12 recently cut wood planks about 10 inches by three-eighths of an inch by 12 feet were propped against the trees. On the patio of the adobe hut, saws and crude homemade machetes and hammers were stained with blood.

Inside, five skulls were strewn among the smashed tiles. The men were carpenters, according to a boy who was working among beehives behind the mud hovel.

Mrs. Amaya said the first column of soldiers arrived in Mozote on foot about 6 P.M. Three times during the next 24 hours, she said, helicopters landed with more soldiers.

She said the soldiers told the villagers they were from the Atlacatl Battalion. "They said they wanted our weapons. But we said we didn't have any. That made them angry, and they started killing us."

Many of the peasants were shot while in their homes, but the soldiers dragged others from their houses and the church and put them in lines, women in one, men in another, Mrs. Amaya said. It was during this confusion that she managed to escape, she said.

She said about 25 young girls were separated from the other women and taken to the edge of the tiny village. She said she heard them screaming.

"We trusted the army," Mrs. Amaya said when asked why the villagers had not fled. She said that from October 1980 to August 1981, there had been a regular contingent of soldiers in Mozote, often from the National Guard. She said that they had not abused the peasants and that the villagers often fed them.

Rebel leaders in this region said Mozote was not considered a prorebel village. But the guerrillas did say that 3,000 of their supporters had fled the area when the army came in.

MEN AND BOYS FLED

When the soldiers and helicopters began arriving in the village of La Joya, the older boys and men fled, said 46-year-old Cesar Martinez.

"We didn't think they would kill children, women and old people, so they remained," he explained. But, he said, the soldiers killed his mother, his sister and his sister's two children, ages 5 and 8 years. He said that among the others the soldiers killed were a 70-year-old woman and another woman and her 3-day-old baby.

On the wall of one house, Mr. Martinez said the soldiers scrawled "the Atlacatl Battallion will return to kill the rest." Sitting next to Mr. Martinez as he talked was 15-year-old Julio. Julio said his mother, father, 9-year-old brother and two sisters, ages 7 and 5 years, had been killed by the soldiers in La Joya. He said that when he heard the first shooting, he ran and hid in a gulley.

Julio said that he has returned to his village once since the massacre, to bury his family and two of his friends, ages 7 and 10 years.

WHETHER TO LEARN OR FIGHT

Julio has never been to school, and unlike many boys his age in this area, he had not been involved in the revolutionary movement. Now he is confused: He doesn't know whether to attend the school for children that is operated by the guerrillas or learn to use a rifle so "I can fight against the enemy," he said.

Another La Joya peasant, 39-year-old Gumersindo Lucas, said that before he fled with his wife, children and other relatives, he took his 62-year-old mother, who was too sick to walk, to a neighbor's house and hid her under some blankets. He said the soldiers shot her there and then burned the house.

Holding his half-naked chubby-cheeked 4-month-old daughter, who was wearing a red T-shirt and a tiny red bracelet, Mr. Lucas said that he had not sympathized
with the rebels. Now, he said, "I want my wife and children to go to Honduras, but
I am going to stay and fight."

Mrs. Amaya said she has not been able to return to Mozote since the massacre.
"If I return, I will hear my children crying."

Salvadoran Peasants Describe Mass Killing; Woman Tells of Children's Death

ALMA GUILLERMOPRIETO, special to the *Washington Post*

Several hundred civilians, including women and children, were taken from their
homes in and around this village and killed by Salvadoran Army troops during a
December offensive against leftist guerrillas, according to three survivors who say
they witnessed the alleged massacres.

Reporters taken to tour the region and speak to the survivors by guerrilla soldiers, who control large areas of Morazán Province, were shown the rubble of
scores of adobe houses they and the survivors said were destroyed by the troops in
the now deserted village community. Dozens of decomposing bodies still were seen
beneath the rubble and lying in nearby fields, despite the month that has passed
since the incident.

In Washington, Salvadoran Ambassador Ernesto Rivas Gallont said, "I reject
emphatically that the Army of El Salvador" was engaged in "killing women and children. It is not within the armed institutions' philosophy to act like that." He
acknowledged that the "armed forces have been active in that part of the country,"
particularly during a December offensive against the guerrillas, but said that their
actions had "definitely not been against the civilian populations."

The survivors, including a woman who said her husband and four of her six
children were killed, maintained that no battle was under way during the second
week in December when the alleged massacre took place.

The woman, Rufina Amaya, a 38-year-old housewife, said that the troops
entered the village one morning and, after herding the residents into two separate
groups—men divided from women and children—took them off and shot them.
Amaya said she had hidden during the shooting and later escaped to the guerrilla-
protected camp where she was interviewed.

At the same time, troops allegedly spread into the nearby countryside and
smaller surrounding villages. Jose Marcial Martinez, 14, from nearby La Joya, said he
had hidden in a cornfield and watched his parents, brothers and sisters killed. Jose

---

Washington Post, January 27, 1982, p. A1. Copyright © the *Washington Post*.

Santos, 15, said he had witnessed the similar slaying of his parents, three younger brothers and two grandparents.

A dozen other persons from the area interviewed by this correspondent said they had fled their homes during the December offensive and claimed to have lost family members in the military assault.

To reach the heart of Morazán Province from the north, it is necessary to walk for several days, passing through villages and guerrilla camps. After several months of requests, the Farabundo Marti Liberation Front agreed to take this correspondent into the province in early January, two weeks after the guerrillas' clandestine radio station first reported the alleged massacres in Morazán. It was clear that the guerrillas' purpose was not only to demonstrate to journalists their control of the region, but also to provide what they said was evidence of the alleged massacre in December.

As we neared Mozote, the group of young guerrillas who were my guides and I passed on foot through the village of Arambala, whose pretty, whitewashed adobe houses appeared to have been looted of all contents. The village was deserted.

About 45 minutes farther down the road, we entered another small town. Here the houses also were gutted and looted, but the overwhelming initial impression was of the sickly sweet smell of decomposing bodies. This was Mozote.

The muchachos boys, as the guerrillas are called, walked us toward the central square where the ruins of what had been a small, whitewashed church stood. The smaller sacristy beside it also appeared to have had its adobe walls pushed in. Inside, the stench was overpowering, and countless bits of bones—skulls, rib cages, femurs, a spinal column—poked out of the rubble.

The 15 houses on the main village street had been smashed. In two of them, as in the sacristy, the rubble was filled with bones. All of the buildings, including the three in which body parts could be seen, appeared to have been set on fire, and the remains of the people were as charred as the remaining beams.

Several small rural roads led away from the village to other groups of houses that collectively are known as the Mozote community. We walked down one, an idyllic path where every house had a grove of fruit trees, a small chicken pen and at least one beehive. Only the fruit trees were intact; the hives were overturned, the bees buzzing everywhere. The houses were destroyed and looted.

The road was littered with animal corpses, cows and horses. In the cornfields behind the houses were more bodies, these unburned by fire but baked by the sun. In one grouping in a clearing in a field were 10 bodies: two elderly people, two children, one infant—a bullet hole in the head—in the arms of a woman, and the rest adults. Although local peasants later said they had buried some of the bodies in the area, the guerrilla youths acknowledged they had asked that the corpses be left until someone from the outside could be brought to see them.

It was getting dark, and we traveled to a guerrilla military encampment.

The camp was populated by about 20 young guerrillas, all armed and obviously under military discipline. Farther down the road was a civilian camp, like the other a collection of small adobe houses, with about 80 peasants, refugees and guerrilla sympathizers. It was from this camp the next morning that the guerrillas sent for Amaya, who said she was the only survivor she knew of from Mozote.

The guerrillas left me alone to talk to her. She said that it was on the evening of Dec. 11, although she spoke more of days of the week than dates, that troops of the Atlacatl Brigade had come to Mozote. The brigade is an elite, 1,000-man unit of the Salvadoran Army, well known at least by name to most Salvadorans, that has been trained for rapid deployment and antiguerrilla offensives by U.S. military advisers here.

"The Army people had warned Marcos Diaz, a friend of theirs from our village, that an offensive was coming and that there would be no more traffic allowed from San Francisco Gotera [the provincial capital] in December and that we should all stay in Mozote where no one would harm us. So we did. There were about 500 of us in all living in the village."

The soldiers, she said, took those villagers who were in their homes and made them stand outside "in the road for about 1½ hours. They took our money, searched the houses, ate our food, asked us where the guns were and went away. We were happy then. 'The repression is over,' we said. They didn't kill anybody."

Amaya spoke with what appeared to be controlled hysteria. During our conversation, she broke down only when speaking of what she said were the deaths of her children. She said that while her two surviving sons have joined the guerrillas since the December incident, Mozote was not predominantly proguerrilla, although it is in the heart of a rebel zone.

She said the guerrillas had gone around the villages in early December warning the population of an impending government offensive and instructing civilians to head for towns and refugee camps outside the area.

"But because we knew the Army people, we felt safe," she said. Her husband, who Amaya said was on very good terms with the local military, "had a military safe conduct [pass]."

At around 5:30 the morning after their initial visit, she said, the troops, headed by the same officer she called Lt. Ortega, returned to Mozote. She said they herded the people into the tiny village square in front of the church, men in one line and women and children in another.

"Marcos Diaz, who had been told by the Army we would be safe, and my husband were in the men's line. I counted about 80 men and 90 women not including the children."

She said the women were herded with their children into a house on the square. From there they saw the men being blindfolded and bound, kicked and thrown against each other, then taken away in groups of four and shot.

"The soldiers had no fury," she said. "They just observed the lieutenant's orders. They were cold. It wasn't a battle.

"Around noon they began with the women. First they picked out the young girls and took them away to the hills. Then they picked out the old women and took them to Israel Marquez's house on the square. We heard the shots there. Then they started with us in groups. When my turn came and I was being led away to Israel Marquez's house I slipped behind a tree and climbed up. I saw the lieutenant then. He was personally machine-gunning people."

"I heard the soldiers talking," she continued tonelessly. "An order arrived from a Lt. Caceres to Lt. Ortega to go ahead and kill the children too. A soldier said, 'Lieutenant, somebody here says he won't kill children.' 'Who's the sonofabitch who said that?' the lieutenant answered. 'I am going to kill him.' I could hear them shouting from where I was crouching in the tree.

"I could hear the children crying. I heard my own children. When it was all over late at night the lieutenant ordered the soldiers to put a torch to the corpses. There was a great fire in the night."

Amaya said she escaped while the fire was still burning. "I heard the soldiers say 'Let's go. Witches could come out of the fire.' Then they left to go on what they called a 'combing operation' in the houses on the hills. I started walking and walked for three nights. In the daytime I hid because there were troops everywhere."

Amaya, as well as the two boys who said they witnessed their families being killed, emphasized that the troops appeared to be in regular radio contact with someone.

I later saw Amaya in the civilian camp down the road, where I also met the two boys. Although they were the only ones who claimed to have witnessed the killing, nearly everyone in the camp said they had come there because of "the repression in December" and claimed to have lost members of their families.

In Washington, Ambassador Rivas, in denying the accuracy of this account Tuesday, said that "serious efforts" were being made to stem armed forces abuses and that this was the "type of story that leads us to believe there is a plan" to discredit the ongoing electoral process in El Salvador, and to discredit the armed forces "or to take credit away from the certification President Reagan must make to Congress."

This week the Reagan administration must by law certify to Congress that the Salvadoran leadership "is achieving substantial control over all elements of its own armed forces, so as to bring to an end the indiscriminate torture and murder of Salvadoran citizens by these forces," or risk a cutoff of aid to El Salvador under congressional restrictions.

Excerpt from the Report of the Commission on Truth in El Salvador

C. MASSACRES OF PEASANTS BY THE ARMED FORCES

In 1980, 1981 and 1982, several massacres of peasants were carried out by troops of the armed forces of El Salvador. An account of three of them follows.

1. ILLUSTRATIVE CASE: EL MOZOTE

Summary of the Case

On 10 December 1981, in the village of El Mozote in the Department of Morazán, units of the Atlacatl Battalion detained, without resistance, all the men, women and children who were in the place. The following day, 11 December, after spending the night locked in their homes, they were deliberately and systematically executed in groups. First, the men were tortured and executed, then the women were executed and, lastly, the children, in the place where they had been locked up. The number of victims identified was over 200. The figure is higher if other unidentified victims are taken into account.

These events occurred in the course of an anti-guerrilla action known as "Operación Rescate" in which, in addition to the Atlacatl Battalion, units from the Third Infantry Brigade and the San Francisco Gotera Commando Training Center took part.

In the course of "Operación Rescate," massacres of civilians also occurred in the following places: 11 December, more than 20 people in La Joya canton; 12 December, some 30 people in the village of La Ranchería; the same day, by units of the Atlacatl Battalion, the inhabitants of the village of Los Toriles; and 13 December, the inhabitants of the village of Jocote Amarillo and Cerro Pando canton. More than 500 identified victims perished at El Mozote and in the other villages. Many other victims have not been identified.

We have accounts of these massacres provided by eyewitnesses and by other witnesses who later saw the bodies, which were left unburied. In the case of El Mozote, the accounts were fully corroborated by the results of the 1992 exhumation of the remains.

Despite the public complaints of a massacre and the ease with which they could have been verified, the Salvadoran authorities did not order an investigation and consistently denied that the massacre had taken place.

The Minister of Defense and the Chief of the Armed Forces Joint Staff have denied to the Commission on Truth that they have any information that would make it possible to identify the units and officers who participated in "Operación Rescate." They say that there are no records for the period.

From *From Madness to Hope: The 12-Year War in El Salvador,* Report of the Commission on Truth in El Salvador, United Nations Security Council Document S/25500, April 1, 1993, pp. 114–26.

The President of the Supreme Court has interfered in a biased and political way in the judicial proceedings on the massacre instituted in 1990.

Description of the Facts
Village of El Mozote

On the afternoon of 10 December 1981, units of the Atlacatl Rapid Deployment Infantry Battalion (BIRI) arrived in the village of El Mozote, Department of Morazán, after a clash with guerrillas in the vicinity.

The village consisted of about 20 houses situated on open ground around a square. Facing onto the square was a church and behind it a small building known as "the convent," used by the priest to change into his vestments when he came to the village to celebrate mass. Not far from the village was a school, the Grupo Escolar.

When the soldiers arrived in the village they found, in addition to the residents, other peasants who were refugees from the surrounding areas. They ordered everyone out of the houses and into the square; they made them lie face down, searched them and asked them about the guerrillas. They then ordered them to lock themselves in their houses until the next day, warning that anyone coming out would be shot. The soldiers remained in the village during the night.

Early next morning, 11 December, the soldiers reassembled the entire population in the square. They separated the men from the women and children and locked everyone up in different groups in the church, the convent and various houses.

During the morning, they proceeded to interrogate, torture and execute the men in various locations. Around noon, they began taking out the women in groups, separating them from their children and machine-gunning them. Finally, they killed the children. A group of children who had been locked in the convent were machine-gunned through the windows. After exterminating the entire population, the soldiers set fire to the buildings.

The soldiers remained in El Mozote that night. The next day, they went through the village of Los Toriles, situated 2 kilometers away. Some of the inhabitants managed to escape. The others, men, women and children, were taken from their homes, lined up and machine-gunned.

The victims at El Mozote were left unburied. During the weeks that followed the bodies were seen by many people who passed by there. In Los Toriles, the survivors subsequently buried the bodies.

Background

The Atlacatl Battalion arrived at El Mozote in the course of a military action known as "Operación Rescate," which had begun two days earlier on 6 December and also involved units from the Third Brigade and the San Francisco Gotera Commando Training Center.

The Atlacatl Battalion was a "Rapid Deployment Infantry Battalion" or "BIRI," that is, a unit specially trained for "counter-insurgency" warfare. It was the first unit of its kind in the armed forces and had completed its training, under the supervision of United States military advisers, at the beginning of that year, 1981.

Nine months before "Operación Rescate" took place, a company of the Atlacatl Battalion, under the command of Captain Juan Ernesto Méndez, had taken part in an anti-guerrilla operation in the same northern zone of Morazán. On that occasion, it had come under heavy attack from guerrillas and had had to withdraw with heavy casualties without achieving its military objective. This setback for the brand new "Rapid Deployment Infantry Battalion" made it the butt of criticism and jokes by officers of other units, who nicknamed it the "Rapid Retreat Infantry Battalion."

The goal of "Operación Rescate" was to eliminate the guerrilla presence in a small sector in northern Morazán, where the guerrillas had a camp and a training Center at a place called La Guacamaya.

Colonel Jaime Flórez Grijalva, Commander of the Third Brigade, was responsible for overseeing the operation. Lieutenant Colonel Domingo Monterrosa Barrios, Commander of the Atlacatl BIRI, was in command of the units taking part.

On 9 December, clashes took place between Government troops and the guerrillas. That same day, a company of the Atlacatl BIRI entered the town of Arambala. They rounded up the population in the town square and separated the men from the women and children. They locked the women and children in the church and ordered the men to lie face down in the square. A number of men were accused of being guerrilla collaborators. They were tied up, blindfolded and tortured. Residents later found the bodies of three of them, stabbed to death.

In Cumaro canton as well, residents were rounded up in the main square by Atlacatl units on the morning of 10 December. There, however, no one was killed.

There is sufficient evidence that units of the Atlacatl BIRI participated in all these actions. In the course of "Operación Rescate," however, other mass executions were carried out by units which it has not been possible to identify with certainty.

In all instances, troops acted in the same way: they killed anyone they came across, men, women and children, and then set fire to the houses. This is what happened in La Joya canton on 11 December, in the village of La Ranchería on 12 December, and in the village of Jocote Amarillo and Cerro Pando canton on 13 December.

Subsequent Events

The El Mozote massacre became public knowledge on 27 January 1982, when the *New York Times* and the *Washington Post* published articles by Raymond Bonner and Alma Guillermoprieto, respectively, reporting the massacre. In January, they had visited the scene of the massacre and had seen the bodies and the ruined houses.

In the course of the year, a number of human rights organizations denounced the massacre. The Salvadoran authorities categorically denied that a massacre had taken place. No judicial investigation was launched and there was no word of any investigation by the Government or the armed forces.

On 26 October 1990, on a criminal complaint brought by Pedro Chicas Romero, criminal proceedings were instituted in the San Francisco Gotera Court of the First Instance. During the trial, which is still going on, statements were taken from witnesses for the prosecution; eventually, the remains were ordered exhumed, and this provided irrefutable evidence of the El Mozote massacre. The judge asked the Government repeatedly for a list of the officers who took part in the military operation. He received the reply that the Government did not have such information.

The Results of the Exhumation

The exhumation of the remains in the ruins of the little building known as the convent, adjacent to the El Mozote church, took place between 13 and 17 November 1992.

The material found in the convent was analyzed by expert anthropologists and then studied in minute detail in the laboratories of the Santa Tecla Institute of Forensic Medicine and of the Commission for the Investigation of Criminal Acts by Dr. Clyde Snow (forensic anthropologist), Dr. Robert H. Kirschner (forensic pathologist), Dr. Douglas Scott (archaeologist and ballistics analyst), and Dr. John Fitzpatrick (radiologist), in collaboration with the Argentine Team of Forensic Anthropologists made up of Patricia Bernardi, Mercedes Doretti and Luis Fondebrider.

The study made by the experts led to the following conclusions:

1. "All the skeletons recovered from the site and the associated evidence were deposited during the same temporal event." The physical evidence recovered in the site excludes the possibility that the site could have been used as a clandestine cemetery in which the dead were placed at different times.

2. "The events under investigation are unlikely to have occurred later than 1981." Coins and bullet cartridges bearing their date of manufacture were found in the convent. In no case was this date later than 1981.

3. In the convent, bone remains of at least 143 people were found. However, the laboratory analysis indicates that "there may, in fact, have been a greater number of deaths. This uncertainty regarding the number of skeletons is a reflection of the extensive perimortem skeletal injuries, postmortem skeletal damage and associated commingling. Many young infants may have been entirely cremated; other children may not have been counted because of extensive fragmentation of body parts."

4. The bone remains and other evidence found in the convent show numerous signs of damage caused by crushing and by fire.

5. Most of the victims were minors.

   The experts determined, initially, after the exhumation, that "approximately 85 percent of the 117 victims were children under 12 years of age," and indicated that a more precise estimate of the victims' ages would be made in the laboratory.

   In the laboratory, the skeletal remains of 143 bodies were identified, including 131 children under the age of 12, 5 adolescents and 7 adults. The experts noted, in addition, that "the average age of the children was approximately 6 years."

6. One of the victims was a pregnant woman.

7. Although it could not be determined with certainty that all the victims were alive when they were brought into the convent, "it can be concluded that at least some of the victims were struck by bullets, with an effect that may well have been lethal, inside the building."

This conclusion is based on various factors:

1. A "large quantity of bullet fragments [were] found inside the building." "Virtually all the ballistic evidence was found at level 3, in direct contact with or imbedded in the bone remains, clothing, household goods and floor of the building." Moreover, "the spatial distribution of most of the bullet fragments coincides with the area of greatest concentration of skeletons and with concentrations of bone remains." Also, the second and third areas of concentration of bullet fragments coincide with the second and third areas of concentration of skeletons, respectively.

2. "Of 117 skeletons identified in the field, 67 were associated with bullet fragments. In 43 out of this subtotal of 67, the fragments were found in the areas of the skull and/or the thorax, i.e., parts of the body where they could have been the cause of death."

3. "In at least nine cases, the victims were shot inside the building while lying in a horizontal position on the floor. The shots were fired downwards. In at least six of the nine cases mentioned, these shots could have caused the victims' deaths."

4. "Direct skeletal examination showed intact gunshot wounds of entrance in only a few skulls because of the extensive fracturing that is characteristically associated with such high-velocity injuries. Skull reconstruction identified many more entrance wounds, but relatively few exit wounds. This is consistent with the ballistic evidence that the ammunition involved in the shootings was of a type likely to fragment upon impact, becoming essentially frangible bullets. Radiologic examination of skull bones demonstrated small metallic densities consistent with bullet fragments in 45.2 percent (51/115).

   In long bones, vertebrae, pelvis and ribs there were defects characteristic of high velocity gunshot wounds."

5. The weapons used to fire at the victims were M-16 rifles.

   As the ballistics analyst described, "two hundred forty-five cartridge cases recovered from the El Mozote site were studied. Of these, 184 had discernible headstamps, identifying the ammunition as having been manufactured for the United States Government at Lake City, Missouri. Thirty-four cartridges were sufficiently well preserved to analyze for individual as well as class characteristics. All of the projectiles except one appear to have been fired from United States-manufactured M-16 rifles."

6. At least 24 people participated in the shooting. They fired "from within the house, from the doorway, and probably through a window to the right of the door."

An important point that emerges from the results of the observations is that "no bullet fragments were found in the outside west facade of the stone wall."

The evidence presented above is full proof that the victims were summarily executed, as the witnesses have testified.

The experts who carried out the exhumation reached the following conclusion: "All these facts tend to indicate the perpetration of a massive crime, there being no evidence to support the theory of a confrontation between two groups."

For their part, the experts who conducted the laboratory analysis said that "the physical evidence from the exhumation of the convent house at El Mozote confirms the allegations of a mass murder." They went on to say, on the same point: "There is no evidence to support the contention that these victims, almost all young children, were involved in combat or were caught in the crossfire of combat forces. Rather the evidence strongly supports the conclusion that they were the intentional victims of a mass extra-judicial execution."

Action by the Commission

Before the Commission on the Truth began its work, the Director of the Human Rights Division of the United Nations Observer Mission in El Salvador (ONUSAL) brought a motion before the judge hearing the case to have qualified foreign experts appointed.

The Commission on the Truth, from the moment it was set up, took a special interest in having the exhumation conducted under conditions that guaranteed the necessary scientific rigor and impartiality.

The Commission also reviewed the available publications, documentation and court records. It took testimony directly from eyewitnesses and was present at the exhumation site.

The Commission wrote three times to the Minister of Defense and once to the Chief of the Armed Forces Joint Staff requesting information about the units and officers who took part in "Operación Rescate," and about any orders, reports or other documents relating to that operation that might be in the archives. The only response it received was that there were no records for that period.

Special mention must be made of the interference in the case by the President of the Supreme Court of El Salvador, Mr. Mauricio Gutiérrez Castro. When on 17 July 1991 representatives of the Legal Protection Office asked the trial judge to appoint qualified foreign experts to conduct the exhumations, he told them that this would require the approval of Mr. Gutiérrez Castro. It was not until nine months later, on 29 April 1992, after ONUSAL stepped in, that he proceeded to appoint them.

On 16 July 1992, when the members of the Commission on the Truth went to see him, Mr. Gutiérrez Castro said that the exhumation ordered by the trial judge would prove that "only dead guerrillas are buried" at El Mozote.

A few days later, the court hearing the case ruled that its appointment of foreign experts was not valid without a complicated procedure of consultation with
foreign Governments through the Supreme Court of Justice, with the result that the
exhumation was on the point of going ahead without the presence of such experts.

On 21 October, Mr. Mauricio Gutiérrez Castro came to the exhumation site
and, in giving his opinion on how future excavations in the zone should be carried
out, said that care should be taken not to "favor one of the parties" (presumably the
Government and FMLN) "because of the political implications of this process,
which override legal considerations."

Findings

There is full proof that on 11 December 1981, in the village of El Mozote, units of
the Atlacatl Battalion deliberately and systematically killed a group of more than
200 men, women and children, constituting the entire civilian population that they
had found there the previous day and had since been holding prisoner.

The officers in command of the Atlacatl Battalion at the time of the operation
whom the Commission has managed to identify are the following: Battalion Commander: Lieutenant Colonel Domingo Monterrosa Barrios (deceased); Com-
manding Officer: Major Natividad de Jesús Cáceres Cabrera (now Colonel); Chief of
Operations: Major José Armando Azmitia Melara (deceased); Company Commanders: Juan Ernesto Méndez Rodríguez (now Colonel); Roberto Alfonso Men-
doza Portillo (deceased); José Antonio Rodríguez Molina (now Lieutenant Colonel),
Captain Walter Oswaldo Salazar (now Lieutenant Colonel) and José Alfredo Jiménez
(currently a fugitive from justice).

There is sufficient evidence that in the days preceding and following the El
Mozote massacre, troops participating in "Operación Rescate" massacred the non-
combatant civilian population in La Joya canton, in the villages of La Ranchería,
Jocote Amarillo y Los Toriles, and in Cerro Pando canton.

Participating in this operation, in addition to the Atlacatl Battalion, were units
of the Third Infantry Brigade, commanded by Colonel Jaime Flórez Grijalba
(now retired) who was also responsible for supervising the operation, and units from
the San Francisco Gotera Commando Training Center commanded by Colonel Ale-
jandro Cisneros (now retired).

Although it received news of the massacre, which would have been easy to corroborate because of the profusion of unburied bodies, the Armed Forces High
Command did not conduct or did not give any word of an investigation and repeatedly denied that the massacre had occurred. There is full evidence that General José
Guillermo García, then Minister of Defense, initiated no investigations that might
have enabled the facts to be established. There is sufficient evidence that General
Rafael Flórez Lima, Chief of the Armed Forces Joint Staff at the time, was aware
that the massacre had occurred and also failed to undertake any investigation.

The High Command also took no steps whatsoever to prevent the repetition of
such acts, with the result that the same units were used in other operations and followed the same procedures.

The El Mozote massacre was a serious violation of international humanitarian law and international human rights law.

The President of the Supreme Court of Justice of El Salvador, Mr. Mauricio Gutiérrez Castro, has interfered unduly and prejudicially, for biased political reasons, in the ongoing judicial proceedings on the case.

The Commission recommends that the competent authorities implement the recommendations made in the experts' reports.

2. SUMPUL RIVER

Summary of the Case

On 14 May 1990, units of Military Detachment No. 1, the National Guard and the paramilitary Organización Nacional Democrática (ORDEN) deliberately killed at least 300 non-combatants, including women and children, who were trying to flee to Honduras across the Sumpul River beside the hamlet of Las Aradas, Department of Chalatenango. The massacre was made possible by the cooperation of the Honduran armed forces, who prevented the Salvadoran villagers from landing on the other side.

The Salvadoran military operation had begun the previous day as an anti-guerrilla operation. Troops advanced from various points, gradually converging on the hamlet of Las Aradas on the banks of the Sumpul River. In the course of the operation, there had been a number of encounters with the guerrillas.

There is sufficient evidence that, as they advanced, Government forces committed acts of violence against the population, and this caused numerous people to flee, many of whom congregated in the hamlet, consisting of some dozen houses.

Troops attacked the hamlet with artillery and fire from two helicopters. The villagers and other people displaced by the operation attempted to cross the Sumpul River to take refuge in Honduras. Honduran troops deployed on the opposite bank of the river barred their way. They were then killed by Salvadoran troops who fired on them in cold blood.

Description of the Facts
Background

In 1970, when the so-called Soccer War between Honduras and El Salvador ended, a demilitarized zone was established comprising a strip of land three kilometers wide on each side of the border. The zone was monitored by an observer mission of the Organization of American States. The armed forces of both countries were prohibited from entering the zone.

When the conflict in El Salvador began, many Salvadoran peasants took refuge in Honduras, where they set up camps. When anti-guerrilla actions increased in early 1980, a large number of Salvadoran peasants crossed the border, leaving a number of villages, including Las Aradas, almost deserted. The Honduran Government became increasingly concerned as Salvadoran refugees entered and remained in

Honduras. It should be recalled that one of the reasons for the war between the two countries had been the settlement of Salvadoran peasants in border areas in Honduran territory.

The Salvadoran Government, for its part, believed that the demilitarized zone and Honduran territory were serving as a base of operations and a refuge for guerrillas whose activities had intensified in the adjacent area, in the north of the Department of Chalatenango.

A large part of the peasant population in the zone also belonged to the Federación de Trabajadores del Campo, which had joined the struggle for agrarian reform and was viewed by the Salvadoran government as a guerrilla support organization.

In the last two weeks of March 1980, Honduran authorities put pressure on the refugees to return to their country. A group of refugees returned to Las Aradas.

Anti-guerrilla operations by the Government of El Salvador continued in the zone. After the villagers' return to Las Aradas and before the May massacre, National Guard and ORDEN troops, who were able to enter the zone freely, twice advanced as far as Las Aradas. On both occasions, residents fled across the river to Honduran territory.

On 5 May, nine days before the massacre, Honduran and Salvadoran military leaders met on the border, according to the Honduran press, to work out a way of preventing Salvadoran guerrillas from entering Honduras. A few days later, Honduran soldiers again put pressure on Salvadoran refugees and a group of them returned to Las Aradas.

When the operation which would lead to the massacre began a week later, many fleeing peasants converged on Las Aradas, confident that from there they would be able to cross the hanging bridge over the Sumpul River, which was running high because of the rainy season, and take refuge in Honduran territory. They also hoped that Salvadoran soldiers would not enter the demilitarized zone.

Subsequent Events

The armies of the two countries left the zone that same day. The National Guard continued to patrol the area to prevent residents from returning. The bodies were not buried.

In Honduras, the massacre received extensive media coverage. The first news report was transmitted on 21 May by a morning news program on Radio Noticias del Continente, which operates out of Costa Rica. A few days later, the newspaper *Tiempo* published an interview with Father Roberto Yalaga, a priest in the diocese of Santa Rosa de Copán, who confirmed that at least 325 Salvadorans had been killed by the army and that a Honduran military detachment had cordoned off the bank of the Sumpul River.

Two foreign journalists, Gabriel Sanhuesa and Ursula Ferdinand, managed to get to Las Aradas from the Honduran side and obtain visual evidence of the massacre. They also managed to interview a number of survivors who had taken refuge in Honduran border villages. They published a leaflet on the incident.

A formal complaint about the massacre was filed by the priests and nuns of the Honduran diocese of Santa Rosa de Copán on 19 June 1980, signed by the diocese's 38 pastoral workers. The complaint was based on the visual evidence and the testimony gathered by the diocese as part of its investigations.

The complaint accused the Government and the armed forces of the Republic of Honduras of complicity in the massacre and in the subsequent cover-up and the Organization of American States (OAS) of complicity in covering up the tragic event. This accusation was endorsed by the entire Honduran Conference of Bishops, headed by the Archbishop of Tegucigalpa, Monsignor Héctor E. Santos, in a statement published by the press on 1 July 1980. From El Salvador, the Archdiocese of San Salvador endorsed and associated itself with the complaint by the diocese of Santa Rosa de Copán, in a communiqué published on 29 June 1980.

The Minister of Defense of El Salvador, General José Guillermo García, denied that the massacre had occurred. A year later, in an interview, he admitted that a number of people had died in a clash on 14 May 1980 at the Sumpul River, but said that the number of deaths had been greatly exaggerated.

In October 1980, President José Napoleón Duarte, in an interview with the Canadian publication *United Church Observer*, acknowledged that a military operation had taken place in the Sumpul River area and said that some 300 people, all of them "communist guerrillas," had died.

The charges made by the diocese of Santa Rosa de Copán were also denied in an official statement issued by the Government and armed forces of Honduras describing the accusations as libelous and irresponsible. The Honduran President, Policarpo Paz, denied the truth of the complaint in a speech broadcast on national radio and television. The Minister of Government, Colonel Cristóbal Díaz García, told the press that Honduras would not set up any commission of investigation. Replying to a question, he said that no one doubted that there had been a massacre on the other side of the river, but that Honduras had not been involved.

Colonel Alfonso Rodríguez Rincón, Chief of the OAS observers, dismissed the accusation by the Honduran Church as the product of an overactive imagination. He said that as chief of the observers, he could confirm that they had known nothing about the incident. He added that there were numerous operations on the Salvadoran side and it was conceivable that many guerrillas had been killed; he wondered whether the incident was perhaps being confused with another one.

However, the Commission found out that OAS observers did report a major clash between Salvadoran troops and FMLN guerrillas as having occurred between 14 and 16 May 1980 on the border in that region. According to their report, over 200 people had been killed and some civilians had been caught in the crossfire, but there was no evidence that innocent civilians had been massacred.

On 26 October 1992, surviving witnesses of the Sumpul River massacre filed a judicial complaint with the Chalatenango Court of First Instance, which was declared admissible under the title "on verifying the murder of 600 people."

Action Taken by the Commission

The Commission received some 100 direct testimonies on the incident and examined an equivalent number of testimonies presented to other organizations. It examined the documentation available, including photographs, and interviewed the original complainants. A Commission official traveled to Honduras to gather direct testimony. Members of the Commission personally inspected the scene of the massacre.

The Commission repeatedly requested the cooperation of the Salvadoran military authorities in conducting the investigation, but the only reply it received was that there were no records for that period. The Commander of Military Detachment No. 1 at the time, Colonel Ricardo Augusto Peña Arbaiza, was summoned to testify but did not appear.

Findings

There is substantial evidence that on 13 and 14 May 1980, troops from Military Detachment No. 1 and members of the National Guard and of the paramilitary Organización Nacional Democrática (ORDEN), backed by the air force, massacred no less than 300 unarmed civilians on the banks of the Sumpul River.

The Commission believes that the Salvadoran military authorities were guilty of a cover-up of the incident. There is sufficient evidence that Colonel Ricardo Augusto Peña Arbaiza, Commander of Military Detachment No. 1 in May 1980, made no serious investigation of the incident.

The Sumpul River massacre was a serious violation of international humanitarian law and international human rights law.

3. EL CALABOZO

Summary of the Case

On 22 August 1982, in the place known as El Calabozo, situated beside the Amatitán River in the north of the Department of San Vicente, troops of the Atlacatl Rapid Deployment Infantry Battalion (BIRI) killed over 200 men, women and children whom they were holding prisoner.

The victims had converged on El Calabozo from various directions, fleeing a vast anti-guerrilla military operation which had begun three days earlier in the area of Los Cerros de San Pedro and which involved, in addition to the Atlacatl BIRI, other infantry, artillery and aerial support units.

There was a major guerrilla presence, supported by the local population, in the area of the operation. Government forces had penetrated the area on earlier occasions, but the guerrillas had avoided combat. This time the operation, which bore the name "Teniente Coronel Mario Azenón Palma," involved some 6,000 troops and was designed to clear the area of guerrillas. As the troops advanced, the civilian population fled, fearing the shelling and the soldiers' violence. One of the places where a large number of fugitives congregated was El Calabozo.

According to witnesses, the fugitives were surprised by the Atlacatl Battalion unit. Some of them managed to escape; the rest were rounded up and machine-gunned.

The military operation continued for several more days. The Government informed the public that it had been a success: many guerrillas had been killed, camps had been destroyed and weapons and other supplies had been seized.

On 8 September, two weeks after the incident, the massacre was reported in the *Washington Post*. The Minister of Defense, General José Guillermo García, said that an investigation had been made and that no massacre had occurred. He repeated this assertion in an interview with the Commission.

In July 1992, the San Sebastián Mixed Court of First Instance launched a judicial investigation of the incident on the basis of a private complaint.

The Commission received eyewitness testimony and examined available documentation. Commission members inspected the scene of the massacre. When the Commission requested information on the military operation, the units which had taken part in it and the outcome of the alleged investigation, the Minister of Defense replied that there were no records for that period.

Findings

There is sufficient evidence that on 22 August 1982, troops of the Atlacatl Battalion deliberately killed over 200 civilians—men, women and children—who had been taken prisoner without offering any resistance. The incident occurred at the place known as El Calabozo, near the canton of Amatitán Abajo, Department of San Vicente.

Although the massacre was reported publicly, the Salvadoran authorities denied it. Despite their claim to have made an investigation, there is absolutely no evidence that such an investigation took place.

The El Calabozo massacre was a serious violation of international humanitarian law and international human rights law.

4. PATTERN OF CONDUCT

In addition to the massacres described here, the Commission received direct testimony concerning numerous other mass executions that occurred during the years 1980, 1981 and 1982, in which members of the armed forces, in the course of anti-guerrilla operations, executed peasants—men, women and children who had offered no resistance—simply because they considered them to be guerrilla collaborators.

Because the number of such individual and group executions is so high and the reports are so thoroughly substantiated, the Commission rules out any possibility that these might have been isolated incidents where soldiers or their immediate superiors went to extremes.

Everything points to the fact that these deaths formed part of a pattern of conduct, a deliberate strategy of eliminating or terrifying the peasant population in areas where the guerrillas were active, the purpose being to deprive the guerrilla forces of this source of supplies and information and of the possibility of hiding or concealing themselves among that population.

It is impossible to blame this pattern of conduct on local commanders and to claim that senior commanders did not know anything about it. As we have described, massacres of the peasant population were reported repeatedly. There is no evidence that any effort was made to investigate them. The authorities dismissed these reports as enemy propaganda. Were it not for the children's skeletons at El Mozote, some people would still be disputing that such massacres took place.

Those small skeletons are proof not only of the existence of the cold-blooded massacre at El Mozote but also of the collusion of senior commanders of the armed forces, for they show that the evidence of the unburied bodies was there for a long time for anyone who wanted to investigate the facts. In this case, we cannot accept the excuse that senior commanders knew nothing of what had happened.

No action was taken to avoid incidents such as this. On the contrary, the deliberate, systematic and indiscriminate violence against the peasant population in areas of military operations went on for years.

─6─

Watergate

James M. Perry

EDITORS' NOTE

Watergate may be the most famous story in American investigative journalism. It led to impeachment hearings, President Richard Nixon's resignation from office, and a spate of new political ethics laws. It also had an enormous impact on the practice of investigative journalism. Bob Woodward and Carl Bernstein wrote two best-selling books (one of which is quoted at length in this case) on the affair, and it became the basis of a popular movie starring Robert Redford and Dustin Hoffman. Enrollments in journalism schools skyrocketed. Some observers have also suggested that the affair tipped the attitude of journalists toward public officials from usually healthy skepticism to often unhealthy cynicism.

The episode offers a variety of rich journalistic issues to explore. This case has been written to focus on two:

1. Why was one news organization, the *Washington Post,* able to keep the story alive while just about everyone else gave up? This was true even though the *Post's* two lead reporters were much less experienced than those assigned to the story at other papers. Author James Perry, who spent thirty years as a Washington reporter for the *National Observer* and the *Wall Street Journal,* explores this issue in the context of the early investigative reporting that led to the discovery of the Dahlberg check—a key turning point in the case.

2. When is a story considered verified, and what is the real meaning of getting the facts right? Woodward and Bernstein made a mistake in covering the questioning of Hugh Sloan, former treasurer for the Committee for the Re-election of the President. But the mistake was technical in nature and their story still held true. Is being wrong in only the technical sense still being wrong?

The answers reveal a great deal about why some newspapers succeed and why others fail, why some reporters bring to a story the skills and perseverance that others seem to lack. The lessons of Watergate about verification and the meaning of accuracy remain just as instructive today as they were in 1972.

Beginnings

Readers of the *Washington Post* awoke on Sunday morning, June 18, 1972, to discover on the front page a story by veteran police reporter Alfred E. Lewis, with the following lead: "Five men, one of whom said he is a former employee of the Central Intelligence Agency, were arrested at 2:30 A.M. yesterday in what authorities described as an elaborate plot to bug the offices of the Democratic National Committee here."

The five men, Lewis wrote, "were surprised at gunpoint by three plain-clothes officers of the metropolitan police department in a sixth floor office at the plush Watergate, 2600 Virginia Ave., NW, where the Democratic National Committee occupies the entire floor."

Watergate.

The name still reverberates as one of the greatest domestic scandals in American political history, leading to the resignation of President Richard M. Nixon and the trial and conviction of many of the men closest to him. It echoes, too, as the most daring and exciting story in the history of American journalism.

Barry Sussman, the *Post*'s city editor in 1972, asserts in a recent interview that he never thought of the story in cosmic terms; he just thought it was a good yarn that needed good reporting. He remembers that at about 8:30 A.M. on Saturday, June 17, he received a phone call from his boss, Harry M. Rosenfeld, the metropolitan editor. Rosenfeld said five men had been arrested for a break-in at Democratic Party headquarters and asked him to get into the office on what was normally his day off to supervise the coverage.

Before doing anything else—before even getting out of bed—Sussman called two reporters to get on the story. One choice was predictable—Al Lewis, the *Post*'s legendary police reporter, a man who had been on the beat so long (36 years) that he thought like a cop. Lewis arrived at the Watergate complex with the city's acting police chief. They walked through the police lines and into the building—passing dozens of frustrated and curious reporters—and took the elevator straight up to the party's headquarters.

The other reporter summoned by Sussman was not so predictable a choice. His name was Bob Woodward. Thirty years old, he had worked for the *Post* on the metro desk for just eight months.

With more than eighty metro reporters at his beck and call, why did Sussman pick Woodward?

"You could see he was good," Sussman recalls. "Though he'd only been at the *Post* a short time, he'd been on page one as much as anyone else." That was partly because he never seemed to leave the building.

"I worked the police beat all night," Woodward says, "and then I'd go home—I had an apartment five blocks from the *Post*—and sleep for a while. I'd show up in the newsroom around 10 or 11 [in the morning] and work all day too. People complained I was working too hard."

He says he just couldn't help himself. "I loved the place. I loved the feel of the newsroom—the intensity, the mystery, the unexpected things that happened."

"He really had his shit together," recalls Ben Bradlee, the *Post*'s executive editor at the time of the break-in, in an interview. "He was tenacious and worked hard," says Harry Rosenfeld, the metro editor at the time of the burglary. "He had already impressed me by the work he did on the George Wallace shooting." Wallace, a presidential candidate, had been shot and seriously wounded on May 15 of that year at a suburban shopping mall in Laurel, Maryland, by Arthur Bremer. At the time, according to Sussman and Rosenfeld, Woodward said he had "a friend" who might be able to help. Woodward says his "friend" filled him in on Bremer's background and revealed that Bremer had also been stalking other presidential candidates.

The Importance of a "Friend"

Woodward, interviewed in his beautiful home in Georgetown, the capital's poshest neighborhood, says that even after all these years he will not say anything more. But that "friend" of Woodward's became the most mysterious of all the figures in the Watergate drama: the source known only as "Deep Throat."

Woodward was dispatched that Saturday to cover the court arraignment of the five Watergate burglars. He squeezed into a front-row seat and heard James W. McCord, one of the defendants, describe himself as a retired government worker. "What agency?" he was asked. "The CIA," McCord replied in what was almost a whisper. "Holy shit," Woodward remembers saying to himself, half-aloud.

Wandering around the newsroom that Saturday was the newspaper's Peck's Bad Boy, the official office hippie, a long-haired, 29-year-old metro reporter who played the guitar and never turned his expense accounts in on time: Carl Bernstein.

As the *Post*'s publisher in 1972, Katharine Graham, wrote in her autobiography, *Personal History*, Bernstein had been at the *Post* since the fall of 1966, "but had *not* distinguished himself. He was a good writer, but his poor work-habits were well known throughout the city room even then, as was his famous roving eye. In fact, one thing that stood in the way of Carl's being put on the story was that Ben Bradlee was about to fire him. Carl was notorious for an irresponsible expense account and numerous other delinquencies—including having rented a car and abandoned it in a parking lot, presenting the company with an enormous bill."

But Sussman liked Bernstein and thought he might be helpful. Anyway, there he was, ready and willing to go to work. He was assigned to the story.

Woodward was a wealthy young man from the Midwest who had attended private schools and Yale University. He had served five years as an officer and a gentleman in the U.S. Navy. Bernstein was that rare species in the *Post* newsroom—a D.C. native. He had grown up in metropolitan Washington and spent some time at the University of Maryland before dropping out. Both reporters had been married, but Woodward was divorced and Bernstein was separated from his wife. Without family obligations, they were able to devote almost all of their waking hours to the story.

By late afternoon on that first day, the *Post*'s Watergate team was already shaping up. Next up the ladder from the two young reporters was Sussman, 38, the city editor (responsible for District of Columbia news), an introspective fellow who had grown up in Brooklyn and had been something of a vagabond before settling in at the *Post*. Sussman's boss was Harry Rosenfeld, 43, who had been foreign editor at the *New York Herald Tribune* when it folded. He was the *Post*'s metropolitan editor (in charge of the news from the city and its suburbs). Day by day, these were the people who worked on the Watergate story.

They all reported to Howard Simons, 43, the *Post*'s highly competent managing editor: a one-time science editor chosen by Bradlee to run the paper day to day. Simons, in turn, reported to Bradlee, 51 years old in June of 1972. That Saturday, when the story broke, he was at his cabin in West Virginia, where the phone, as usual, was not working. And at the very top was Mrs. Graham, the paper's well-bred, gutsy publisher.

THEIR FIRST PAIRED BYLINE

Sunday's story in the *Post* described the break-in and identified one of the defendants as James McCord, a retired CIA agent. Monday's story—it carried the bylines of Bob Woodward and Carl Bernstein, their first of many byline pairings—reported that McCord was not only a retired CIA agent, but also "the salaried security coordinator for President Nixon's re-election commit-tee." And that was not all, they reported: he also was under contract to pro-vide security services to the Republican National Committee.

The reporters were able to pin down McCord's campaign connections because the paper's regular White House reporter, Carroll Kilpatrick, had spotted McCord's name in Sunday's story. "I know that man," he said, and he called the news desk to inform them that McCord was on the re-election com-mittee's payroll.

In the first of the many lies that were to follow, former Attorney General John Mitchell, head of the Committee for the Re-election of the President (which came to be known as CREEP by reporters) said that McCord's only role with the campaign was to install a security system at campaign head-quarters. As for the four other defendants (all residents of Miami with anti-Castro backgrounds), Mitchell claimed that they "were not operating either in our behalf or with our consent."

Rosenfeld recalled that by late Sunday afternoon Bernstein had concluded that Nixon and his long-time political "hatchet" man, Murray Chotiner, were behind Watergate. (This time, though, Chotiner, who had performed any number of questionable chores for Nixon over the years, was in fact innocent.) Bernstein wrote a five-page memo expounding his "Chotiner Theory" and sent it to Woodward, Sussman, and Rosenfeld. "It scared the marrow out of my bones," Rosenfeld remembers. For many reporters and editors at the *Post*—and for almost everyone else at other media outlets—the idea that the president could be involved in such activities was simply ludicrous.

Sussman says he did not want to think about any of those things. He sim-ply wanted to keep the story going day by day, and see where it finally led. Tuesday's story, though, kept the ball rolling nicely—and in the direction of 1600 Pennsylvania Avenue.

Address Book Provides Break

The break came from the *Post*'s night police reporter, Eugene Bachinski. On Monday, a friendly police officer allowed him to browse through the note-books and papers confiscated from the five suspects. In one address book, he found the notation "W.H." In another, he found the listing "W. House." The name connected to both of them was Howard Hunt. Bachinski arrived at the newsroom shortly before noon on Monday and told Sussman what he had discovered.

Sussman gave Hunt's name to Woodward (in the book he wrote with Bernstein, *All the President's Men,* Woodward says he already knew about Hunt because Bachinski had called him at home late Sunday night). Woodward called the White House switchboard and the telephone operator put him through to an extension, but there was no answer. Just as Woodward was about to hang up, the operator came back on the line and told him, "There is one other place he might be. In Mr. Colson's office." Hunt wasn't there either, but the secretary answering the phone suggested that he might be reached at Robert R. Mullen and Company, a public relations firm. She said he worked there as a writer.

Nearly everybody on the *Post*'s national staff knew who Colson was. He was Charles W. Colson, special counsel to the President of the United States, and he was a major figure in the White House. But Woodward had no idea. He asked an editor on the news desk if he had heard of someone named Colson. Sure, the editor replied: Chuck Colson, like Murray Chotiner, was one of Nixon's "hatchet" men. Woodward called the White House back and confirmed that Hunt was on the payroll as a consultant working for Colson.

Armed with all this information, he called Hunt at his P.R. firm. "Howard Hunt here." Woodward identified himself and then asked why Hunt's name and phone number were in the address books of two of the burglars arrested at the Watergate.

"Good God!" Hunt replied, as Woodward and Bernstein recalled in their book. He paused for a moment before going on. "In view that the matter is under adjudication, I have no comment." He then slammed the phone down, according to Woodward.

In the book, Woodward recounted that he telephoned his special "friend" who worked for the government—the legendary anonymous source dubbed Deep Throat—and was reassured that the FBI considered Hunt a prime suspect in its Watergate investigation. Woodward and Bernstein also said in their book that Sussman, invariably referred to as a master of detail, remembered Colson, and pulled clips about him from the *Post*'s library. Sussman still bristles at the idea that he was not much more than a master of detail. He argues that he was the editor with the broadest overview of the whole story and that, time and time again, it was he who whipped the stories into shape, often rewriting the leads. Sussman says in an interview that he has no recollection of pulling those clips from the library.

Tied to the White House

Yet someone pulled the Colson clips, because the information in them became part of the unfolding story. One of the pieces in the clips was written by a *Post* reporter named Kenneth W. Clawson. Clawson had left the paper earlier in 1972 to become the White House deputy director of communications. He had quoted an anonymous source describing Colson as "one of the original back room boys—the guys who fix things when they broke [*sic*] down and do the dirty work when it's necessary." Somebody slipped that lovely quote into the story, taking careful note to mention that Clawson was now working at the White House. Tuesday's story was headlined, "White House Consultant Linked to Bugging Suspects."

"Three days into the story," recalled Ben Bradlee, "and we're already into the White House. Not bad for those two kids."

The fact that four of the Watergate burglars were anti-Castro partisans from Miami led some reporters and investigators to the conclusion that Cuba had something to do with the break-in. The *New York Times* had sent reporter Walter Rugaber to Miami, and he was filing some interesting stories about how the Watergate burglars had been financed. Rugaber's contact seemed to be Dade County state's attorney (prosecutor) Richard Gerstein, who was running for re-election and had opened his own Watergate investigation.

At this point, the *Post,* in fact, went into something of a funk. The root of the problem was the paper's massive commitment to coverage of the presidential election. More than forty reporters were preparing to cover the summer's political conventions, and there was not much time for other news. In his book *The Great Cover-Up: Nixon and the Scandal of Watergate,* Sussman said that to the paper's political writers the Watergate story was "like a leaky faucet—something to think about when you stood near the sink, easy to forget when you were out covering the election campaign."

The news staff's focus had turned to the election, although the big conventions were still weeks away. For now, the newsroom seemed to experience the same summer slowdown as the rest of Washington. Sussman took his wife and two daughters to the beach for a holiday starting the last day of June. He was there on Saturday, July 1, when Mitchell announced that he was stepping down as the president's campaign manager to be with his family. He was succeeded by former Minnesota Congressman Clark MacGregor. When he returned from vacation, Sussman was called into managing editor Simons's office and told that the paper had to do more with the Watergate story. Simons pointed to the *New York Times* on his desk, carrying one of Rugaber's reports. Other papers were getting into the act as well. On July 22, the Long Island daily *Newsday* reported that a former White House aide named G. Gordon Liddy had been fired in June for refusing to cooperate with the FBI. Simons told Sussman to work full time on the story, along with Woodward and Bernstein.

THE DAHLBERG LINK

Bernstein tried to play catch-up with the *Times'* reporting—a job loathed by every good reporter. He learned from reading the *Times* and by making his own phone calls that the Miami investigators had subpoenaed the bank records of one of the burglars, Bernard L. Barker, and had begun turning up provocative information. From the *Times* Bernstein learned that $89,000 had been both deposited in Barker's account and then withdrawn from it in April. He reached the Dade County prosecutor's chief investigator, Martin Dardis, and asked him about the money. "It's a little more than $89,000," Dardis said. It was, in fact, a little more than $100,000, and most of the money had been laundered in Mexico, so no one could trace where it came from. But Dardis did not tell Bernstein this.

Bernstein was given permission to get on a plane to Miami to learn more about the cash. As he boarded the plane on Monday, July 31, he glanced for the first time at the front page of his copy of the *New York Times*. "Cash in Capital Raid Traced to Mexico," read a headline. "Bernstein directed his ugliest thoughts to Gerstein and Dardis," the two reporters later wrote in their book. Upon his arrival in Miami, Bernstein checked in at the Sheraton Four Ambassadors, the city's most elegant. He asked about Rugaber's whereabouts. "He checked out over the week-end," the desk clerk told him.

At about 8:00 P.M. on Monday, Bernstein called from Miami to report that, after a long game of cat and mouse, Dardis—unable to shake the persistent reporter—had finally let him see the actual checks. "There's a check for $25,000 signed by someone named Kenneth Dahlberg," Bernstein said. He had no idea who Dahlberg was, and neither did Woodward or Sussman.

In their book, the two reporters recount how Bernstein started working the phones furiously, calling police investigators and bank officials in Florida. One of the bankers, James Collins, said that, yes, he knew Dahlberg—he was one of the bank's directors. He added, gratuitously, that Dahlberg had been head of Nixon's Midwest campaign in 1968. The two reporters wrote in their book that Bernstein called Sussman with his scoop; that Sussman told him that Woodward was at that very moment on the phone with Dahlberg. "For Christ's sake!" Bernstein screamed, "Tell him Dahlberg was head of Nixon's Midwest campaign in 1968!"

"I think he knows something about it," Sussman is reported to have replied, according to the Woodward-Bernstein book.

Woodward, working on the story in the *Post* newsroom in Washington, had traced a Kenneth H. Dahlberg to two addresses, one in Boca Raton, Florida, the other in Minneapolis. Woodward tracked his man down at his home in Minneapolis. They chatted for a few minutes. Yes, said Dahlberg, he also had a home in Boca Raton. And what did he do? Well, among other things, said Dahlberg, he was a fundraiser for Richard Nixon.

Dahlberg called back later to confirm that Woodward really was a *Post* reporter. And he spilled more of the beans. He had raised so much money in cash, he said, that he had become worried about carrying it around. So he would deposit the money in the First Bank and Trust Company, in Boca Raton, in exchange for a cashier's check. When he got to Washington, he would give each cashier's check either to Hugh Sloan, treasurer of the campaign finance committee, or to the top man himself, Maurice Stans, the former secretary of commerce and head of the finance committee. He told Woodward he had already talked to the FBI three times and had no idea how the money ended up in Barker's bank account. Or, he might have added, how fifty-three $100 bills drawn from Barker's account had ended up in the pockets of the Watergate burglars.

"Never a Story Like This"

The story ran in the *Post* on Tuesday, August 1, below the fold. It would have received better play that day were it not for the fact that another story led the page with an eight-column banner: "Eagleton Bows Out of '72 Race; McGovern Weighs Replacement." Thomas Eagleton, a well-respected U.S. senator from Missouri, had withdrawn as George McGovern's vice presidential running mate when it became public knowledge that he had been hospitalized three times with mental problems and had undergone shock therapy on two of those occasions.

The *Post's* August 1 Watergate story began with these words:

A $25,000 cashier's check, apparently earmarked for President Nixon's re-election campaign, was deposited in April in a bank account of one of the five men arrested in the break-in at Democratic National Headquarters here June 17.

The check was made out by a Florida bank to Kenneth H. Dahlberg, the president's campaign finance chairman for the Midwest. Dahlberg said last night that in early April he turned the check over to "the treasurer of the Committee [for the Re-election of the President] or to Maurice Stans himself."

Woodward remembers that when Sussman finished editing the story—right on deadline, as usual—he put his pencil and his pipe down on his desk and told his ace reporter, "We've never had a story like this. Just never."

That night, Woodward says, he had dinner with the man he considers a mentor, the late Jerry Landauer, the *Wall Street Journal*'s legendary investigative reporter (who had broken the story that led to the resignation of Nixon's first vice president, Spiro Agnew). "Bob," Landauer said, "I would have given my left arm for that Dahlberg story today."

Looking back at all the *Post*'s Watergate stories, Sussman believes that this one, the August 1 story, was the most significant because it showed more clearly than anything else that the Watergate burglars were a part of Nixon's re-election campaign. It gave the lie to the campaign's contention that the Watergate break-in was carried out by zealots operating independently—Gordon Liddy chief among them—who were simply out of control. It set in motion the official inquiries that led to Nixon's resignation.

All these years later, Ben Bradlee still revels in the *Post*'s Watergate coverage, and especially that August 1 story. "We had street reporters," he says. "Over at the *New York Times,* they had Max Frankel [the Washington bureau chief] and he spent most of the day talking on the phone with Henry Kissinger."

Certainly luck had been a part of the *Post*'s success in nailing down the Dahlberg story. Rugaber missed the check; Bernstein found it. But that wonderful *Post* passion—the sheer doggedness of the coverage—played a part too. Bernstein had been given the runaround in Miami. He met delay after delay. Maybe he could see the checks, maybe not. But he persisted. He didn't give up. He didn't call the office and say he was coming home because the authorities weren't cooperating. In the end, he got the single biggest, most important of all the Watergate stories. It was at this point that the *Times* and the rest of the *Post*'s opposition began to fade away. The August 1 story marked the beginning of the *Post*'s ascension.

It is difficult to exaggerate just how hard Bernstein and Woodward worked on the Watergate story. They made phone calls; they knocked on doors. Each developed his own thick list of sources. They worked around the clock—and they believed in what they were doing.

THE STORY GETS BIGGER

Suspicions were now growing that prosecutor Earl Silbert and the Justice Department, heavily influenced by the Nixon White House, hoped to restrict the investigation to the burglars themselves. The August 1 story about the $25,000 Dahlberg check demonstrated that it was a much bigger story than that. The wheels began to turn.

The most important wheel was a little-known agency in the General Accounting Office called the Federal Elections Division, headed by Philip S. "Sam" Hughes, a veteran bureaucrat who had helped write the GI Bill of Rights following World War II. The agency had set up shop on April 7, charged by a recently enacted campaign reform act to tighten up the reporting of campaign contributions. Best of all, it was a part of the legislative, rather than the executive, branch. Hughes told Woodward that there was no mention of the Dahlberg check in any of the finance filings by the Nixon committee. He pledged he would take a serious look—perform a full audit—to see what was going on.

At the same time, Congressman Wright Patman, the 79-year-old chairman of the House Banking and Currency Committee, directed his staff to see if there had been any violations of banking law in the handling of the Dahlberg check and the laundered Mexican cash. That investigation never really got off the ground, partly because on some days Patman could not assemble a quorum of committee members, but it was a start. On the Senate side, Edward M. Kennedy, chairman of the Judiciary Committee's Subcommittee on Administrative Practices and Procedure, began another investigation.

But it was Sam Hughes and his little agency that were to cause the White House the most trouble. Woodward's editors told him to make absolutely certain that no other paper beat the *Post* on the agency's findings. Woodward called someone in Hughes's office every day.

On August 22, the second day of the GOP national convention in Miami, Woodward and Bernstein reported that Hughes's election office was preparing to release its report documenting illegal activities by Nixon's re-election committee. But, just hours before the final report was to be released, Maurice Stans, for whom Hughes had once worked, summoned Hughes to Miami to talk things over. He made the flight, even though he knew it might look improper if the press got wind of the meeting. Word did leak out—it almost always does in situations like this—and Democratic National Chairman Lawrence O'Brien charged that it was "the most outrageous conspiracy of suppression that I have witnessed in a generation of political activity."

The Nixon campaign knew it could not suppress Hughes's report, but it did manage to keep it from coming out while Nixon was celebrating his triumphal re-nomination. The report was finally published on August 26, after the convention had adjourned.

A SLUSH FUND REVEALED

In the short time he was in Miami, Hughes managed to track down Hugh Sloan, the one-time Nixon finance committee treasurer. It was at that time, Woodward and Bernstein say, that Sloan revealed to Hughes that the Dahlberg check and the Mexican money were a part of a larger cash fund kept in two safes at CRP headquarters—one in Sloan's old office and one in Stans's office. This was the secret campaign fund—the slush fund—that the P.R. officials at the White House and at campaign headquarters had insisted did not exist.

Senator Bob Dole, the Republican national chairman and a major White House mouthpiece, argued that George McGovern's Democratic finance committee had committed many more serious violations of campaign finance laws—he cited fourteen of them—and demanded that Hughes investigate the Democrats too. The *Post* published this story on September 13, reporting that the "General Accounting Office investigators have found only technical violations of the new campaign finance law [by] George McGovern's election committee, according to reliable sources."

The findings were in sharp contrast to those from Hughes's inquiry into the Nixon re-election committee, which led the GAO to refer its audit to the Justice Department for criminal investigation. But, of course, the Justice Department was moving at a glacial pace in its Watergate investigation, saying frequently that it would be a disservice to the system and to the defendants to comment on the various allegations.

Sussman says he often wondered why the *Post* had so little media competition in the Watergate story. No other paper, he points out, took the time to investigate Dole's allegations of impropriety in the financial affairs of the McGovern campaign. There was even a little skepticism at the *Post,* especially among members of the national staff. "'Be careful,' they kept telling us, 'don't go overboard. These things happen in all campaigns.'"

Metro editor Rosenfeld claims that the lack of competition didn't bother him a bit. "I was happy to be alone on the story," he recalled in a long telephone interview for this case study. "We all know what happens when one paper gets ahead of everybody else. The other guys gang up and piss on your story. Journalists are always denigrating one another."

FORTRESS CRP

By mid-August, Woodward, Bernstein, Simons, Sussman, and others directly connected to the Watergate story were convinced that senior officials at the White House—perhaps even the president himself—had to be involved. Checks for $25,000 did not move around by themselves; somebody with influence had to authorize them. One of the obstacles in pinning the story down was the campaign headquarters itself. It was like a bunker, with uniformed guards at the door. Interviews with the people inside were hard to set up, and when a reporter was allowed past the gates he was always accompanied by someone to the office of the person he or she had arranged to interview, and then, when the interview was over, taken in hand and led back to the gate and out the front door.

Who were all those people working at CRP headquarters? What were their telephone numbers and where did they live? Woodward and Bernstein wrote that a *Washington Post* researcher obtained a list of a hundred CRP employees from a friend. Another list, containing even more names, was published by Sam Hughes's agency.

"Studying the roster became a devotional exercise not unlike reading tea leaves," Bernstein and Woodward wrote in their book. "Divining names from the list, Bernstein and Woodward, in mid-August, began visiting CRP people at their homes in the evenings," they wrote, using the third person. "The first-edition deadline was 7:45 P.M., and each night they would set out soon afterward, sometimes separately, sometimes together in Woodward's 1970 Karmann Ghia. When traveling alone, Bernstein used a company car or rode his bicycle."

They had not known each other very well when they began working on the story. And, in the early days, they viewed each other with a little bit of suspicion. By now, though, they had become a team. This is how they described their working relationship in their book: "They realized the advantages of working together, particularly because their temperaments were so dissimilar. . . . Each kept a master list of telephone numbers. The numbers were called at least twice a week. . . . Eventually, the combined total of names on their lists swelled to several hundred, yet fewer than 50 were duplicated."

Bernstein and Woodward had developed their own style of working together. Their book continues:

To those who sat nearby in the newsroom, it was obvious that Woodstein [Woodward-Bernstein] was not always a smoothly operating piece of journalistic machinery. The two fought, often openly. Sometimes they battled for fifteen minutes over a single word or sentence. Nuances were critically important; the emphasis had to be just right. The search for the journalistic mean was frequently conducted at full volume, and it was not uncommon to see one stalk away from the other's desk. Sooner or later, however (usually later), the story was hammered out.

Each developed his own filing system; oddly, it was Bernstein, far the least organized of the two, who kept records neatly arranged in manila folders labeled with the names of virtually everyone they encountered. Subject files were kept as well. Woodward's record-keeping was more informal, but they both adhered to one inviolate rule: they threw nothing out and kept all their notes, as well as the early drafts of stories. Soon they had filled four filing cabinets.

Usually, Woodward, the faster writer, would do a first draft, then Bernstein would rewrite. Often, Bernstein would have time to rewrite only the first half of the story, leaving Woodward's second half hanging like a shirttail. The process often consumed most of the night.

Sussman claims that the procedure did not always work exactly as the two reporters describe it. Often, he recalls, there was heavy editing and rewriting: "These two guys were good leg men, but they weren't much better than okay in putting their thoughts together."

The door-to-door canvassing began paying off, in bits and pieces. "It was all part of a mosaic," Woodward explains. One CRP employee told the reporters, in tears, that she was scared of what was happening, and that all kinds of documents were being shredded. Another said that Frederic LaRue, Herbert L. Porter, and Jeb Stuart Magruder—all former White House employees working at campaign headquarters—knew about the bugging of the Democratic headquarters. What amazed both reporters was the fact that federal investigators had not interviewed many of these people. Woodward remembers Earl Silbert, the chief prosecutor, asking him, "Why are you believing all these women?" Even at the time he considered it a sexist remark.

Deep Throat

Lurking in the background was Woodward's special friend, the man managing editor Simons had christened Deep Throat (the title of a pornographic movie popular at the time). In their book, Woodward and Bernstein described Deep

Throat as a member of the executive branch who had access to information at both CRP and the White House. He had agreed to talk to Woodward on "deep background" with a guarantee that neither his name nor his title would ever be revealed without his permission.

At first Deep Throat and Woodward talked on the telephone, Woodward says. But, as the story became hotter, Deep Throat insisted on other arrangements. He suggested that Woodward open the drapes in his apartment at 17th and P Streets as a signal. Deep Throat would check the drapes every day. If they were open, they would meet that night. There was one problem with the arrangement—Woodward liked to open the drapes to let the sun in. So they refined the procedure. Woodward had an old flowerpot with a red flag on a stick, and he placed it at the front of his balcony. If he wanted to see Deep Throat, he would move the flowerpot and the stick with the red flag to the rear of the balcony. If the pot had been moved, Woodward and Deep Throat would meet at 2:00 A.M.—an hour when downtown Washington was quiet and even a little eerie—in an underground parking garage.

In those rare instances when Deep Throat wanted to initiate a meeting with Woodward, he would somehow circle page 20 in Woodward's copy of the *New York Times,* which was delivered to his apartment house every day a little before 7:00 A.M. In the lower corner of the page there would be a hand-drawn clock, the hands pointing to the hour when Deep Throat wanted to meet Woodward in the garage. Woodward says he still has no idea how Deep Throat got hold of the newspaper to make those markings.

Sussman suggests that Deep Throat made for good drama but was not really that important as a source. The problem was that he often spoke in riddles, like the oracle at Delphi. No, he would say, you can go higher to incriminate people at a still more important level of responsibility in the campaign. Yes, you should look harder at who had access to the money.

On September 15, the five Watergate burglars, plus Hunt and Liddy, were indicted by the grand jury. According to Attorney General Richard Kleindienst, the indictments represented the culmination of "one of the most intensive, objective, and thorough investigations in many years, reaching out to cities all across the United States as well as into foreign countries."

At the *Post,* Woodward and Bernstein wrote in their book, there was the gnawing suspicion that this was as far as the federal prosecutors intended to take the case. After all, they noted, the Mexican checks, the $25,000 Dahlberg check, and the slush fund stashed away in Stans's safe were not even mentioned in the indictments.

PUSHING ON

So—by now mostly out on a limb by themselves—they pushed on.

The very next day, September 16, they reported that funds used in the Watergate bugging and break-in had been "controlled by several assistants of John N. Mitchell" when he was the campaign boss. Then, on September 29, they delivered a stunner: John Mitchell, while serving as U.S. attorney general, had personally controlled a secret Republican fund that was used to gather information about the Democrats, according to sources involved in the Watergate investigation.

Four other persons, they reported, were eventually given authorization to approve payments from the secret fund. They identified two of them as former Secretary of Commerce Stans, the campaign's finance chairman, and Jeb Magruder, the deputy director of the campaign. The other two were unnamed.

In putting the story together, Bernstein called Mitchell at his apartment in New York at about 11:00 P.M. and read him the lead. "Jesus," Mitchell told Bernstein. "All that crap, you're putting it in the paper? It's been denied. Jesus. Katie Graham [the *Post*'s publisher] is gonna get her tit caught in a big fat wringer if that's published. Good Christ. That's the most sickening thing I've ever heard."

In the story, the quote was cleaned up to eliminate any mention of the publisher's anatomy. (Although it did not bother Mrs. Graham much. A dentist in California made a little wringer, with a working crank, out of gold he normally used for fillings and sent it to her. Later her friend the humorist Art Buchwald gave her a tiny gold breast to go with it. "I occasionally wore them on a chain around my neck," she wrote in her autobiography.)

One result of what Woodward calls "incremental reporting"—taking one step at a time, day after day, big stories and small ones—is that potential sources become acquainted with your work and know whom to call when they think they have something worthwhile to offer. Other papers—the *Los Angeles Times,* the *Washington Star-News,* the *New York Times*—did good work on Watergate, but only the *Post* did the kind of incremental reporting that made people aware that it was the paper with the biggest stake in the story.

Thus, on the night of September 28, Bernstein received a phone call from a government lawyer with an interesting story. The caller said that he had a friend named Alex Shipley who had been approached "to go to work for the Nixon campaign in a very unusual way." How unusual? Bernstein asked. Well, the caller said, his friend had been asked to join the Nixon team in the summer of 1971 to work with "a crew of people whose job it would be to disrupt the Democratic campaign during the primaries. This guy told Shipley there would be virtually unlimited money available."

Woodward and Bernstein had believed all along that the bugging and break-in at the Watergate had not been an isolated event; it must have been, they thought, a part of a larger campaign of sabotage and obstruction. Bernstein ran down Shipley, a Democrat and an assistant attorney general in Tennessee, who identified the man who had tried to hire him to do dirty tricks as Donald H. Segretti, a 31-year-old lawyer in Marina del Rey, California.

Bernstein and Woodward broke this blockbuster on the front page on October 10:

> FBI agents have established that the Watergate bugging incident stemmed from a massive campaign of political spying and sabotage conducted on behalf of President Nixon's re-election and directed by officials of the White House and the Committee for the Re-election of the President.
>
> The activities, according to information in FBI and Department of Justice files, were aimed at all the major Democratic presidential contenders and— since 1971—represented a basic strategy of the Nixon re-election effort.

Woodward and Bernstein had not actually gotten anything from Segretti, who refused to talk to them, but from three different people he had tried to recruit for his dirty-tricks operation they had learned the broad outlines of what he was trying to accomplish.

SABOTAGE DETAILED

The two reporters had also stumbled onto what they described as the best example they had seen so far of the kind of sabotage carried out by the Nixon re-election committee. It involved a letter to the editor published in the *Manchester (N.H.) Union Leader* on February 24, alleging that Senator Edmund S. Muskie of Maine, at that time the leading contender for the Democratic presidential nomination, had condoned the use of the derogatory word *Canucks* to describe Americans with French-Canadian roots (who vote in large numbers in New Hampshire elections). The letter, signed by a fictional Paul Morrison of Deerfield Beach, Florida, deeply disturbed the thin-skinned Muskie, and he ended up—in what many reporters present thought were tears—talking about his troubles in a campaign speech in Manchester. It marked the beginning of the end for his campaign. Muskie's withdrawal was a coup for the Nixon strategists; they had believed from the start that he would be their most challenging opponent.

In their October 10 story, Bernstein and Woodward reported that Ken Clawson, the White House press officer who had once been a reporter at the *Post,* had told *Post* reporter Marilyn Berger that he was the author of the Canuck letter. Maybe he was, maybe he wasn't—Woodward says he still isn't sure—but the damage was done. Two days later, Bernstein wrote a story detailing more dirty tricks played on Muskie and his campaign. They included stolen documents, faked literature, canceled rallies, and mysterious telephone calls. The whole business seemed bizarre, but Deep Throat put it all in perspective. "These are not very bright guys," he told Woodward.

Both the *Post* and *Time* magazine, whose Washington bureau had good sources at the Justice Department, reported on Sunday and Monday, October 15 and 16, that Segretti had been hired for the dirty tricks job by Dwight Chapin, Nixon's appointments secretary. At Sussman's request, Bernstein and Woodward noted that Chapin met the president on a daily basis and "is one of a handful of White House staff members with easy access to the President." In their story on October 16, Bernstein and Woodward reported that Segretti had been paid to do his dirty tricks by Herbert Kalmbach, Nixon's lawyer.

One step at a time, the reporting was taking the *Post* closer and closer to the Oval Office itself.

It was at this point that Sussman began to think he was being pushed aside by Rosenfeld and other top editors at the *Post.* "I began to feel somewhat sorry for myself," Sussman wrote in his book, "and for the first time in a long while, I left the office in the midst of a Watergate story."

The next morning, Rosenfeld complained that Woodward and Bernstein had been difficult to work with the night before. Woodward and Bernstein in turn griped that Rosenfeld had been a problem. That afternoon, they all met in managing editor Simons's office. Simons told them that the *Post* was putting together a Watergate task force, with Sussman still in charge. But Sussman realized that things would never be quite the same. The bureaucracy was moving in on the story.

THE HUGH SLOAN STORY

Sussman arrived for work in the newsroom at about 9:30 A.M. on October 24, to find Woodward already talking to a source on his telephone. He gave Sussman the thumbs-up signal, covered the phone, and announced, "We've got Haldeman." H. R. "Bob" Haldeman and his sidekick, John Ehrlichman, were

Nixon's two top aides and advisers. They were the team that ran the White House. Haldeman, Nixon's chief of staff, would be the biggest catch of all.

Sources were telling the two reporters that Chapin would never have hired or paid Segretti without the approval of his boss, Haldeman. Their most important source was Hugh Sloan, the former CRP treasurer who had resigned weeks earlier, apparently because he disapproved of what was going on at the re-election committee. They talked to him time and time again, and they became convinced that he had hinted to them that Haldeman was one of the handful of Nixon operatives with access to the famous slush fund in Stans's safe. They also understood that Sloan had told them he had testified to that effect before the grand jury. Other sources seemed to confirm the story.

At about 6:00 P.M., the two reporters, along with Sussman, Rosenfeld, and Simons, met in Bradlee's office. "Bradlee began asking questions the way a prosecutor would," Sussman remembered. This was something new; story sessions on Watergate had never been handled like this before. For the first time, too, lawyers were called in to read the copy.

In the end, Bradlee said, "OK, go." The story appeared on the *Post*'s front page the morning of October 25, saying that Sloan had testified before the grand jury that Haldeman was one of the men who had access to the secret campaign fund.

The story was wrong.

Throughout the Watergate affair, Nixon Administration officials had been criticizing stories by attacking them without actually denying them. These official statements at first sounded like denials, but when they were carefully parsed, they did not actually contradict the allegations made in the stories. Reporters even coined a term for these statements: they called them "non-denial denials." At times, when the administration was shown to have in fact done what they had seemingly denied doing, officials would quietly back away from those earlier statements. At one point, White House press secretary Ron Ziegler even said that one former non-denial denial was "no longer operative."

When the Hugh Sloan story hit, Woodward, Bernstein, and others at the *Post* knew there were problems because the administration's denials were the real thing.

"I watched the shit hit the fan on the *CBS Morning News*," Bradlee recalled in his book. "To my eternal horror, there was correspondent Dan Schorr with a microphone jammed in the face of Hugh Sloan and his lawyer. And the lawyer was categorical in his denial: Sloan had not testified to the grand jury that Haldeman controlled the secret fund."

Even now, Bradlee shudders at the thought. "It was terrible," he recalls. "So many people had been waiting for us to get it wrong, and here we did it. When you pick yourself off first base, and that's what we did, you can't pretend it didn't happen."

Sussman says the story was wrong on three points: "Sloan hadn't told the grand jury about Haldeman, Haldeman hadn't been interviewed by the FBI as we said he had, and we had his age wrong. He was 46, not 47."

In the past, the White House had been forced to waffle on most of its explanations about the *Post*'s stories. This time, Nixon's spokesmen jumped all over the *Post* with both feet. No, said Ron Ziegler at his regular morning press conference, the story was not true. "I personally feel," he said, "that this is shabby journalism by the *Washington Post*. . . . It is a blatant effort at character assassination that I do not think has been witnessed in the political process in some time."

As it turned out, Bernstein and Woodward had the main point right— Haldeman was deeply involved with the slush fund. But they had the details wrong. For this, they paid a heavy price.

CAUTIONARY LIGHTS ALONG THE WAY

How did these two young reporters—so far ahead of everyone else on this story that no one could even see their dust—get the October 25 story so wrong?

In fact there had been cautionary yellow lights all along the way. According to Sussman's book, for example, one of the sources, an unidentified FBI agent, was asked by Bernstein "Are you sure it's Haldeman?" in a phone call with Woodward listening in on another line. "Yeah," he replied, "John Haldeman." After they hung up, the two reporters looked at each other. "John Haldeman?" Haldeman's first name, of course, was Bob. So Bernstein called the source back. "You said John Haldeman, but his name is Bob." Not to worry, the agent said, it's Haldeman. "I can never remember first names."

There were more problems. Woodward and Bernstein had spent hours with Sloan, who was still reluctant to tattle on his old colleagues. He was "elliptical" in what he told the two reporters, Sussman said in his book. It was not a clean story that was easy to write.

The two reporters knew who their sources were—even though what they had said came up short—and they had more problems in figuring out how to handle the story's attribution. They were faced with finding a way to make the story sound authoritative without exposing their reluctant or maybe confused sources.

Howard Simons, the managing editor, was uneasy. He suggested, according to Sussman, that Woodward and Bernstein try to come up with another source. Sussman recalled that Bernstein piped up that he knew a source in the Justice Department who might be willing to confirm such an important story. But the source was skittish, and in the end Bernstein suggested a novel arrangement in which the source would say nothing if the story was right and hang up if it was wrong. The source agreed and used the signal that Bernstein understood meant that the story about Haldeman's involvement was correct.

In his book, Sussman told what happened next: "'That's madness, Carl,' I said. 'Don't ever do anything like that.' Bernstein and Woodward knew a lot more about the details of what they were reporting than I did. But here was Bernstein saying that he was able to confirm a story damaging to the President of the United States and his chief of staff through the silence of a balky source. Maybe that could work in the movies, but not in the *Washington Post*."

The story ran on schedule in the *Post*. A year later, Sussman bumped into the balky Justice Department source. He told Sussman, "Carl got his own signals mixed up. I didn't give him the 'confirm' signal, I gave him the 'deny.'"

Bernstein's arrangement with his source was highly unusual. Yet no one blew the whistle on the story. Everyone wanted the story to be right. Everyone wanted to nail Nixon's chief of staff.

Publicly, the *Post*'s initial reaction was a statement from Bradlee that the *Post* stood behind its story. Internally, however, the editors and reporters knew better. They did argue that the story was "basically true" because Haldeman was really involved, even though Sloan had not explicitly said so in his appearance before the grand jury. Yet they admitted to themselves, and later publicly—and still believe, even to this day—that they blew the story. They knew that if the details were wrong, the story was inaccurate. And they vowed to examine where they had gone wrong and do better in the future. None of the principals involved in the story defends those mistakes as involving mere details.

It's Retribution Time

Two weeks later, on November 7, Nixon was re-elected president, defeating McGovern by eighteen million votes (60.7 percent to 37.5 percent).

For the White House, it was retribution time. No more stories for the *Post*; the White House dumped them all into the laps of the *Washington Star-*

News. Even Dorothy McCardle, the nice 68-year-old lady who covered social events at the White House for the *Post,* was cut off. The *Post* could not help but notice, too, that two of its television stations in Florida suddenly had their licenses challenged.

Worst of all, the *Post* fell into what Bradlee called a "black hole." "We couldn't get a smell of a story," he wrote.

Desperate to make some news, Bernstein and Woodward tried to get in touch with the grand jurors handling the Watergate investigation in late November. They came very close to being thrown in jail for their efforts. "I am sure we were all influenced by Nixon's overwhelming re-election win, on top of our own inability to break new ground in the Watergate story," Bradlee wrote. He went on to defend the exercise, but without very much enthusiasm. Bernstein and Woodward, in their book, conceded that it was "a seedy venture" and said they wished they had never thought of it.

Early in December, *Post* reporter Lawrence Meyer discovered that a White House phone used by Howard Hunt had been installed in a woman's home in Alexandria. The telephone company said that it had never seen an arrangement quite like it. It was not much of a story, but it put the *Post* back in the game. "We won a $2 bet," Woodward says. But, for all the *Post*'s gloom, the cavalry was on the way.

"What you have to remember," says Woodward, "is that while maybe everyone wasn't reading about Watergate, we had two subscribers who were reading every word." One of them was John Sirica, the chief judge of the United States District Court for the District of Columbia, a tough jurist known, not always affectionately, as "Maximum John." The other was Democratic Senator Sam Ervin of North Carolina, one very smart country lawyer.

THE TRIAL

The trial of the five Watergate burglars and Liddy and McCord began in Judge Sirica's courtroom on Monday, January 8, 1973. It marked the end of the *Post*'s Lone Ranger coverage of the Watergate story. Now, with an actual trial under way, with real people doing real things, reporters from other newspapers and magazines as well as radio and television could finally get their teeth into the story.

Bradlee wrote that he was actually pleased to be beaten on an important story by his old friend Seymour M. "Sy" Hersh and the *New York Times,* "because it meant the *Post* was no longer alone in alleging obstruction of justice by the administration." Hersh had reported that the Watergate defendants were being paid hush money with funds that appeared to have been raised for the Nixon re-election campaign. Bradlee said one story like that was fine, "as long as we didn't get beaten again."

Sirica was not pleased with the way the trial was progressing. He had read all those *Post* stories, and he was convinced there was a lot more at stake than a bugging and burglary at Democratic Party headquarters. He got the break he needed when McCord wrote him a letter saying pressure had been applied to keep the defendants quiet and that perjury had been committed.

More damaging information came from the hearings to confirm L. Patrick Gray's appointment as FBI director. On February 5, Senator Ervin introduced a resolution calling for an allocation of $500,000 to fund the operation of a Special Senate Committee to investigate Watergate. The resolution passed 77–0. Woodward interpreted that to mean that possibly Nixon's support on Capitol Hill was beginning to erode.

On April 30, Haldeman, Ehrlichman, and Attorney General Kleindienst resigned, and White House Counsel John Dean was fired. James McCartney, the respected national correspondent for Knight Newspapers, was in Bradlee's office when the news came in, interviewing the editor for a long freelance piece in the *Columbia Journalism Review*. McCartney wrote:

> Howard Simons, the *Post*'s managing editor, slipped into the room. "Nixon has accepted the resignations of Ehrlichman and Haldeman and Dean," he said. "Kleindienst is out and [Elliot] Richardson is the new attorney general." For a split second, Ben Bradlee's mouth dropped open with an expression of sheer delight. Then he put one cheek on the desk, eyes closed, and banged the desk repeatedly with his right fist. "How do you like them apples?" he said to the grinning Simons. "Not a bad start." Then, addressing the visitor: "The White Hats Win."
>
> Bradlee couldn't restrain himself. He strode into the *Post*'s vast fifth-floor newsroom, and shouted across rows of desks to reporter Bob Woodward. "Not bad, Bob! Not half bad."

NIXON'S UNLUCKIEST DAY

Still, it wasn't over. Everything around him was collapsing, but Nixon was still standing. It needed something more. By May 17, when the Watergate committee began its televised hearings, there was only one name left in their files that Bernstein and Woodward had never thoroughly checked out— presidential aide Alexander P. Butterfield. Sloan had once told them that Butterfield was involved in "internal security." Deep Throat had said he might be interesting. Woodward passed the word to investigators for Ervin's Watergate committee. Maybe, he said, it would be a good idea to interview Butterfield. Sam Dash, the committee counsel, set up the interview for Friday, July 13, 1973—surely the unluckiest day of all for Richard Nixon.

The next morning, Woodward received a phone call from a senior investigator. "We interviewed Butterfield," he said. "He told the whole story."

What whole story? Woodward asked.

"Nixon bugged himself," the investigator replied.

Woodward called Bradlee at home on Saturday night and told him what he had learned. Bradlee, half asleep, did not seem very interested.

"How would you rate the story?" Woodward asked.

"B-plus," Bradlee replied.

On Monday, before a national television audience, Butterfield laid out the whole story about how the President of the United States had recorded all those terribly incriminating conversations in his own office.

"OK," Bradlee said the next day, "it's more than a B-plus."

Woodward says it was the only time during the whole pursuit of the story that Bradlee was wrong.

Events now moved slowly but inexorably.

On July 23, Nixon refused to turn over the tape recordings to the Senate committee. On October 20, in what became known as the "Saturday Night Massacre," he fired Archibald Cox as the Watergate special prosecutor and abolished his office. Attorney General Richardson and Deputy Attorney General William D. Ruckelshaus resigned in protest.

It wasn't until July 24, 1974, that the Supreme Court ruled, unanimously, that Nixon had to turn over the tapes, in which investigators finally found the "smoking gun." Three days later, the House Judiciary Committee passed the first of three impeachment articles, obstruction of justice. On August 8, 1974, Nixon resigned as president. His vice president, Gerald R. Ford, succeeded him.

DISCUSSION QUESTIONS

1. What were the steps that Woodward and Bernstein took that led them to the Dahlberg check, the slush fund, and the Nixon connection? Were there some steps in the sequence that other journalists might not have taken?

2. How were the two reporters supervised day-to-day by their editors? What was the relationship between reporters and editors?

3. What steps can a news organization take to correct a mistake? Should the steps vary according to the seriousness of the error?

SOURCES

The information for this case came from a variety of sources. The original news articles can be found on the *Washington Post*'s Web site, at www.washingtonpost.com/wp-srv/ national/longterm/watergate/front.htm, a page commemorating the twenty-fifth anniversary of Watergate, or on microfilm at the Library of Congress.

Many quotations are based on personal interviews with Ben Bradlee, Harry Rosenfeld, Barry Sussman, and Bob Woodward in the fall of 1999.

Several books are referenced, including the following:

Bernstein, Carl, and Bob Woodward. *All the President's Men.* New York: Simon and Schuster/Touchstone, 1994.

Bradlee, Ben. *A Good Life: Newspapering and Other Adventures.* New York: Simon and Schuster, 1995.

Graham, Katharine. *Personal History.* New York: Knopf, 1997.

Lukas, J. Anthony. *Nightmare, The Underside of the Nixon Years.* New York: Viking, 1976.

McCartney, James. "The *Washington Post* and Watergate": How Two Davids Slew Goliath," *Columbia Journalism Review* 12 (July/August 1973): 8–22.

Sussman, Barry. *The Great Cover-Up: Nixon and the Scandal of Watergate.* New York: Crowell, 1974.

Woodward, Bob, and Carl Bernstein. *The Final Days.* New York: Simon and Schuster, 1996.

Appendix

Bug Suspect Got Campaign Funds

CARL BERNSTEIN and BOB WOODWARD, staff writers

A $25,000 cashier's check, apparently earmarked for President Nixon's re-election campaign, was deposited in April in a bank account of one of the five men arrested in the break-in at Democratic National Headquarters here June 17.

The check was made out by a Florida bank to Kenneth H. Dahlberg, the President's campaign finance chairman for the Midwest. Dahlberg said last night that in early April he turned the check over to "the treasurer of the Committee [for the Re-election of the President] or to Maurice Stans himself."

Stans, formerly secretary of Commerce under Mr. Nixon, is now the finance chief of the President's re-election effort.

Dahlberg said he didn't have "the vaguest idea" how the check got into the bank account of the real estate firm owned by Bernard L. Barker, one of the break-in suspects. Stans could not be reached for comment.

Reached by telephone at his home in a Minneapolis suburb, Dahlberg explained the existence of the check this way: "In the process of fund-raising I had accumulated some cash . . . so I recall making a cash deposit while I was in Florida and getting a cashier's check made out to myself. I didn't want to carry all that cash into Washington."

A photostatic copy of the front of the check was examined by a *Washington Post* reporter yesterday. It was made out by the First Bank and Trust Co. of Boca Raton, Fla., to Dahlberg.

Thomas Monohan, the assistant vice president of the Boca Raton bank, who signed the check authorization, said the FBI had questioned him about it three weeks ago.

According to court testimony by government prosecutors, Barker's bank account in which the $25,000 was deposited was the same account from which Barker later withdrew a large number of hundred-dollar bills. About 53 of these $100 bills were found on the five men after they were arrested at the Watergate.

Dahlberg has contributed $7,000 to the GOP since 1968, records show, and in 1970 he was finance chairman for Clark MacGregor when MacGregor ran unsuccessfully against Hubert H. Humphrey for a U.S. Senate seat in Minnesota.

MacGregor, who replaced John N. Mitchell as Mr. Nixon's campaign chief on July 1, could offer no explanation as to how the $25,000 got from the campaign finance committee to Barker's account.

He told a *Post* reporter last night: "I know nothing about it . . . these events took place before I came aboard. Mitchell and Stans would presumably know."

Washington Post, August 1, 1972, page A1. Copyright © 1972 the *Washington Post* Company.

MacGregor said he would attempt this morning to determine what happened.

Powell Moore, director of press relations for the Committee for the Re-election of the President, told a reporter that Stans was unavailable for comment last night. Mitchell also could not be reached for comment.

In a related development, records made available to the *Post* yesterday show that another $89,000 in four separate checks was deposited during May in Barker's Miami bank account by a well-known Mexican lawyer.

The deposits were made in the form of checks made out to the lawyer, Manual Ogarrio Daguerre, 68, by the Banco Internacional of Mexico City.

Ogarrio could not be reached for comment and there was no immediate explanation as to why the $89,000 was transferred to Barker's account.

This makes a total of $114,000 deposited in Barker's account in the Republic National Bank of Miami, all on April 20.

The same amount—$114,000—was withdrawn on three separate dates, April 24, May 2 and May 8.

Since the arrest of the suspects at 2:30 A.M. inside the sixth floor suite of the Democratic headquarters in the Watergate, Democrats have tried to lay the incident at the doorstep of the White House or at least to the Nixon re-election committee.

One day after the arrests, it was learned that one of the suspects, James W. McCord Jr., a former FBI and CIA agent, was the security chief to the Nixon committee and a security consultant to the Republican National Committee. McCord, now free on bond, was fired from both posts.

The next day it was revealed that a mysterious White House consultant, E. Howard Hunt Jr., was known by at least two of the suspects. Hunt immediately dropped from sight and became involved in an extended court battle to avoid testimony before the federal grand jury investigating the case.

Ten days ago it was revealed that a Nixon re-election committee official was fired because he had refused to answer questions about the incident by the FBI. The official, G. Gordon Liddy, was serving as financial counsel to the Nixon committee when he was dismissed on June 28.

In the midst of this, former Democratic National Chairman Lawrence F. O'Brien filed a $1 million civil suit against the Nixon committee and the five suspects charging that the break-in and alleged attempted bugging violated the constitutional rights of all Democrats.

O'Brien charged that there is "a developing clear line to the White House" and emphasized what he called the "potential involvement" of special counsel to the President, Charles Colson.

Colson had recommended that the White House hire Hunt, also a former CIA agent and prolific novelist, as a consultant.

While he was Nixon campaign chief, Mitchell repeatedly and categorically denied any involvement or knowledge of the break-in incident.

When first contacted last night about the $25,000 check, Dahlberg said that he didn't "have the vaguest idea about it . . . I turn all my money over to the [Nixon] committee."

Asked if he had been contacted by the FBI and questioned about the check, Dahlberg said: "I'm a proper citizen. What I do is proper."

Dahlberg later called a reporter back and said he first denied any knowledge of the $25,000 check because he was not sure the caller was really a reporter for the *Washington Post*.

He said that he had just gone through an ordeal because his "dear friend and neighbor," Virginia Piper, had been kidnapped and held for two days.

Mrs. Piper's husband reportedly paid $1 million ransom last week to recover his wife in the highest payment to kidnapers in U.S. history.

Dahlberg, 54, was President Nixon's Minnesota finance chairman in 1968. The decision to appoint him to that post was announced by then-Rep. MacGregor and Stans.

In 1970, Mr. Nixon appointed Dahlberg, who has a distinguished war record, to the board of visitors at the U.S. Air Force Academy.

A native of St. Paul, Minn., Dahlberg has apparently made his money through Dahlberg Electronics, Inc., a suburban Minneapolis firm that sells miniature hearing aids.

In 1959, the company was sold to Motorola, and Dahlberg continued to operate it. In 1964, he repurchased it.

In 1966, the company established a subsidiary to distribute hearing aids in Latin America. The subsidiary had offices in Mexico City. Three years later, Dahlberg Electronics was named the exclusive United States and Mexican distributor for an acoustical medical device manufactured in Denmark.

Active in Minneapolis affairs, Dahlberg is a director of the National City Bank & Trust Co. of Fort Lauderdale. In 1969, he was named Minneapolis' "Swede of the Year."

Mitchell Controlled Secret GOP Fund

CARL BERNSTEIN and BOB WOODWARD, staff writers

John N. Mitchell, while serving as U.S. Attorney General, personally controlled a secret Republican fund that was used to gather information about the Democrats, according to sources involved in the Watergate investigation.

Beginning in the spring of 1971, almost a year before he left the Justice Department to become President Nixon's campaign manager on March 1, Mitchell personally approved withdrawals from the fund, several reliable sources have told the *Washington Post*.

Those sources have provided almost identical, detailed accounts of Mitchell's role as comptroller of the secret intelligence fund and its fluctuating $350,000–$700,000 balance.

Four persons other than Mitchell were later authorized to approve payments from the secret fund, the sources said.

Two of them were identified as former Secretary of Commerce Maurice H. Stans, now finance chairman of the President's campaign, and Jeb Stuart Magruder, manager of the Nixon campaign before Mitchell took over and now a deputy director of the campaign. The other two, according to the sources, are a high White House official now involved in the campaign and a campaign aide outside of Washington.

The sources of the *Post*'s information on the secret fund and its relationship to Mitchell and other campaign officials include law enforcement officers and persons on the staff of the Committee for the Re-election of the President.

Last night, Mitchell was reached by telephone in New York and read the beginning of the *Post*'s story. He said: "All that crap, you're putting it in the paper? It's all been denied. Jesus. Katie Graham [Katharine Graham, publisher of the *Washington Post*] is gonna get caught in a big fat wringer if that's published. Good Christ. That's the most sickening thing I've ever heard."

Told that the Committee for the Re-election of the President had issued a statement about the story, Mitchell interjected: "Did the committee tell you to go ahead and publish that story? You fellows got a great ball game going. As soon as you're through paying Williams [Edward Bennett Williams, whose law firm represents the Democratic Party, as well as the *Washington Post*], we're going to do a story on all of you." Mitchell then hung up the phone.

Asked to comment on the *Post* report, a spokesman for President Nixon's re-election committee, Powell Moore, said, "I think your sources are bad; they're providing misinformation. We're not going to comment beyond that."

Asked if the committee was therefore denying the contents of the story, Moore responded: "We're just not going to comment."

Later, Moore issued a formal statement that read: "There is absolutely no truth to the charges in the *Post* story. Neither Mr. Mitchell nor Mr. Stans has any knowledge of any disbursement from an alleged fund as described by the *Post* and neither of them controlled any committee expenditures while serving as government officials."

Asked to discuss specific allegations in the story, Moore declined, saying: "The statement speaks for itself."

According to the *Post*'s sources, the federal grand jury that investigated the alleged bugging of the Democrats' Watergate headquarters did not establish that the intelligence-gathering fund directly financed the illegal eavesdropping.

Investigators have been told that the only record of the secret fund—a single sheet of lined ledger paper, listing the names of about 15 persons who received payments and how much each received—was destroyed by Nixon campaign officials after the June 17 break-in at the Watergate.

It has been established, however, that G. Gordon Liddy, the former Nixon finance committee counsel who was one of the seven men indicted in the Watergate case, withdrew well in excess of $50,000 in cash from the fund, the sources said.

Some of the still-unrevealed intelligence activities for which the secret fund was used were described by one federal source as potentially "very embarrassing" to the Nixon campaign if publicly disclosed. Other sources said they expect these activities to be revealed during the trial of the seven men indicted in the Watergate case.

Mitchell served as the President's campaign manager for three months and resigned on July 1, citing an ultimatum from his wife that he leave politics.

The former attorney general has repeatedly denied that his resignation was related in any way to the Watergate bugging or that he had any knowledge of it.

When asked whether it would be illegal for an incumbent attorney general to control disbursements from a political campaign fund, one federal attorney involved in the Watergate case said yesterday: "I don't know. There's a question."

A spokesman for the Justice Department said there is no law prohibiting the political activity of a member of the President's cabinet.

Last month, the existence of the secret fund was cited as a "possible and apparent" violation of a new, stricter campaign finance disclosure law in a report by the General Accounting Office, the investigative arm of Congress.

The GAO said the fund contained $350,000 as of May 25 and was possibly illegal, because receipts and expenditures were not publicly reported for a six-week period after the new disclosure law took effect on April 7.

The fund, which was kept in a safe in Stans' office, primarily consisted of cash contributions made to the Nixon campaign over an 18-month period, according to sources.

Although the only record of the fund was destroyed, it is known that investigators were able to reconstruct at least a partial list of recipients.

In addition to Liddy, those who received payments included Magruder, who withdrew about $25,000 from the fund; Herbert L. Porter, scheduling director of the Nixon committee, who received at least $50,000; several White House officials and thus-far unidentified persons who were not on the regular Nixon campaign or White House payroll.

Magruder has denied he received any money from the fund, and Porter has not commented.

At its inception, the secret intelligence fund was wholly controlled by Mitchell, the sources said, with the other four officials gaining authority to approve disbursements later on.

According to the *Post*'s sources, the primary purpose of the secret fund was to finance widespread intelligence-gathering operations against the Democrats. It could not be determined yesterday exactly what individual projects were funded by the secret account.

FBI Finds Nixon Aides Sabotaged Democrats

CARL BERNSTEIN and **BOB WOODWARD,** *Washington Post* writers

FBI agents have established that the Watergate bugging incident stemmed from a massive campaign of political spying and sabotage conducted on behalf of President Nixon's re-election and directed by officials of the White House and the Committee for the Re-election of the President.

The activities, according to information in FBI and Department of Justice files, were aimed at all the major Democratic presidential contenders and—since 1971— represented a basic strategy of the Nixon re-election effort.

During their Watergate investigation, federal agents established that hundreds of thousands of dollars in Nixon campaign contributions had been set aside to pay for an extensive undercover campaign aimed at discrediting individual Democratic presidential candidates and disrupting their campaigns.

"Intelligence work" is normal during a campaign and is said to be carried out by both political parties. But federal investigators said what they uncovered being done by the Nixon forces is unprecedented in scope and intensity.

They said it included:

Following members of Democratic candidates' families and assembling dossiers on their personal lives; forging letters and distributing them under the candidates' letterheads; leaking false and manufactured items to the press; throwing campaign schedules into disarray; seizing confidential campaign files; and investigating the lives of dozens of Democratic campaign workers.

In addition, investigators said the activities included planting provocateurs in the ranks of organizations expected to demonstrate at the Republican and Democratic conventions; and investigating potential donors to the Nixon campaign before their contributions were solicited.

Informed of the general contents of this article, the White House referred all comment to the Committee for the Re-election of the President. A spokesman there said, "The *Post* story is not only fiction but a collection of absurdities." Asked to discuss the specific points raised in the story, the spokesman, DeVan L. Shumway, refused on grounds that "the entire matter is in the hands of the authorities."

Law enforcement sources said that probably the best example of the sabotage was the fabrication by a White House aide—of a celebrated letter to the editor alleging that Sen. Edmund S. Muskie (D-Maine) condoned a racial slur on Americans of French-Canadian descent as "Canucks."

The letter was published in the *Manchester Union Leader* Feb. 24, less than two weeks before the New Hampshire primary. It in part triggered Muskie's politically damaging "crying speech" in front of the newspaper's office.

Washington Post staff writer Marilyn Berger reported that Ken W. Clawson, deputy director of White House communications, told her in a conversation on September 25th that, "I wrote the letter."

Interviewed again yesterday, Clawson denied that he had claimed authorship of the "Canuck" letter, saying the reporter must have misunderstood him. "I know nothing about it," Clawson said.

William Loeb, publisher of the Manchester paper, said yesterday that although the person who signed the letter—a Paul Morrison of Deerfield Beach, Fla.—has never been located, "I am convinced that it is authentic."

However, Loeb said he is investigating the possibility that the letter is a fabrication because of another letter he received about two weeks ago. The recent letter, Loeb said, maintains that another person was paid $1,000 to assist with the "Canuck" hoax.

B. J. McQuaid, Editor-in-Chief of the *Union-Leader,* said earlier this year that Clawson had been "useful" to the paper in connection with the "Canuck" letter. Though McQuaid did not elaborate, he too said that he believed the original letter was authentic.

Clawson, a former *Washington Post* reporter, said yesterday that he met McQuaid only briefly during the New Hampshire primary while lunching in the state with editors of the newspaper.

He denied that he provided any assistance with the letter. Clawson said the first time he heard of the "Canuck" letter was when "I saw it on television" following the Muskie speech.

Immediately following his "crying speech," Muskie's standing in the New Hampshire primary polls began to slip and he finished with only 48 percent of the Democratic primary vote—far short of his expectations.

Three attorneys have told the *Washington Post* that, as early as mid-1971, they were asked to work as agents provocateurs on behalf of the Nixon campaign. They said they were asked to undermine the primary campaigns of Democratic candidates by a man who has been identified in FBI reports as an operative of the Nixon re-election organization.

All three lawyers, including one who is an assistant attorney general of Tennessee, said they turned down the offers, which purportedly included the promise of "big jobs" in Washington after President Nixon's re-election. They said the overtures were made by Donald H. Segretti, 31, a former Treasury Department lawyer who lives in Marina Del Ray [*sic*], Calif.

Segretti denied making the offers and refused to answer a reporter's questions.

One federal investigative official said that Segretti played the role of "just a small fish in a big pond." According to FBI reports, at least 50 undercover Nixon operatives traveled throughout the country trying to disrupt and spy on Democratic campaigns.

Both at the White House and within the President's re-election committee, the intelligence-sabotage operation was commonly called the "offensive security" program of the Nixon forces, according to investigators.

Perhaps the most significant finding of the whole Watergate investigation, the investigators say, was that numerous specific acts of political sabotage and spying were all traced to this "offensive security," which was conceived and directed in the White House and by President Nixon's re-election committee.

The investigators said that a major purpose of the sub rosa activities was to create so much confusion, suspicion and dissension that the Democrats would be incapable of uniting after choosing a presidential nominee.

The FBI's investigation of the Watergate established that virtually all the acts against the Democrats were financed by a secret, fluctuating $350,000–$700,000 campaign fund that was controlled by former Attorney General John N. Mitchell while he headed the Justice Department. Later, when he served as President Nixon's campaign manager, Mitchell shared control of the fund with others. The money was kept in a safe in the office of the President's chief fundraiser, former Secretary of Commerce Maurice Stans.

According to sources close to the Watergate investigation, much of the FBI's information is expected to be revealed at the trial of the seven men indicted on charges of conspiring to eavesdrop on Democratic headquarters at the Watergate.

"There is some very powerful information," said one federal official, "especially if it becomes known before Nov. 7."

A glimpse of the Nixon campaign's spying and disruptions are to be found in the activities of Segretti. According to investigators, Segretti's work was financed through middlemen by the $350,000–$700,000 fund.

Asked by the Washington *Post* to discuss Segretti, three FBI and Justice Department officials involved in the Watergate probe refused. At the mention of Segretti's name, each said—in the words of one—"That's part of the Watergate investigation." One of the officials, however, became angry at the mention of Segretti's name and characterized his activities as "indescribable."

Segretti, visited in his West Coast apartment last week by *Washington Post* special correspondent Robert Meyers, repeatedly answered questions by saying, "I don't know." "I don't have to answer that." And "No comment." After 15 minutes, he said: "This is material for a good novel, it's ridiculous," and chased the reporter outside when he attempted to take a picture.

According to the three attorneys interviewed by the *Post,* Segretti attempted to hire them in 1971 as undercover agents working on behalf of President Nixon's re-election. All three said they first met Segretti in 1968, when they served together in Vietnam as captains in the Army Judge Advocate General Corps.

One of the lawyers, Alex B. Shipley, a Democrat who is now assistant attorney general of Tennessee, said Segretti told him, "Money would be no problem, but the people we would be working for wanted results for the cash that would be spent."

Shipley, 30, added: "He [Segretti] also told me that we would be taken care of after Nixon's re-election, that I would get a good job in the government."

According to Shipley, Segretti said that the undercover work would require false identification papers under an assumed name; that Shipley recruit five more per-

sons, preferably lawyers, for the job; that they would attempt to disrupt the schedules of Democratic candidates and obtain information from their campaign organizations; that Shipley would not reveal to Segretti the names of the men he would
hire; and that Segretti could never reveal to Shipley specifically who was supplying
the money for the operation.

Shipley recalled in a telephone interview: "I said, 'How in hell are we going to
be taken care of if no one knows what we're doing?' and Segretti said: 'Nixon knows
that something is being done. It's a typical deal.' Segretti said, 'Don't-tell-me-
anything-and-I-won't-know.'"

Segretti's first approach, said Shipley, came on June 27, 1971. "He called me
before then and told me he would be in Washington and he came to a dinner party
at my apartment at South Four Towers [4600 S. Four Mile Run Drive, Arlington] the
night before," said Shipley. "Nothing was said about it then. The next morning I met
him for breakfast and drove him to the airport—Dulles."

According to Shipley, he picked Segretti up that morning, a Sunday, at the
Georgetown Inn, where—hotel records show—a Donald H. Segretti stayed in room
402 on June 25, and June 26, 1971 (total bill $54.75, including $2.25 in telephone calls).
In addition, travel records obtained by the *Washington Post* show that Segretti bought
a Washington–San Francisco–Monterey (Calif.) airline ticket on June 27 (departure
Dulles).

On the way to Dulles, said Shipley, Segretti "first mentioned the deal. He asked
would I be interested because I was getting out of the Army. We were both setting
out shortly . . . and didn't have anything lined up. He mentioned on the way to
Dulles that we would do a little political espionage."

Shipley continued: "I said, 'What are you talking about?' He [Segretti] said: 'For
instance, we'll go to a Kennedy rally and find an ardent Kennedy worker. Then
you say that you're a Kennedy man too but you're working behind the scenes; you
get them to help you. You send them to work for Muskie, stuffing envelopes or
whatever, and you get them to pass you the information. They'll think that they are
helping Kennedy against Muskie. But actually you're using the information for
something else.'

"It was very strange," Shipley recalled. "Three quarters of the way to the airport I said, 'Well, who will we be working for?' He said, 'Nixon,' and I was really
taken aback, because all the actions he had talked about would have taken place in
the Democratic primaries. He [Segretti] said the main purpose was that the Democrats have an ability to get back together after a knockdown, drag-out campaign.
What we want to do is wreak enough havoc so they can't."

Shipley said he told Segretti, "Well, it sounds interesting; let me think about it."

In addition to Shipley, Roger Lee Nixt of Dennison, Iowa, and Kenneth Griffiths
of Atlanta, Ga., said they turned down similar offers from Segretti, with whom they
served in Vietnam. Both declined to discuss the offers in detail, but they acknowledged that Segretti had told them they would be engaged in sub rosa activities—
similar to those described by Shipley—to aid President Nixon's re-election.

Still another lawyer who served with Segretti in Vietnam, Peter Dixon of San Francisco, also said Segretti made him an offer. However, Dixon said he told Segretti, "No thanks," before any details of the job were revealed. I said, "Gee, I'm not interested in political matters, and I'm not a Republican anyway," said Dixon.

The most detailed account of Segretti's activities was given by Shipley, who said he wrote a memorandum to himself about the episode, "because it all seemed so strange."

At one point during the four-month period when Segretti was trying to recruit him, said Shipley, he approached a friend who worked for Sen. Albert Gore (D-Tenn.) and was advised to try and "string him [Segretti] out to see what he's up to." Although "I don't like these type of shenanigans," Shipley said, he never subsequently contacted anyone else about the matter and said he has not been questioned by the FBI about Segretti.

During a meeting on July 25, said Shipley, Segretti "didn't go into much detail because it was mostly 'Are you with me or not?'" When he asked Segretti exactly what would be expected of him, in participating in clandestine activities, Shipley said he was told: "'Enlist people, be imaginative.' One thing he stressed was asking lawyers because he didn't want to do anything illegal. It wasn't represented as a strictly strong-arm operation. He stressed what fun we could have."

As an example, he gave this situation: "When a rally is scheduled at 7 P.M. at a local coliseum by a particular candidate, you call up and represent to the manager that you're the field manager for this candidate and you have some information that some rowdies, some hippies or what-have-you are going to cause trouble. So you ask him to move the rally up to 9 o'clock—thereby insuring that the place would be padlocked when the candidate showed up at 7."

Shipley said he was asked by Segretti to fly to Atlanta to enlist their Army colleague, Kenneth Griffiths, in the project, but that he never made the trip. However, when visiting Griffiths last Christmas, said Shipley, "Griffiths mentioned to me that Segretti had been in contact with him and that Griffiths had expressed absolutely no interest at all."

The last time he heard from Segretti, said Shipley, was on Oct. 23, 1971, when "he called from California and asked me to check into Muskie's operation in Tennessee . . . I just never did anything about it."

"At one time during these conjectural discussions," Shipley continued, "Segretti said it might be good to get a false ID to travel under, that it would be harder for anyone to catch up with us. He mentioned he might use the pseudonym Bill Mooney for himself. . . .

"Segretti said he wanted to cover the country," Shipley continued, "that he would be more or less the head coordinator for the country. But some of the things he proposed to do didn't seem that damaging, like getting a post office box in the name of the Massachusetts Safe Driving Committee and awarding a medal to Teddy Kennedy—with announcements sent to the press."

"The one important thing that struck me was that he seemed to be well-financed," Shipley said. "He was always flying across the country. When he came to Washington in June he said he had an appointment at the Treasury Department and that the Treasury Department was picking up the tab on this—his plane and hotel bill."

Segretti later told him, Shipley said that "it wasn't the Treasury Department that had paid the bill, it was the Nixon people. He said, 'Don't ask me any names.'"

(According to travel records, Segretti crisscrossed the country at least half of 1971. Stops included Miami, Houston, Manchester, N.H., Knoxville, Los Angeles, New York, Washington, Salt Lake City, Chicago, Portland, Ore., Albuquerque, Tucson, San Francisco, Monterey and several other California cities.)

(Federal investigators identified the following jurisdictions as the locations of the most concentrated Nixon undercover activity: Illinois, New York, New Hampshire, Massachusetts, California, Texas, Florida, and Washington, D.C.)

Segretti told him one other major element about his covert work, said Shipley: "He intended to go into a law firm near Los Angeles by the name of Young and Segretti—he said it was a cover, that he would be doing only political work."

According to the California Bar Association, Segretti's law office is at 14013 West Captain's Row, Marina Del Rey, California.

There in an apartment surrounded by comfortable furniture, piles of photograph records, tomato plants, a stereo receiver, a tape deck and a lo-speed bike, Segretti was found last week by *Post* special correspondent Myers.

Questioned whether he knew Alex Shipley, Roger Lee Nixt, Kenneth Griffiths, or Peter Dixon, Segretti asked, "Why?" Informed that they had said Segretti attempted to recruit them for undercover political work, he replied "I don't believe it." Then he declined to answer a series of questions except to say either, "I don't know," "No comment," or some similar response.

At one point, Segretti said: "This is all ridiculous and I don't know anything about this." At another point he said: "The Treasury Department never paid my way to Washington or anywhere else." Biographical details about Segretti, who stands about 5 feet 8 and weighs about 150 pounds, are minimal.

From Army colleagues and classmates at the Boalt Hall School of Law at the University of California in Berkeley, it is known that he was raised on the West Coast.

After receiving his law degree, he served as a Treasury Department attorney in Washington for less than a year, according to friends, and then entered the Army as an officer in the Army Judge Advocate General Corps.

A Treasury Department spokesman confirmed that Segretti, in 1966 and 1967, worked as an attorney in the office of the Comptroller of the Currency here.

About a year of Segretti's Army service, friends said, was spent in Vietnam, with American Division headquarters in Chulai and U.S. Army Vietnam headquarters at Longbinh.

—7—

New Orleans Times-Picayune
Series on Racism

>-+>-0-<+-<

JACK NELSON

EDITORS' NOTE

In 1993 the *New Orleans Times-Picayune* published a trail-blazing series of articles on race relations that, among other things, documented the paper's own racist past. No other newspaper had ever taken such a searing look at its own role in perpetuating segregation and white domination.

The project rocked New Orleans and sparked controversy not only in the community, but also within the paper's own editorial ranks. Work on the race relations series was emotionally wrenching for both white and black staffers, and it resulted in heated arguments and frayed or broken friendships. Some staffers described the many months they spent on the project as traumatic and all-consuming. And although most agreed that they were proud to have played a role in the project, they were almost unanimous in saying they would not want to go through it again.

Based on interviews with many of the journalists involved, Jack Nelson, former Washington bureau chief of the *Los Angeles Times* and a regular on *Washington Week in Review,* narrates the series and depicts the newsroom environment that accompanied it.

Nelson's narrative asks whether journalists can ever fully separate themselves from their personal and cultural predilections, and, if not, how these are best handled. The case also explores how one measures success in journalism: in the end, was the series worth it, both financially and journalistically? And it suggests a broader question: where is the line at which the writing of journalism ends and the writing of history begins?

Staff members at the *New Orleans Times-Picayune* had anguished over the idea of a series on race relations for almost two years. It had been stewing ever since their controversial coverage of a bruising, racially charged 1991 governor's race that pitted former Klansman David Duke against former governor Edwin Edwards. The editors and reporters had been so concerned that Duke might defeat Edwards that they had taken the extraordinary step of abandoning traditional journalistic neutrality and aggressively using news columns as well as editorials in a concerted campaign to defeat Duke.

Edwards, boosted by the newspaper's campaign, rolled on to a landslide victory. He defeated Duke 61 percent to 39 percent and drew more votes than any gubernatorial candidate in Louisiana history. Later, analysts would say that without the newspaper's explicit crusading in its news columns—including its investigations of Duke at every opportunity—the Klansman would have won.

Duke drew 680,070 votes, an impressive total that reflected deep racial polarization in the state. That result convinced some black staffers, including city editor Keith Woods, that the newspaper needed to address the problem in a major way.

Two days after the election, Woods, 33, took the lead in proposing that the newspaper launch a project on race. He felt that the *Times-Picayune* had not given adequate coverage to racial problems and that an in-depth series on the subject might lead to greater understanding of the issue and ultimately to better race relations. The paper's 46-year-old editor, Jim Amoss, a Yale graduate and Rhodes scholar, thought the idea had merit. Amoss, a native of New Orleans, had closely monitored Duke's career as a Klansman and thought the proposal for a series on race was especially relevant in the aftermath of his strong showing in the election. But he and other white editors ultimately thought it would consume too much time and energy when the paper could be focusing on projects that could bear fruit more quickly.

Ashton Phelps Jr., the 47-year-old publisher, proposed a series on crime. This too was a hot issue in New Orleans at the time. Woods objected. He felt that such a series would inevitably end up offending blacks and be seen as nothing more than white journalists examining black pathology. He had no doubt that a series on crime would invariably carry the message that it was a black problem, that blacks were inherently more disposed to criminal activity, that they did not seem capable of escaping the housing projects and a criminal environment. Undertaking a series on crime might also, he thought, preclude a race relations series. Phelps claims that, although he had suggested that the newspaper look at ways of helping reduce crime, which was rampant in New Orleans, "the idea of a crime series never precluded or competed" with the race relations series.

In time, the suggestion of a crime series faded. Yet tackling race relations remained a topic of discussion, gaining momentum the following year when racial rancor disrupted the traditionally all-white New Orleans Mardi Gras parade. The predominantly African American city council passed an ordinance forcing Carnival Krewes—clubs that run the parades and other social events—to integrate. For the city's African American population—which accounted for 55 percent of its citizens—it was a measure long overdue. Yet some wealthy white families who had opposed the ordinance decided to stop parading rather than integrate.

TRAINING FOR DIVERSITY

Times-Picayune employees had recently gone through diversity workshops dealing with both racial and gender attitudes. These gave further traction to the idea for a project on race. The workshops raised the racial consciousness not only of the rank and file, but also of the editor and publisher. Amoss believed that the workshops forced him to examine his own feelings on race and made him much more sensitive to issues with racial overtones. Phelps—who is especially sensitive about any criticism of the paper's coverage of racial issues in the 1960s and 1970s, when his father was the publisher—said that the experience made him examine his own "internal feelings."

"One of the realizations I came to," he recalled, "was that growing up in the 1950s and '60s in New Orleans, I never heard a racially prejudiced remark from either of my parents."

For weeks Woods continued to press the idea of a race relations project on Amoss and two other white editors—Peter Kovacs, the managing editor, and Kristin Gilger, assistant to the editor. Gilger, who was 39 at the time, served in various editing positions at the *Times-Picayune* from 1984 to 1993, when she became managing editor of the *Salem (Ore.) Statesman-Journal*. Since 1998 she has been a senior editor on the *Arizona Republic*'s metropolitan desk. All agreed that a race series would make a worthy project, but they seemed unable to agree on how to proceed.

Should it be a single series run on consecutive days or a series that would run periodically? How many staffers should be assigned, and who among them would be best qualified to work on the project? How much space would it require? What specific topics should be covered? Was the subject so sensitive that it might provoke a race riot? The editors debated these and other questions repeatedly.

Not until March 1992 did the four editors, meeting over lunch, finally agree to assemble a biracial team to discuss ways to carry out the project. After lunch, they sat in a car in the newspaper's parking lot and selected reporters, a photographer, a copy editor, and a graphic artist for the eighteen-member project staff.

Gilger was named project editor and, after calling the first staff meeting in the newspaper's conference room, she got an early taste of how difficult it would be to carry out the assignment.

"I started out," she remembered, "by saying we would do a project on race and asked 'What do you want to do?' The meeting quickly degenerated; there was so much hostility in the room. Black reporters immediately challenged the assumption that whites could do a project on race in the first place. 'Suspicious,' 'hostile' are not too strong words to use. Oh my God, we were so far apart we couldn't even talk about it! The distrust! I ended the meeting as quickly as I could."

SUSPICIONS AROUSED

Black staffers were suspicious that their white colleagues had an agenda—they wanted to report on black pathology. What's wrong with blacks? Can't they get out of the projects? Why are so many of them into crime?

Amoss recalls "a grudging feeling" at the meeting on the part of some white editors who did not like the way the discussions were going. "In the end, it just fizzled, was a disaster," he said. "Blacks sensed that we were treating the whole thing as just another topic coming down the pike, not with the seriousness with which they thought it should be invested. They became silent, sullen. The project seemed to be stillborn."

Afterwards, Gilger and Woods told Amoss that they were concerned it would not work. Woods, however, suggested that it might work if Amoss could get Nelson Hewitt—an African American diversity consultant, whom staffers of both races had come to trust during the diversity workshops—to return for more intensive diversity sessions with the project team.

Amoss, a big supporter of the earlier diversity workshops, seized on the idea and proposed it to Phelps. The publisher, whose staunch support for the project was essential, never blinked. "Go ahead," he told Amoss, and he authorized $30,000 for the sessions. Phelps, a lawyer, had been publisher since 1979 and had served on the business side of the paper since 1971, when his father, then the publisher, had appointed him as his assistant.

For two days, Amoss recalls, he and the project staff were closeted with Hewitt, the facilitator, in a hotel room, where "he got us to talk about race relations and what our opinions were and helped us break down some barriers."

The sessions were wrenching, especially for white staffers, who recall either expressing or repressing feelings of guilt. "White women admitted that if a black man was walking down the street in their direction, they might hold their purse and cross the street," said Paula Devlin, the copy desk chief. "Some wouldn't admit that in their hearts they felt the same way."

Like many of the staffers of both races, Devlin, who is white, said that the diversity sessions and working on the race relations project "literally changed my life." She recalled the reaction when Stephen Casmier, an African American reporter, said he would "pay a million dollars to have skin that was white."

"The mouths of all the whites in the room dropped," she said, "but the other blacks nodded their heads up and down. It made me ashamed of my skin. My life changed. My husband's life changed. Race is everything in this country; I'm much more aware of it now."

Kevin Bell, then a young black reporter and seven years later a graduate student at New York University, studying for a Ph.D. in comparative literature, recalls that "racist attitudes, some that were unconscious, emerged, and I don't think you would have had the race relations series without the diversity sessions."

Not all the diversity sessions went smoothly. After one exploded in arguments and bitter recriminations, Amoss called a meeting of the staff and explained why white employees had to change their attitudes toward black co-workers and why the newspaper had to do a better job of writing for all its readers, not just whites. The paper quoted Amoss as later saying, "To the extent that readers don't see themselves and don't see their lives, their friends, their children and their activities reflected in the paper, they feel shut out. And if people feel shut out, a newspaper is failing in its mission, and ultimately will fail altogether."

A Front-Burner Issue

For all of the diversity sessions, white and black staffers sometimes found it difficult to work together. But in discussions of the race relations project in which whites and blacks generally split along racial lines, some whites could be found on the mostly black side, and vice versa. In fact, James O'Byrne, a white reporter who had grown up in Denver and New Orleans, aligned himself so regularly with Woods and other blacks that the project staff, after attending the movie *Malcolm X*, nicknamed him "James O'X." O'Byrne recalls the staff's diversity sessions as "a real defining moment in building the team."

"Blacks had the courage to talk in a friendly and honest way and their brutal honesty commanded an honest response," he says. "Black folks face the race issue as a fact on the front burner every day of their lives. And they brought that home to us."

The team building and discussions about what the project would cover and how it would be handled went on for four to five months. Would it cover only current race relations? And if it delved into the past, how far back would it go? As far back as the Jim Crow era, when laws sanctioned segregation? Back to the era of slavery? Would it involve investigative reporting, digging into specific cases of discrimination? According to Amoss, a crucial rule, proposed by Woods, came out of the discussions: *From then on, every article on race would have to be "reviewed by a pair of African American eyes before publication."* Some editors "didn't take kindly" to the rule, Amoss said. But the editor, described by his staff as soft-spoken but with a tough streak, was determined to enforce it.

Some black staffers argued that, in reporting on institutional racism, the project team would have to take a serious look at the *Times-Picayune*'s own racist past. Amoss's reaction, he recalls, was a gulp, followed by "Of course."

A LOOK INWARD

It was not an easy decision for Amoss. The *Times-Picayune,* like most Southern newspapers, had a long history of supporting slavery before the Civil War and backing segregation through the 1950s and into the 1960s. Most members of the relatively young project team had little idea of how racist the newspaper had been until they embarked on the race relations series.

Amoss felt that "The hardest decision was about reporting on the newspaper itself and to be as searingly honest and true to a history that could be seen in different ways, writing about an institution we were part of and could be proud of, and [we] had to be sure of accuracy in reporting on it."

Some staffers expected Phelps, the publisher, to reject the idea of reporting on the newspaper's racist past. Mark Lorando, the entertainment editor and a project team member, recalled that "People in the newsroom were stunned that Phelps gave it the green light." Keith Woods believed that "The publisher must have lost consciousness when he learned we were planning to do that story."

Could the paper really report on itself fairly? Could it have done the series without publicly probing its own past?

It remains a sensitive subject for Ashton Phelps Jr.—especially because his father was publisher in the late 1960s, when the *Times-Picayune* gave short shrift to the civil rights movement. He stresses that his father—who had been the newspaper's attorney until he was named publisher in 1967—"didn't control the editorial policy until he became publisher." But the *Times-Picayune,* in its own article on institutional racism, faulted itself for not providing any leadership on race until the 1970s when it "made its first halting changes."

Bill Minor, a white columnist who was the paper's correspondent in Jackson, Mississippi, for thirty years, was quoted in the *Times-Picayune*'s story on the newspaper's record of covering race: "The *Picayune* had a great opportunity and we didn't take it. Civil rights was the biggest story of the day, and the *Picayune* didn't understand it." Minor pointed out that, although ten *New York Times* reporters were present, he was the sole *Times-Picayune* reporter on the scene when President John F. Kennedy sent in federal marshals to control the riots that broke out in 1962 when James Meredith became the first black to enter the University of Mississippi at Oxford. Minor, widely acclaimed for his own coverage of civil rights, said that he had begged for additional help, to no avail. As a stringer, he wrote several articles that made big splashes in *Newsweek* and the *New York Times,* but aroused little or no interest at his own paper.

Before the 1970s the *Times-Picayune* had only one black writer, who occasionally submitted stories about the black community. Recalls Joyce Davis, a black woman hired as a reporter in 1972 who became an editor at the *Times-Picayune* before leaving in 1990 to become a National Public Radio editor in New York, "I got the sense I was just there to fill a space, and they were content just to ignore me."

The paper hired a few more black reporters in the early 1970s and was required to hire more black workers in several departments under a consent decree it signed with the Equal Employment Opportunity Commission to settle a job discrimination suit brought against it.

Regardless of the paper's record on race during his father's reign, Ashton Phelps Jr. stood solidly behind the race relations project, even as it took a hard look at the *Times-Picayune* itself. "The only sit-down meeting I had with him on the project was over the story on the paper," said Kristin Gilger, the project editor. "He never questioned whether we should do it; he understood we had to do it. He saw the story before it ran and he had comments about it. But he never tried to soft-pedal anything. We did make a few changes on questions of fact because he knew the paper's history."

Slavery was another subject that Keith Woods and Stephen Casmier argued should be covered in the series. Woods and Casmier—described by colleagues as the moral compasses of the project team—met strong resistance from some white reporters and editors who insisted that slavery was history and did not fit the definition of news. They argued that slavery had been abolished more than a century ago and was not germane to today's relations between the races. Casmier countered that one could not understand race relations without examining them in historic context—including slavery, the Jim Crow era, and the civil rights movement.

Amoss eventually agreed. "We had been underestimating our readers," he now says. "They were interested in the historic context."

THE SERIES RUNS

The series, entitled "Together. . .Apart: The Myth of Race," was published between May and November 1993. The articles, along with more than 1,000 responses by readers, ran in six large installments totaling 105 pages—an extraordinary and expensive allotment of space for any newspaper. The vivid depiction of racial discrimination and rancorous race relations rocked the city. Thousands of phone calls and other messages poured into the *Times-Picayune,* a great majority of them from white critics, many of them attacking the newspaper.

Critics accused the paper of peddling guilt, of opening old wounds, and of stirring racial animosity that could touch off a race riot. The *Times-Picayune* was accused of exploiting the race issue in hopes of winning a Pulitzer Prize. Many hate messages poured into the paper by telephone and mail. A couple of them read as follows:

> Race relations is not the subject; white racism, or perceived racism, is the subject. . . . You should be ashamed of publishing the series. You are furthering the cause of the extremists under the guise of public service. [David H. Lucien, *New Orleans Times-Picayune,* Letters to the Editor, May 16, 1993]

> Surely you realize that [the series] can only serve to exacerbate already strained race relations in this area. I wish you had heeded the sage advice we all received as children: don't pick a bo-bo [*sic*] or it won't heal. [Tom Haney, *New Orleans Times-Picayune,* Letters to the Editor, July 4, 1993]

Undaunted, Phelps published a reprint of the articles and the readers' responses. And in an accompanying letter he and Amoss told readers that the series had been published "in the hope of bringing people together by talking unflinchingly about a subject that has us tongue-tied—race."

"We believe that racial discord remains the gravest threat to the future of our community and nation and that honest dialogue is a remedy to fear, mistrust and rage," Phelps and Amoss wrote. "'Together. . .Apart' is the most difficult story the *Times-Picayune* has ever undertaken to tell. Our readers helped us, responding to our invitation to speak up on race relations. Their 6,500 recorded telephone calls yielded more than 1,000 published comments that appeared in 58 full newspaper pages while the series ran. It is in their voices, presented here with our stories, that we hear proof of the distance to be traveled to bridge the racial divide. The going is painful. But we offer the following pages for those who are willing to begin the journey."

A Painful Self-Critique

The *Times-Picayune*'s report on its own handling of the race question was written by Chris Adams, a white reporter, who has since moved to the *Wall Street Journal*'s Washington bureau. Adams interviewed Phelps for the article, but he found that the publisher "didn't relish talking about it." Phelps, he said, "went off the record forty times in a thirty-five-minute interview to tell me trivial things."

Adams's article cited the report, twenty-five years earlier, of the National Advisory Commission on Civil Disorders (the Kerner Commission), formed by President Lyndon Johnson to investigate the causes of the 1960s civil disorders and racial unrest that rocked American cities. The report concluded that the news media "have failed to analyze and report adequately on racial problems in the United States and, as a related matter, to meet the Negro's legitimate expectations of journalism."

"By and large," the report said, "news organizations have failed to communicate to both their black and white audiences a sense of the problems America faces and the source of potential solutions. The media report and write from the standpoint of a white man's world." The commission went on to observe that "It would be a contribution of inestimable importance to race relations simply to treat ordinary news about Negroes as news of other groups is now treated—in all parts of the paper, from the news, society and club pages to the comic strips."

Adams wrote that complaints were still being lodged against the *Times-Picayune* for not covering African Americans in all parts of the paper. While blacks were covered rather fully in the news and feature sections, other sections were still disproportionately white. A study of a month's worth of society pages, for example, showed that 96 percent of the photos were of whites and 85 percent of the brides and grooms listed were white.

Phelps was quoted as saying that 66 percent of black adults in the New Orleans area read the newspaper, a readership percentage one point less than the figure for all adults and higher than that in other newspaper markets. "I don't know a newspaper in the country that can't improve," he said, "but it would appear our team is doing some things right."

The *Times-Picayune,* 156 years old when the series ran, had a long history of hostility, intolerance, and insensitivity when it came to race, Adams wrote, and the paper gave readers "an image of black people as intellectually and morally inferior, relegated to a lower social caste than white people and often little more than lazy or criminal."

During the 1800s, the newspaper's predecessor, the *Daily Picayune,* habitually demeaned black people as "besotted barbarians full of natural dullness and cowardice." Slave owners were portrayed as providing protection, kindness, and comfort to "inferior Negroes," most of whom were "content with their situation in life."

An Eye-Opener on Slavery

The coverage of slavery in "Together. . .Apart" was just as brutally frank and an eye-opener to many blacks as well as whites. They learned, among other things, that they lived in a city where between 1804 and 1862 some 135,000 Africans had been put on the auction block—more than were auctioned anywhere else in the South.

The *Times-Picayune* published explicit art of the slave trade: an 1850 etching of a slave auction in the rotunda of the former St. Louis Hotel in New Orleans; a photo of a slave showing huge scars from floggings; and an etching of a young black with his neck gripped by a slave collar, described as "an iron band with bells," which made it "painful and difficult for captives to move and enabled owners to track them." The article noted the irony of Louisiana plantations having thrived on slave labor while New Orleans was fostering the largest community of free people in the United States.

The newspaper gave a modern twist to the slavery issue by contrasting the views of a woman whose ancestor had owned slaves with the views of a man whose ancestor was one of those slaves. Mary Flower Pugh Russell, whose ancestor owned the Madewood sugar cane plantation, which 250 slaves had worked to maintain, said the slaves were treated with kindness and provided with adequate food and shelter. But Lionel Tap Sr., related by marriage to Louisa Martin, who was enslaved at Madewood, recounted that before Martin died she told him of whippings and beatings by cruel overseers and owners, and of a life stunted by chains and hard labor.

The Jim Crow era, spanning more than seventy years after the Civil War, was described by the *Times-Picayune* as "a long nightmare for African-Americans in the South and, for white people, at least a partial revival of their slavery-era dominance. The period was marked by lynchings, denial of voting rights and laws segregating everything from water fountains to prostitutes."

CONTEMPORARY DISCRIMINATION

Regarding contemporary discrimination, the newspaper reported that African Americans "cannot go where they want, buy what they want or live where they want without fearing or feeling the sting of discrimination that treats them as paupers and criminals." "Sales clerks, real estate agents, landlords, waiters and other service industry employees," it added, "often ignore, suspect or charge higher prices to African-Americans in an updated form of discrimination that is often subtle yet pervasive."

The paper reported on a pattern of discrimination in house rentals and car sales by sending both black and white reporters out to test the market. But editors chose not to identify the landlords or car dealers who were guilty of discrimination. They explained that they thought it would be unfair to single out individuals who discriminated, since it was believed to be a widespread practice, even though the *Times-Picayune* had not done a comprehensive survey or investigation of the matter. The failure to name names led some staffers to complain that the reports were not tough enough.

The paper also noted that, thirty-nine years after the Supreme Court's desegregation ruling in *Brown v. Board of Education,* New Orleans schools were "integrated in name only." A chart showing the most segregated major U.S. school districts—those in which at least nine of ten students were of a single race—listed New Orleans third with an 88 rating. (Washington, D.C., was first with 96, and Atlanta was second with 92.)

The series included several stories about racial progress, including strides toward interracial communication and cooperation and efforts by some groups to improve racial relations. But black staffers generally were cool to such stories, feeling that they tended to put a happy face on an ugly problem. In any case, such stories amounted to only a small portion of the series.

THE RESPONSE

Although "Together. . .Apart" drew an unprecedented response from readers and was the talk of the town for months, the New Orleans establishment reacted with cold silence. No religious or business group—or indeed any other organized group—spoke up in support of the *Times-Picayune's* argument that New Orleans needed to mount a major dialogue on "the gravest threat to the future of our community and nation." Perhaps, some would think later, the silence was a reaction to the hard look the series had taken at the racism of such institutions as business, industry, religion, and education.

The largely negative reader response shocked Kristin Gilger, the project leader. She read transcripts of all 6,500 "Speak Up" calls recorded by the paper and "felt every day I was being showered with hate, not just transcripts, but letters, tons of letters."

"The level of hatred astonished me," she said. "My father's Archie Bunker; it's not like I wasn't exposed to racism before. Ninety percent of the hatred came from whites. So little of it came from the blacks."

The reaction of the staff was divided, too. Gilger devoted most of her time to reviewing and editing "Speak Up," even though she had been designated editor of the overall project. It was just as well. The publisher, editor, and managing editor were all involved in the series, and the project staff was loosely structured, with other editors, as well as some reporters, taking part in the editing process. Several different people would make small editing decisions on a single article. The group dynamic was "slow and difficult," Gilger said. "You had to reach a consensus on everything and you would get tired of it."

Several other staffers complained that the editing process was cumbersome and frustrating. Coleman Warner, a white reporter from Meridian, Mississippi, felt "Too many people had a say about the tone of the stories, and many changes were made in the stories along the way."

Warner, who wrote the story about contrasting views concerning the treatment of slaves, had what he described as a "heated argument" with Keith Woods about the way his story quoted Mary Flower Pugh Russell, the white woman, in describing her view about slavery. In editing the story, Woods wanted to suggest that the woman's view that owners protected and took good care of slaves could not be true. Warner, who had located the woman and persuaded her to cooperate, thought she was entitled to her unvarnished view and sarcastically suggested that the city editor just call her a "liar" if he did not think she believed what she had said. Warner said that Woods eventually edited the story to his satisfaction, but that he found that incident and other parts of the editing process "physically and mentally exhausting."

Woods agrees that his editing, which juxtaposed slave descendent Lionel Tap's views of harsh treatment with Russell's views, was "a good outcome" to end the dispute with Warner. But Woods says he felt strongly that reporters should "make sure we didn't just allow people to make categorical statements that were immoral and wrong without in some way indicating where we stood on those issues."

At times when the project staff divided pretty much along racial lines, Peter Kovacs, the managing editor, "tried to keep feet in both camps" to avoid being frozen out by either faction. He worried about hard feelings and philosophical differences among the staffers concerning how much hopefulness the series should reflect. And the differences did not cut entirely along racial lines; mostly it was whites who thought the series should have been more hopeful or optimistic than it was.

A Community's Conscience Raised

Although some who worked on the project thought that it resulted in little in the way of concrete changes, the consensus of those looking back on it with six years of hindsight is that, while it was extremely difficult and time consuming to execute, it was a worthy endeavor that raised the community's consciousness on racial issues and to some extent helped change the newsroom culture. As Mark Lorando said, "Now people can approach the race issue with a candor that was not there before."

African Americans are covered more thoroughly throughout much of the paper now. Stories and photographs of African Americans in all walks of life— not just the stereotypical roles of athletes, entertainers, or criminal suspects— now appear throughout the paper. Black business and professional leaders are often quoted and pictured in the paper. While many papers abolished their society pages altogether, Jim Amoss points out that the *Times-Picayune* opted for diversification because it brought higher circulation penetration of the black community.

The perspectives of African American editors or reporters are now sought before publishing stories in which race is an issue. After the series was published the *Times-Picayune* discontinued its policy of publishing photographs of handcuffed prisoners who were regularly paraded in front of news cameras by New Orleans police. A great majority of the prisoners were black; white prisoners usually had lawyers to protect them from having to appear in such staged photographs.

African American editors also began to have more influence over how the *Times-Picayune* played some stories involving blacks. James O'Byrne cites two cases in which stories that had been scheduled to appear inside the paper were instead placed on page one after Terry Baquet, the assistant Sunday editor, argued that they involved news that was important, especially to the black community. One case involved an obituary of Avery Alexander, a militant black civil rights leader, and the other was about the Equal Employment Opportunity Commission charging a white auto dealer with abusing black employees. In both cases, O'Byrne said, the articles would have remained inside the paper, where white editors had consigned them, had Baquet not argued about their importance to black readers.

Editors also now enforce a rule in the *Times-Picayune* stylebook stipulating that people be identified by race or ethnic origin only when such identification is relevant to the story. And when such identifications are used, stories must offer explicit reasons why identifying race or ethnic origin is important.

An Exhausted Staff

Most project staffers, white and black, agree that the series left them feeling exhausted and glad when the project ended. In the words of Lisa Frazier, a black reporter who is now with the *Washington Post,* "Oh God, we were all mentally and emotionally exhausted." Mark Lorando recalls, "I tend to shudder a little when I think back on it. The diversity workshops and the series were all consuming. It created tensions at home and was hard on my marriage. The diversity workshops were valuable, but divided the newsroom between pro-diversity and those who were angry about it and considered the sessions brainwashing. Some people thought the race relations project was a horrible idea."

Coleman Warner and his wife both "wanted it over with." "I wasn't ashamed of the series or my part in it," he said, "but I wanted to put a stake through it. I was proud of most of it and what Amoss and Phelps were willing to attempt in this arena. Execution of it was the problem."

The series caused about 1,000 angry readers to cancel their subscriptions, according to Amoss. Phelps confirms that some subscriptions were canceled, but he downplays the number and significance of any cancellations and says that the series resulted in no loss of advertising.

In the long term, the series had relatively little impact on the newspaper's circulation, but Amoss and Phelps both stress that its circulation penetration in the mostly black community is almost as great as in the mostly white community.

Phelps also tended to downplay threats of one kind or another that some angry critics telephoned to the paper. "Jim Amoss and I were committed to 'Together. . .Apart,' and those who knew us may have known that threats would not produce any desired results. Also, the 'Speak Up' reader feedback feature may have channeled to that source calls that would have normally gone to the editor or publisher. I do not remember any significant threats in spite of the controversial nature of the series."

The *Times-Picayune's* series was a finalist for a Pulitzer Prize, but the prize was awarded to the *Akron (Ohio) Beacon-Journal,* for another series on race relations that was shorter and more analytical. Although the *Times-Picayune* did win a Pulitzer for public service in 1997 for a series on the Gulf of Mexico's pollution problems, Phelps still sees the race relations series as "the most significant work we've ever done."

Phelps also thinks "the most amazing thing" about it was the reader feedback. "Not to take anything away from the fine reporting," he said, "but in twenty-nine years I had never before seen readers read back-to-back pages and respond that way."

Epilogue

Looking back on the *Times-Picayune's* race relations series after six years, it is clear that this was hard-hitting, in-depth journalism that could not have been published without the efforts of a strong-willed editor willing to buck tradition and a supportive publisher willing to incur the expenses the coverage entailed and the wrath of many of the newspaper's readers. The series would never have materialized had it not been for the persistence of Keith Woods, who is now on the staff of the Poynter Institute. According to Amoss, "Keith was the father of this journalistic child; he nurtured it into existence." Gilger called Woods "absolutely essential, a true leader who could navigate between the black world and white world with credibility on both sides."

One of the most wrenching moments for Amoss, who had been with the paper for nineteen years and had been editor for four years, came when Woods and other black staffers argued that the series should report on the *Times-Picayune's* own racist past. Although he agreed with the demand and was supported by Phelps, he admitted that "It was painful for Ashton, and it was painful for me."

On the other hand, the series might have had more impact and been more widely read if it had been much shorter and more focused. It was so massive that even staffers who were enthusiastic about the series suggested that its sheer bulk probably asked too much of the reader.

A major disappointment in the eyes of some staffers was that, after the series was published, the paper produced no follow-up. Editors and reporters talked about such a project, but they could never agree on how to proceed. "I would like to have had a second shot," said Keith Woods. "But to a man and a woman we didn't know enough to turn the corner. Most people involved were happy not to even talk about it very much because the series involved so much personal strain."

At the same time, the series, together with the diversity workshops, created a newsroom atmosphere that became much more conducive to covering race issues effectively. That is the conclusion reached by Stacy A. Teicher, who wrote a comprehensive study of the *Times-Picayune* series for a 1998 master's thesis at the University of Missouri–Columbia Graduate School of Journalism.

Teicher found it difficult to measure the lasting impact of the series, but she concluded that

> At least, individuals learned and say they put into practice some significant lessons about coverage of race issues and ethnic minority groups. Editors in the newsroom say the project created a more open atmosphere and gave journalists a vocabulary for discussing race. Although style policy is constantly evolving, most people believe that the comprehensive racial identification policy took hold because of the lessons learned through the project. The most significant aspect of the racial identification policy, for this study, is the way a rigorous, systematic examination of the relevance of race has replaced what several people referred to as a knee-jerk (in other words, common sense) tendency to apply racial labels, especially in crime stories.

DISCUSSION QUESTIONS

1. What do you think of Amoss's rule that every article on race be "reviewed by a pair of African American eyes before publication?" How might you feel as a reporter if this were a rule where you worked? Would you welcome it? If not, why not?

2. Take a moment to consider the series that ran. What was its news value? Was it too much for a newspaper to tackle or was it fit for the news pages?

3. What about the paper's decision to acknowledge its own faults? Is it more likely to underscore its credibility or to bring more criticism?

SOURCES

The information for this case study was based on a thorough review of the series, an examination of Stacy A. Teicher's excellent master's thesis at the University of Missouri–Columbia, and many hours of interviews with *Times-Picayune* reporters and editors in October–November 1999. Some were in-person interviews and others were carried out by telephone. On October 27–28, the author visited New Orleans and had face-to-face interviews with, among others, editor Jim Amoss and publisher Ashton Phelps Jr.

The author conducted multiple interviews with several principals, who were especially helpful, including Amoss, managing editor Peter Kovacs, and former city editor Keith Woods. Others interviewed included Chris Adams, Kevin Bell, Tammy Carter, Stephen Casmier, Joyce Davis, Paula Devlin, Lisa Frazier, Kristin Gilger, Mark Lorando, James O'Byrne, and Coleman Warner. Unless indicated otherwise, all quotes come from these interviews.

Appendix

Together. . .Apart: The Myth of Race

We live together, black and white, in one community. But in so many ways we remain apart. In our lives, our neighborhoods and our workplaces, divisions exist along racial lines, perpetuating the myth that the color of our skin determines the content of our character.

For the past year, the *Times-Picayune* has examined relations between white people and black people in the metropolitan area. Those relationships, this special report will show, are rooted in our history—one that includes more than two centuries in which white people enslaved black people. Race relations have not completely broken free of that history.

The pain of our past echoes in the present and stifles honest discussion between the races. Today, the *Times-Picayune* begins an effort that will continue throughout the year to open that dialogue, by speaking openly about race, and by giving voice to people, black and white, from all walks of life.

New Orleans Times-Picayune, May 9, 1993, page A1. Copyright © 1993 *New Orleans Times-Picayune.*

Coming Together: Talking to Build Respect

COLEMAN WARNER, staff writer

The classroom full of black students pressed to get to the point.

What was this white man in front of them, they wanted to know, going to do about conditions in the inner city?

Maybe the rioting in Los Angeles was good, they said, because it focused attention on urban problems.

But a lot of people were killed in the process, replied their speaker, August Bailey.

Thus began a dialogue between Bailey and an eighth-grade boys' class at Carter G. Woodson Middle School in New Orleans. It's a discussion that expanded to include workers at the Navy center on Poland Avenue, where Bailey works.

The students took a field trip to the center and met with an assortment of Navy and civilian workers—black and white, men and women.

The adults and teenagers exchanged views about the Rodney King case and the fairness of the criminal justice system.

New Orleans Times-Picayune, May 9, 1993, page A22. Copyright © 1993 *New Orleans Times-Picayune.*

Bailey, 46, was invited to the class by a black friend, Ed LeBlanc, who has struck up a relationship with the class through the Boys To Men program. Through the program, black professionals serve as mentors to boys at Woodson, an Uptown school serving a public housing development.

LeBlanc urged Bailey to speak to the Woodson students, who view the white world as hostile to them.

Bailey said he was stunned at their anger. But now that the conversation has started, he wants it to continue. The students feel the same way. But they aren't making the dialogue easy.

The eighth-graders see themselves in the role of Bailey's teacher—about the world from a black perspective. And they are pulling no punches.

"We tore him up. He tried to tell us his own history," said Meredith Martin, 14. "What he was saying and what we were saying were two different things."

"One of the problems we have right now in race relations is just communication," said Oliver Thomas, a black housing management official who helped launch the Boys To Men program. "With our young people, if they have any differences, we want them to air them."

Double Standard; Many Merchants Overcharge, Overinspect or Overlook Black Customers

STEPHEN CASMIER and COLEMAN WARNER, staff writers

The big black man walked the aisles of the department store.

He wore a black and white bandana, dark sunglasses, black T-shirt, black jeans, an earring in his ear and an electronic device on his hip.

As usual, store workers trailed him to be sure he didn't steal anything.

They didn't know he was a Saint.

"When you go shopping, you go in there just to look, they come following you," said James Williams, a 230-pound linebacker with the New Orleans Saints who makes $325,000 a year.

He pointed to the device on his hip.

"They never think that this thing here goes to my car alarm," said Williams, who drives a white BMW. "They would think it's a beeper or they would automatically think I'm a drug dealer.

"I laugh about it sometimes, but I hate it."

African-Americans cannot go where they want, buy what they want or live where they want without fearing or feeling the sting of a discrimination that treats them as paupers or criminals.

Sales clerks, real estate agents, landlords, waiters and other service industry

New Orleans Times-Picayune, May 10, 1993, page A1. Copyright © 1993 *New Orleans Times-Picayune.*

employees often ignore, suspect or charge higher prices to African-Americans in an updated form of discrimination that is often subtle yet pervasive.

"We're just talking about everyday encounters in which differences are made between black people and white people," said Marsha Houston, a black communications professor at Tulane University.

"You know that is really what the concept of 'niggerizing' someone means," she said. "It means thinking of you as less than a human being, and therefore I don't ever have to treat you with respect or demonstrate everyday human courtesy."

Most white people say they don't see or take part in discrimination against African-Americans.

"I've had some dirty, nasty, repulsive whites come in, and I've been just as leery," said Carol Saunders Jahncke, the white owner of a small Covington gift shop. "You judge a man by his clothes. . . . If a very nice, nice black person comes in my shop, I'm no more nervous than I am when a nice white person comes in."

Other white people argue—usually in private—that it is reasonable to treat black consumers negatively because they commit crimes or act unruly out of proportion to their numbers in the population.

Lawyer John Musser, a white former federal prosecutor, said he believes people of both races view black people as more likely to commit crimes, stemming from crime statistics and news reports.

And Paul Varisco, a white New Orleans retailer, said that while his staff is taught that any customer may shoplift, "I'm sure there is a perception out there that black people do it more." He said black shoppers are more likely to say they want to be left alone by store workers, and such remarks arouse suspicion.

Regardless of the cause, so-called marketplace discrimination occurs on a "massive" scale, said Joe Feagin, a white University of Florida sociologist who studies race relations. Complaints about such treatment were made often in interviews Feagin recently conducted with more than 200 middle-class black Americans in 16 cities.

"Many of them report, as one elderly woman put it, the 'little murders' every day," he said.

These "little murders" occur when white store managers make snap judgments about whether a black customer is a shoplifting threat, or when a black family faces an ordeal in renting or buying a home.

Although African-Americans hold a considerable degree of political power in New Orleans, they are virtually impotent against acts of racism in stores or other public places, Mayor Sidney Barthelemy said.

"In the smaller stuff . . . you're almost powerless really," Barthelemy said. "How can you say how someone treats someone when they're trying to buy a product, or if they're shopping and they're being followed simply because they're black?"

Doors Slam Shut

Incidents of marketplace discrimination are so varied and often so subtle that no single study describes the problem.

But carefully controlled investigations by the U.S. Department of Housing and Urban Development and the American Bar Association found clear evidence of discrimination in areas where consumers spend large chunks of their money: on housing and cars.

One of every two African-Americans who rent an apartment or buy a house faces discrimination, according to a 1989 national study by HUD that included data from the New Orleans area.

The differing treatment often comes at a subtle level: Real estate agents don't call their black customers back or don't show them as many units.

White civil rights lawyer Bill Quigley recalls a complaint brought against a Metairie apartment complex where office workers wrote "very nice person" at the bottom of an application. The notation was a code.

It was used to warn office workers that the applicant was an African-American and should be passed over when a vacancy occurred. The allegation, settled out of court, was made by someone who had worked for the apartment complex, he said.

Barthelemy said his sister-in-law recently had an experience familiar to black renters, "where she talked to the people over the phone and they said the place was available to be rented, and when she went and they saw what she looked like they told her it was rented out."

Landlords can find other ways to discourage African-American renters. They ask for extensive references, require higher security deposits, or hunt for details on applications that can be used to disqualify.

"People are much more sophisticated," said Ron Chisom, a black director of the New Orleans–based People's Institute for Survival and Beyond, which conducts workshops on undoing racism. "They're not as blatant, because there are so many damn laws."

For example, some landlords or sellers use what Feagin calls "runaround discrimination" to deter African-Americans.

"They don't tell you to your face, because you're black you're not going to get this house," he said. "But everything is going great and then all of a sudden, you learn that the owner's not going to send you a contract and you can't find out why, and your real estate agent can't find out why."

Yet many in the real estate community insist fair housing laws, codes of ethics and improved training of sellers have virtually eliminated housing discrimination.

"If it occurs, it occurs at a minimal level," said Conchita Sulli, a Hispanic who is past president of the Jefferson Board of Realtors. "I know that we discourage the practice of discrimination completely."

Another white real estate agent was less sanguine. Many white people associate African-Americans with poverty and fear the change they may bring to a neighborhood, she said.

"Sometimes it's more of a discrimination against poverty than against race, and more of the poor just happen to be black," said the agent, who did not want to be named. "They're scared of the poverty, they're scared of the other things that go with it, the crack dealers, the crime."

But John Yinger, a white Syracuse University economics professor who partici-pated in the HUD study, blames prejudice, not poverty. Many white people don't want to live next to black people of any income level, he said.

"It's still true that many real estate brokers are in a difficult position where they're working in a white community that doesn't want any blacks to move in," Yinger said.

PROFITING FROM PREJUDICE

In the car-buying arena, African-American customers have reason to be on guard during price negotiations. Black customers pay more for their cars than white cus-tomers, a 1990 study of Chicago-area car dealerships by the American Bar Associa-tion concluded. The study also found women pay more than men.

Bob Benson, the white executive vice president of Benson Automotive World and a leader of the Louisiana Automobile Association, said no market-savvy car dealer would quote different prices according to race or gender.

"I can tell you very unequivocally that guy is not going to be around very long in business. The word will get out," he said. "In our own organization we don't dif-ferentiate between classes or races. It's sheer idiocy in today's world."

But the study seems on target to Kevin Williams, a black executive analyst who sold cars in the New Orleans area for four years.

A car seller's livelihood depends on making snap judgments about customers, he said. And salespeople often find it easier to take advantage of an African-American customer, Williams said.

"It's not that they're bigger suckers, it's that they're less educated to the process." Williams said. "They haven't been buying cars in their families for genera-tions. They don't know the terminology sometimes."

Other times, salespeople doubt whether an African-American customer can afford the car, Williams said. It's common when a seller is working with an African-American customer to run a quick credit check before trying to strike a deal, he said. That is done less often with white customers.

In the same way, workers in many retail stores use race to make judgments on who will be a paying customer, a good credit risk or a potential thief.

MAKING JUDGMENTS

When Derrick Taylor, a black engineer, goes to a jewelry counter, clerks often test him before showing the merchandise.

"The first thing they're going to tell me is how much it costs," he said. "They want to know if I can pay for it."

And white sales clerks often are less eager to serve African-American cus-tomers.

This happens all the time in one local upscale department store, said Denese Shervington, a local psychiatrist who is black. "I don't get attended to and I have to almost go and demand it, especially if I go in certain sections of the store and they think I'm not able to afford it."

Black customers say white clerks are especially cautious at the checkout counter, scampering off for managers' approvals or scanning bad-check lists.

"It's like when I go to the supermarket and every time they check the bad-check list, and I'll glance in front and behind and if it's someone white they may not do that," Shervington said.

Some stores have written the race of a customer on a check; some Jefferson Parish merchants said last year that the district attorney's office had told them it would not investigate a bad-check case without the person's race on the check.

Jefferson District Attorney John Mamoulides has said his policy was misunderstood and race was not a mandatory detail. Since the dispute erupted, Rep. Troy Carter, D-Algiers, proposed a law that could send store owners to jail if they ask customers to designate their race on a check.

Check procedures aren't the only worry of black customers. Like actors in an Orwellian nightmare, they are pursued by the stares and glances of clerks and security guards as they walk store aisles.

"Nine times out of 10, if I get the whim to go browsing, I won't indulge it because I have to weigh whether or not I feel like being aggravated by security following my every step," said Chris Harris, 30, who is black and has worked in retail stores.

"It's something that takes an emotional toll on you and it almost affects me physically. Sometimes you just get angry and there's nothing you can really do about it."

Some African-Americans argue that unruly black people are partly to blame for the persistence of marketplace discrimination. The disruptive behavior of a few hurts everybody, they said.

"I've seen a large part of the black community bring racism on themselves," said a black pre-law student at the University of New Orleans. "Just because I'm black, that sticks to me."

Such explanations neglect to mention racism as the root cause of marketplace discrimination, said Houston, the Tulane professor.

White Americans have the same potential for savage acts, for bouncing checks, for theft and murder, she said.

"Society says that it's OK to judge all of us [African-Americans] by the behavior of a few of us, but it doesn't say that about white people," she said. "It doesn't say that we're going to judge all white men by the behavior of serial killers and child molesters, for example, who may be white."

Meanwhile, the shower of daily insults can take a psychological toll, producing stress responses such as depression, dissatisfaction with life and hopelessness, Shervington said.

Shervington said she sometimes screams when she gets home to vent her frustration. Others may scream at clerks before they leave the store.

Many black parents try to steel their children against insults by teaching them that the people who mistreat them are the ones with the problem.

Others take great care to dress up before shopping, even when in the mood for jeans or a sweatsuit, to avoid arousing suspicion or to increase their shot at good service.

As Derrick Taylor, the engineer, shopped at a local department store one day, a security camera observed him deliberately pushing his own parcel away from his body as he bent down to look at some underwear on a bottom shelf. He said he didn't want anyone to suspect him of stuffing shorts in his bag.

"You build an armor around yourself, and it's not really fair," Taylor said.

"I'm still a nigger. That's the way they see me, anyway."

Children of History: A Family Journal

JAMES O'BYRNE, staff writer

When Terrence Duvernay graduated from college with academic honors, the federal government offered him a chance to fulfill a dream.

In exchange for 10 weeks of training out of state, labor department officials promised to hire Duvernay and send him to the impoverished New Orleans neighborhood of his youth. There, he would help people get job training and find work.

But when Duvernay got back to New Orleans in 1964, he faced a different reality.

"I went to the director's office and showed him my certificate and told him what I had learned and how valuable it was," Duvernay recalled. "And he said, 'That's great—except in Louisiana, we're not ready to hire any blacks yet.'"

For Rose Fatima, as for all enslaved women, it was always the same: what the white man came for, the white man got—even if what he came for was her.

Joseph Duvernay was not an unusual Louisiana plantation owner. African slaves were chattel. He could do with them what he liked.

The details of the relationship between Duvernay and Fatima are lost in history. Was it rape? Can a man get consent from a woman who is property, who has no rights? Would he even bother to ask?

From their sexual union came a son, Moliere Duvernay, half European, half African. But not half free.

Because one of his parents was enslaved, so was Moliere. He became free when his white father decided he should be. But his father couldn't make Moliere a white man. That half of him meant nothing. He lived as a black man all his life. And free or not, light-skinned or dark, he was constantly reminded of his place in society. Less than white people. Stained by black blood. Inferior by birth.

Terrence Duvernay learned that he took his name from a white French planter when a fellow employee in City Hall told him they are cousins. Jack Belsom, Duvernay's

New Orleans Times-Picayune, May 11, 1993, page A1. Copyright © 1993 *New Orleans Times-Picayune.*

cousin, was the director of the New Orleans Civil Service Commission before his retirement in 1988. A civil servant by vocation, Belsom, 59, is by avocation a historian and genealogist.

Belsom can trace his roots back to the Duvernay family. Joseph Duvernay's grandfather is Belsom's ancestor, too.

So Belsom and Duvernay share a common ancestry. They grew up in New Orleans. They should have much to talk about, much to find in common about their lives and those of their fathers and grandfathers and relatives back through the years.

But they do not.

That's because the two families, the Belsoms and the Duvernays, have lived distinctly different lives, divided by one inescapable reality of America: Duvernay is descended from a slave. Belsom is not.

It was a critical distinction in Moliere Duvernay's time. It remains one today.

The story of the Duvernays and the Belsoms is the story of race relations in New Orleans. They are blood relatives, and yet family in name only. Because throughout their family histories, from the 1700s to today, racism remains a powerful force, a divide between privilege and punishment.

When Belsom talks about growing up in New Orleans, he talks of living in a neighborhood almost entirely white, attending all-white schools, playing only with white children, going to college at all-white Tulane University and never having close contact with black people until he was an adult. Black people were virtually invisible to him.

"The buses were segregated, the schools were segregated, everything was separate," Belsom recalls about growing up in his Uptown neighborhood. "It wasn't really something we talked about. We could do what we wanted. We never had the feeling of being excluded."

White people were painfully visible to Terrence Duvernay. They were the playmates of his early childhood, white children who reached school age and were ordered by their parents to stop playing with Duvernay because he was black.

They were the students whose names filled the pages of his old textbooks—so many signatures that there was no place left for the names of the black pupils.

"The thing I remember most about going to junior high school was that it was the first time I had ever seen a new textbook, one that hadn't been used by white kids first," Duvernay said.

White folks owned the houses and had the children that were cleaned and cared for by the black women of his neighborhood, who left their Central City homes and families each morning to walk or catch the streetcar heading Uptown, and returned home weary and worn that night to take care of their own.

Questions of Color

The difference between black and white has always been abundantly clear to Greg Osborn.

Growing up in Los Angeles, Osborn, 26, would often be presumed to be white. Other times, people would be puzzled and ask if he was white or black. "Neither," was always his answer. "I'm a Creole."

It is an answer that has not always satisfied. White people often are confused, uncomfortable with the notion of someone who will not choose black or white. Black people often accuse him of betraying his race, of thinking he's better than them because of his light skin and his white ancestry.

Osborn is a cousin to Jack Belsom as well. The two of them share a white ancestor dating back to the earliest years of the Louisiana colony in the late 17th and early 18th centuries. But unlike Belsom, who has lived all his life as a white man, and Duvernay, who has lived all his life black, Osborn spent 19 years trying to live as a Creole, taking haven in the definition that he thought allowed him to live in any world he wished. Neither white, nor black. A mix of both, yet unlike either.

Osborn thought he could stay on the fence, not choose. Hadn't his grandparents done it? In church, as Creoles they had to sit behind the white people. But they got to sit in front of the black people. They were less than the group in power. But at least not at the bottom.

Osborn's family grew up in New Orleans. His parents moved out to the West Coast before he was born. He moved to New Orleans last year because he says it is where he feels at home.

He has discovered New Orleans is an extraordinarily diverse place, where assumptions about what a person is are suspect. It is a place where white people Uptown and black people downtown both call themselves Creoles—and disagree on what that means.

But when it comes to black and white, there is no middle ground. If you're not all white, then you're black. White people even developed a language to describe degrees of blackness. Octoroon. Quadroon. Mulatto. One-eighth, one-fourth, one-half. A little black was the same as being all black.

Today, white people who have African ancestry still are confronted with the racism that makes them view that ancestry as tainted, that gives it the power to obliterate other ethnicities, other colors. And so they do not embrace it as part of themselves.

White people with African ancestry have even fought lengthy court battles to be declared white. There is no evidence of anyone in Louisiana ever going to court to be declared black.

Researchers in genealogy and history in New Orleans know that thousands of people here who consider themselves white have black ancestors. Many of them know it. Yet few will discuss it publicly. For most white people, blackness remains an unspeakable stigma.

FORCED TO CHOOSE

It was a racist white friend who pushed Osborn off the fence, who made him come to terms with America's color line, with the determination of people to force a choice.

"I was black on paper until I was 19," Osborn said. "That means if people assumed I was white, I didn't do anything to dissuade them. But I had a good friend, a white person, who was overtly racist. He would call people nigger. He hated minorities.

"Then when I got accepted to prep school, he told all my friends it was only because I was a minority. That's when it hit me. How can I say it's OK for him to call people with skin darker than mine nigger, but not me? How could I be prejudiced against my own family?"

Since Osborn has moved to New Orleans, he has begun searching for answers to the question, "What am I?" In the search, he has been forced to confront the potency of black ancestry in the American experience.

Indeed, the way white people define blackness has been such a powerful force that a drop of black blood can make a person black, no matter how many white relatives a person has.

White lawmakers in Louisiana legally defined whiteness in terms of how much black ancestry a person had. Until 1983, anyone with 132nd black blood was considered legally black. A single great-great-great grandparent of African ancestry, long since dead, determined what race someone was, even if all 31 other great-great-great grandparents were white.

Most states have had similar standards. There is no other ethnic corollary in America, and few places on earth where such an all-or-nothing racial ideology has endured for so long.

Osborn came to realize that in America, he really didn't have a choice. And he realized that by choosing "Creole," he was obscuring part of who he was.

"When you're mixed, you don't have the stability of knowing what you are and who you are, and having that knowledge seems to be important to people somehow," Osborn said. "I had problems being viewed as black. I needed to be confronted with my own racism, to understand my own blackness."

He also understood that his lack of choice grew out of slavery. And the search for understanding who he is was partly the search for a slave.

"I wanted to know who in my background was all something," Osborn said. "I found her. She's my great-grandmother's great-grandmother. She was a slave."

And since the child of a slave in America was usually a slave, the women's children were born into slavery as well. So were the sons and daughters of white slaveowners, men who impregnated African women, but were repelled enough by African blood often to keep their children in bondage.

Polls confirm that many white people believe slavery is irrelevant to relations today between black people and white people.

And yet the attitude that made slavery possible, the attitude that white people are superior, black people inferior, has a frightening resilience. It has built and maintained separate worlds, black and white, that persist today.

It is the attitude that caused white people for 240 years in America to treat black people as less than human, to enslave them and beat them and rape them and sometimes kill them.

It is an attitude demonstrated in the structure of the white-dominated city in which Jack Belsom grew up, where he always sat in the front of the streetcar, and was allowed to attend the city's best schools, where he got the newest textbooks and gained entry into the city's best university—privileges that white people denied to black people.

It is the same attitude that caused Osborn to recognize instantly the advantages of identifying himself as something other than a black person, that caused him to use his whiteness to his advantage and to feel superior to black people in the process, until he realized it was racist.

And the attitude has changed little between 1863, when slavery ended in New Orleans, and a time less than a century later in Central City, when a little boy taught Terry Duvernay a lesson about race, one that would stay with Duvernay for the rest of his life.

"Vincent was the son of the white store owners of the corner grocery," Duvernay recalled. "He was my friend. And one day he came to me about the time it was time for us to start school and he said, 'I can't play with you anymore because my parents told me black and white kids don't play together.'

"We never played again. And it hurt me. I wasn't mad, but it hurt me. I understood there was a difference between black and white. But I did not know until that moment that it extended that far. That was my first real understanding about how far it would go."

New Orleans' Newspapers Give White View of the City

CHRIS ADAMS, staff writer

On Aug. 12, 1990, Chelita Bolden and Ashley Alldredge made history. In the *Times-Picayune*'s annual debutante section, the photo of Bolden was published next to the photo of Alldredge. Bolden is black, Alldredge is white. And for the 156-year-old newspaper, placing such photos side-by-side was a first.

Until then—128 years after slavery ended, 36 years after the Supreme Court deemed separate-but-equal unacceptable, 27 years after Martin Luther King Jr. talked of little black girls and little white girls playing side-by-side—black debs and white debs came out on separate pages of the *Times-Picayune*.

White debutantes were showcased in a section of the Sunday newspaper devoted just to them; a small biography and picture were included for each white debutante. Black debutantes were shown over several days in regular issues of the newspaper; they never received the full treatment, with the biography, that white debs did.

New Orleans Times-Picayune, June 17, 1993, page A18. Copyright © 1993 *New Orleans Times-Picayune.*

That separate-but-unequal debutante policy is but one part of a long history during which the *Times-Picayune* and its predecessors demonstrated racial hostility, racial intolerance and racial insensitivity. For most of its years, historians and journalists said, the newspaper has been a powerful force in New Orleans, shaping and reflecting racial attitudes and the character of the city. And for the greater part of its years, the newspaper gave readers an image of black people as intellectually and morally inferior, relegated to a lower social caste than white people and often little more than lazy or criminal. It's that image of black people that many people carry today.

But the newspaper has changed, and most people say it has changed dramatically. It has gone from the *Daily Picayune* of the 1880s that referred to black people as "besotted barbarians" to the *Times-Picayune* of the 1990s that at times is praised for coverage of racial issues. Publisher Ashton Phelps Jr., who is white, points out that the 66 percent of black New Orleans area adults reading the daily *Times-Picayune* newspaper is one point less than the figure for all adults—and higher than in other newspaper markets. "I don't know a newspaper in the country that can't improve," he said. "But it would appear our team is doing some things right."

Editor Jim Amoss, who is white, says he is committed to publishing a newspaper that truly reflects the area's racial diversity, and has taken steps to do that. The newspaper has brought in more black journalists and endeavored to make the newsroom a more hospitable place for black employees.

But internal change alone won't alter how readers view the *Times-Picayune*. From many quarters, it is seen as a paper that, through its years, "was never the most hostile to blacks, but never the most friendly," as white University of New Orleans historian Joe Logsdon put it. "It usually spoke for the white business community. And in that sense, it hasn't changed."

Many people remember a newspaper that fought to keep schools segregated, calling integration "evil" and King a "troublemaker." The *Times-Picayune* was a paper with no full-time black reporters until the 1970s, one that rarely wrote about black people unless they committed crimes.

"That history is a burden the *Picayune* will have to bear," said Norman Francis, who is black, president of Xavier University and a member of the *Times-Picayune* Advisory Board. "I do believe the paper is changing. But there are times I read it and realize again that, yes, it still is a white paper."

CONSERVATIVE PAPER BORN DURING SLAVE ERA

What readers grab from their doorstep today began on a rainy winter day in 1837. A small paper named for a Spanish coin took up shop in a cramped office at 38 Gravier St.

From its inception, the *Picayune* was one of the most conservative papers in town, according to white historian Philip Mabe, who wrote his doctoral dissertation on the racial ideology of New Orleans newspapers.

At times, 19th century New Orleans had a dozen newspapers, including several—the *Times*, the *Democrat*, the *Daily States*, the *Daily City Item*—which over the years merged into the *Times-Picayune* that readers see today. Most of those papers were white, conservative and racist like the *Daily Picayune*. At the same time, New Orleans also was home to the first black-owned daily newspaper in the country—the defunct *Tribune*—and to newspapers that advocated an end to slavery, such as the *Republican* and the German-language *Deutsche Zeitung*.

During the late 1800s, the *Daily Picayune* habitually demeaned black people, referring to them as "besotted barbarians" full of "natural dullness and cowardice." Slaveowners, meanwhile, provided "protection, kindness and comfort" to "inferior" Negroes, most of whom were "content with their situation in life," the newspaper said.

"The negro has a long stride to make before he reaches the degree of intelligence of even the most ignorant class of whites," the newspaper said. And of the scholarly abolitionist Frederick Douglass, the paper said: "Douglass is half-white. How are we to be resolved that it is not the white part of his nature that has given him such intellect?"

For historians such as Mabe, the *Daily Picayune* was much more than just a proslavery newspaper making money from runaway slave ads.

Before the Civil War, newspapers paid little attention to slavery. When the North threatened the South, however, white people dug in their heels, determined to preserve the social superiority of white people, Mabe said. With every other institution in town—the banks, the government—controlled by the Union Army, New Orleans newspapers were in a unique position of power.

By 1872, the editor of the *Daily Picayune* crowed that his paper "was the mightiest engine of public opinion in the city."

Mabe agrees. "The *Daily Picayune* and two other conservative white newspapers became the single most important factor in setting the tone for a system of race relations virtually unknown in the city," he said. "The press talked so long and so forcefully about controlling blacks that it confirmed in the public's mind the route they had to take."

"CRAZED NEGROES" POPULATE PAGES

That course was Jim Crow, the set of laws that lasted from the 1880s to the mid-1960s and denied black people basic civil rights.

The *Daily Picayune* pushed for many of those laws, including a poll tax that wiped black voters off the rolls. And when a proposal was introduced to prohibit discrimination in hotels, the newspaper railed against the "inky black," the "Congo kinky heads," the "fat, shapeless Negroes" who supported it. The proposal was defeated.

Then, with Jim Crow firmly in place, the *Daily Picayune* and subsequently the *Times-Picayune* either ignored black people or ridiculed them. To the reading public of New Orleans it must have appeared as though black people were either "crazed" or simply crazy.

- April 28, 1931: "Girl Is Slashed with Jackknife by Crazed Negro"
- April 6, 1930: "Seven-Foot Alligator Shares Bed with Negro Woman Who Has Trained Creature as Pet"
- Aug. 16, 1923: "Negro in Hospital after Exchanging Kicks with Mule"

Even when black people made advances in intellectual or artistic circles, the *Times-Picayune* berated them. For example, in the city generally considered the birthplace of jazz, the *Times-Picayune* of the 1920s "portrayed jazz as a noisy art, as non-musical jungle music," said Luther Williams, a Xavier University journalism professor, who is black. "News of jazz stars as late as 1965 wasn't even mentioned."

In 1954, a young white reporter named Fritz Harsdorff joined the paper. One night, when a local sailor was killed, the editors asked Harsdorff to work up a story.

"I sent a cab to get a photo," Harsdorff said. "We didn't know he was black. The cab driver took every picture the family had. But when we saw the pictures, we didn't run even one of them.

"Black people just weren't covered," Harsdorff said. "You've got to understand that down here the Civil War was still on the minds of the people, and those attitudes were just embedded into the operation of the paper."

The other papers that eventually became part of the *Times-Picayune* said much the same things. In a 1947 investigation, for example, the *New Orleans Item* seemed, for the first time, to uncover an alien culture in its midst: "The New Orleans Negro has a strong strain of nature worship in his blood which accounts for his rich emotionalism. . . . By nature, too, the Negro is a vegetarian."

KEEPING UP WITH KING AND THE COMMUNISTS

But with the 1954 *Brown vs. Board of Education* decision, the U.S. Supreme Court ushered in the civil rights era. Many white newspapers led the resistance, stirring up the defiant feelings of the Old South. A few bucked popular opinion, saying it was time for the South to change its Jim Crow ways.

The *Times-Picayune* stood in the middle. The paper wasn't for integration, but it asked the people of Louisiana to obey the law.

"The *Picayune* had a great opportunity and we didn't take it," said Bill Minor, a white columnist who was the *Times-Picayune*'s correspondent in Jackson, Miss., for 30 years. "Civil rights was the biggest story of the day, and the *Picayune* didn't understand it."

An example, Minor said, was the coverage of James Meredith's bid to enter the University of Mississippi in Oxford in 1962. As riots swept the campus, President John F. Kennedy sent in federal marshals. Minor begged his editors for extra help.

"The *New York Times* had 10 reporters there. *Newsweek* had another 10," Minor said. "I had to cover it for the *Picayune* all by myself."

In time, the *Times-Picayune* did go along with integration, and like many Southern papers, gave adequate if uninspired coverage of the civil rights movement. In its news pages, the paper wrote about laws that were being changed in Washington, but little else. And the paper often didn't agree with civil rights activists or their methods.

In 1962, for example, the *Times-Picayune* and four other newspapers ran a story about how the new executive director of the Southern Christian Leadership Council was a communist. The story—which was false—had been planted in all five papers by the FBI, which was trying to discredit the movement by painting SCLC founder King as a communist, according to King biographer David Garrow.

School Integration: "The Dreadful Day"

The *Times-Picayune* also battled school integration, the biggest civil rights issue of the day. Between 1954, when the U.S. Supreme Court delivered its landmark *Brown vs. Board of Education* decision, and 1960, when the first trickle of integration started, the *Times-Picayune* used its editorial pages to help the state resist federal integration orders.

The day after the *Brown* decision, the *Times-Picayune*'s editorial said the decision would "do no service either to education or racial accommodation." In 1956, it ran a lengthy editorial detailing how the state could use legal technicalities to resist the Supreme Court's decision. In 1960, a front-page editorial endorsed a candidate for School Board, partly because he "has proved himself an ardent opponent of forced integration."

As it sometimes referred to integration as an "evil," the *Times-Picayune* said its only choice was to pick the lesser of "two evils."

In its editorial headlines, it called the coming of integration "A Time for Sorrow" and "The Dreadful Day."

"The day most New Orleanians had dreaded came Monday," the newspaper said after integration was a fait accompli. "So far as we are concerned, we don't like school integration any better in 1960 than we did in 1954, when we urged a relentless legal fight against it."

"Other newspapers in the South did a much better job on this issue," said Logsdon, the UNO professor and author of *Crescent City Schools*. "When desegregation came, everybody thought New Orleans would be a good place to start. But the newspaper didn't give any leadership."

Changes Slow to Come in Newsroom

Joyce Davis started at the *Times-Picayune* in 1972, just as the newspaper made its first halting changes.

Still a student at Loyola University, Davis was hired as one of the *Times-Picayune*'s first full-time black reporters. Before the 1970s, there had been only one black writer, the late Marcus Neustadter, who occasionally submitted stories about the black community. In the late 1960s, there had been public protests against the *Times-Picayune* because it had no fulltime black reporters. The newspaper hired a few black reporters in the early 1970s, and those numbers gradually increased during the decade. Also during that time, a lawsuit against the newspaper led to the eventual signing of a consent decree with the federal Equal Employment Opportunity Commission that required the *Times-Picayune* to hire more black workers in several areas, including photography.

"I got the sense I was just there to fill a space, and they were intent just to ignore me," said Davis, who became an editor at the *Times-Picayune* before leaving in 1990 to be an editor at National Public Radio in Washington, D.C.

Davis said she endured her share of racist jokes and slurs. One editor would come to work drunk, hurling racist insults at her, she said. At the same time, however, there were other people, mostly young, "who went out of their way to help me. Without them, I never would have stood a chance," she said.

Black reporters, for the most part, kept those incidents to themselves. By the time Davis broke into the reporting ranks, Harsdorff was associate editor, news. He was specifically mentioned by black reporters for his friendly ways. But he still didn't see the hostility the black reporters were encountering.

"The first black reporters we hired, hell, they were accepted right away," Harsdorff recalled. "I had some trepidation about it, to tell the truth. In the beginning, there was a little hesitation to assign black reporters to black stories, because I guess there was a fear it might be slanted. But that didn't happen.

"I think it was just great the way it worked."

Black Journalists Feel Isolated

But just as disturbing to Davis, and to some white reporters at the newspaper, was the *Times-Picayune*'s approach to news.

"The thing that was really oppressive was having to be the sole source of dissension at every meeting," Davis said. "I didn't have anybody who supported me. If I constantly spoke up, I'd feel like I was on the outside. If I didn't speak up, I'd feel I was betraying my mission for being there."

In 1978, Paul Lester, a white *Times-Picayune* photographer and now a journalism professor at California State University, Fullerton, started working on a new picture page called "Tuesday." Lester proposed a story and pictures about a Magazine Street gym that trained boxers, most of whom were black.

"I was told, 'No, that can't be the first story because it's too black,'" Lester said. "It would give people and the advertisers the idea that's what the magazine was all about."

Merger Brings Coverage Changes

In 1980, the *Times-Picayune* and the *States-Item* merged. Although the *Times-Picayune* was the larger of the two newspapers, *States-Item* editor Charles A. Ferguson became editor of the merged paper.

At the time, the *States-Item* was suffering the fate of many afternoon papers: It was losing readers and advertisers to the *Times-Picayune,* which came out in the morning. The *Times-Picayune* was read by more than twice the number of both black and white adults as the *States-Item.*

Even so, most black people interviewed today said the *States-Item,* although still clearly a white paper, had been less hostile to the city's black population than the *Times-Picayune.*

In 1969, the *States-Item* had been granted editorial independence from the *Times-Picayune* by then-publisher Ashton Phelps Sr., and was allowed to distinguish itself from the *Times-Picayune.* The *States-Item* was more likely to write stories about black people, such as a series of vignettes about famous African-Americans that ran during Black History Month. The newspaper also did special series on the emerging black middle class and on the new group of black politicians who were taking power.

"So when it became the *Times-Picayune* alone [in 1980], the feelings were, 'Oh my God, we've lost our voice,'" said Francis, Xavier's president. "That's not to say the *States-Item* ever really helped black people much, but at least it didn't hurt us."

Since then—in the view of Francis and others—the *Times-Picayune* has attempted to cover issues important to the black community. Sometimes they're covered well, sometimes poorly. Arnold Hirsch, a white University of New Orleans historian, cited the paper's coverage of Ernest "Dutch" Morial, the city's first black mayor.

The *Times-Picayune* did endorse Morial—a position decidedly unpopular among most white New Orleanians. In 1978, when he first ran for mayor, the newspaper endorsed a white candidate in the primary, but Morial in the runoff. In 1982, it endorsed Morial for reelection against white state Rep. Ron Faucheux.

At the same time, however, Hirsch contends the paper treated Morial differently than it would have a white politician. He said the paper overplayed the brash and aggressive aspects of Morial's personality without addressing the issues he pushed.

"The *Picayune* was not quite ready to deal with the phenomenon Dutch was at the time," Hirsch said. "I don't think the ownership or staff displayed knowledge of—or concern for—Morial's constituency."

Dwight Webster, who is black, is minister of the Christian Unity Baptist Church in New Orleans. He said he is starting to see reporting in the *Times-Picayune* that he considers fair, important and balanced.

"So we know there's some pretty outstanding black people there, and some whites, but it's still nothing that the black community has any partnership with," Webster said. "I can't tell you how many black people have told me they were so disgusted with the *Times-Picayune* that they canceled their subscriptions. I've done so twice myself. It's almost a ritual."

Amoss, the *Times-Picayune*'s editor, recognizes the position the newspaper is in.

"Until the 1960s, the newspaper didn't run photos of black people on page one," said Amoss, who has been editor since 1990. "If that's part of your experience as a reader, it's not something you can just purge from your system and say, 'Oh, yes, they've turned over a new leaf.' I think it's a long, long evolutionary process, and I suppose some black people will never embrace us as their newspaper."

Attention to Race Brings Reader Backlash

At the same time, the *Times-Picayune* is under fire by some white readers.

During David Duke's campaign for governor, for example, many readers praised the *Times-Picayune*'s reporting on Duke's white supremacist past. But the newspaper also was deluged with complaints from white readers that it was going overboard, unfairly harping on Duke's past and letting opinion creep into its news stories.

Likewise, the appearance of the paper's first local black columnist three years ago was praised by many as positive and long overdue. But not everybody agrees. As one white reader wrote columnist Lisa Frazier: "Do you expect a black woman to be impartial and unbiased? All you're going to get is black, black, black. . . . Too bad there are more no-good blacks than good ones."

That same sentiment prompted a white Metairie reader to write: "We only wish you would leave the black people's news out. You do remember why we moved to Metairie from N.O., don't you?"

Such complaints aside, if the *Times-Picayune* is to be a mirror of the New Orleans area, as editor Amoss hopes it will be, it has a ways to go. The reflection the area sees today is still out of focus.

Although black people are featured in the news pages far more than they used to be, the vast majority of photos and stories are of white people: white people getting married, white people shopping, white people as advertising models.

Why is that? History plays a large part.

For example, the newspaper publishes all the wedding photos it gets from readers. But because many black readers remember when the newspaper wouldn't publish their wedding photos, they are less inclined to drop the photos off, Amoss said.

Such largely white images can be seen in other historically white papers across the country. Lester, the California professor, conducted a 1990 study in which he counted the photos in the *Times-Picayune* and other large metropolitan newspapers. The results show the *Times-Picayune* fares as well as other large papers in the percentage of its photos that are of African-Americans. Especially considering its past, the *Times-Picayune* should be commended, Lester said. But when taking into account the large black population the newspaper serves, he said, the *Times-Picayune* continues to give its readers an out-of-focus picture of African-Americans.

As in other large papers, a large percentage of the photos in the *Times-Picayune* were what Lester considered "stereotypical": black people as entertainers, athletes or criminals.

"If all a white reader sees is African-Americans who are criminals and entertainers and sports figures, then that's the impression they'll develop about African-Americans," Lester said.

That was the conclusion of the Kerner Commission, formed 25 years ago by President Lyndon Johnson to investigate the causes of riots and racial unrest that rocked American cities in the 1960s. One cause, the commission said, was American newspapers.

"It would be a contribution of inestimable importance to race relations," the commission concluded, "simply to treat ordinary news about Negroes as news of other groups is now treated—in all parts of the paper, from the news, society and club pages to the comic strips."

Those same complaints are made against the *Times-Picayune* today. Since the Kerner Commission, the *Times-Picayune* has fully integrated black people into some aspects of the news pages; the news sections and feature sections reflect a range of African-American people and interests. But other sections are still disproportionately white: In a recent month of society pages, for example, 96 percent of the photos were of white people; 85 percent of the brides and grooms were white.

And a recent Sunday comics section had 58 white characters and four black characters. There were more animal characters—two dogs, two cats, one tiger, one bird and one penguin—than black characters.

Newspaper Has Instituted Change

The *Times-Picayune* has undertaken several changes in the past few years in an attempt to better serve its market.

For example, the newspaper is trying to increase the number of African-American reporters and editors on its staff through recruiting efforts such as a minority job fair the paper held earlier this year, its second in four years.

Further, the paper is engaged in an intensive series of sessions designed to help employees work in a multicultural environment. It's the culmination of a process begun in 1989 when former assistant metro editor Davis started a support group for black journalists, and a similar group for female journalists began to meet.

Both groups of journalists felt they were being ignored, passed over for promotions and forced to work amid hostility. When their complaints reached top management at the paper, a consultant was brought in to provide diversity training.

Many of the sessions have been productive, and some employees have come out of the sessions asking that the paper do more to increase coverage of race and gender issues and hire more black and female employees.

When one meeting in April exploded in bitter feelings and harsh words Amoss called a staff meeting to try to smooth the waters. Reporters and editors packed the newspaper's second-floor meeting room. Amoss explained why the newspaper was engaging in the diversity project, why white employees had to change their attitudes toward black co-workers, why the newspaper had to change—why it had to do a better job writing for all its readers in the New Orleans area, not just white, male readers.

"To the extent that readers don't see themselves and don't see their lives, their friends, their children and their activities reflected in the paper, they feel shut out," Amoss said later. "And if people feel shut out, a newspaper is failing in it's mission, and ultimately will fail altogether."

—8—

John McCain's 2000 Presidential Campaign: Political Reporting

Jon Margolis

EDITORS' NOTE

On Monday, February 28, 2000, Senator John McCain of Arizona, a candidate for the Republican presidential nomination, made one of the most important speeches of his campaign. In a high school auditorium in Virginia Beach, Virginia, McCain took the high-stakes gamble of criticizing two influential figures in his own party, Pat Robertson and Jerry Falwell. These men were not only important Republican fund-raisers; they were prominent members of the religious right—and both were from Virginia.

The setting of the speech and the circumstances surrounding its delivery were politically challenging—which made them journalistically challenging, too. Exacerbating the challenge for journalists was the fact that reporters had little time to write the story before they hopped on an airplane and switched gears to cover the Western states' primaries.

Jon Margolis left the *Chicago Tribune* early in 1995 after twenty-two years as Washington correspondent, sportswriter, correspondent at large, and general columnist. He had spent the bulk of his time there as chief national political correspondent. Margolis led the *Tribune*'s coverage of all the presidential elections from 1976 through 1988, and also covered other major national stories, including the impeachment proceedings against President Richard Nixon.

Margolis approached this case by studying the coverage of McCain's speech in sixteen different newspapers and the Associated Press (see note 1), as well as on network television. After looking at the various elements of each of the stories, Margolis divides them into four different approaches to covering the story and explains the basis of each approach. He then poses these broad questions: Was there a right way to cover the speech? If so, was it represented by one of the four approaches offered here?

This case study allows students to grapple with the issues related to the hurried news judgments reporters have to make and the considered analysis they have to provide on deadline. Students will be encouraged to consider the apparently contradictory requirements of contemplating issues on the run and understanding the full implications of what a candidate has done—even if, perhaps, the candidate does not.

In late February of 2000, John McCain was hot stuff. He was getting the kind of attention—often adulation—usually reserved for rock stars or ballplayers. His presidential candidacy was topic one on radio and television talk shows. People who had not voted in years were registering as Republicans to support him in the primaries, and someone had come up with the word *McCainiacs* to describe his followers.

The proximate cause of this frenzy was McCain's upset victory over Governor George W. Bush of Texas in the New Hampshire primary on February 1.

More than a year earlier, Bush had been all but anointed by the Republican establishment as the party's nominee. Governors and senators had raced to endorse him, and he had sopped up so much of the supply of GOP donations that two of his best-known challengers, former vice president Dan Quayle and former labor secretary and Red Cross director Elizabeth Dole, had had to drop out long before the first primary vote was cast because they could not raise enough money.

Most of the others in the race, such as financial magazine publisher Steve Forbes, conservative Christian activist Gary Bauer, and radio personality Alan Keyes, were running mostly to get their voices heard, though they had no expectation of winning the nomination. By the time the voting had begun in the Iowa precinct caucuses on January 24, McCain was Bush's only real challenger, and he did not seem to be much of a threat. Bush won Iowa easily.

But the next day, when the campaigns moved to New Hampshire for the first primary, experienced observers could feel the political ground shifting under their feet. The polls put Bush in the lead. The energy, however, was all with the McCain campaign; enthusiastic crowds cheered his vows to reform the campaign finance system and to "change Washington"—with a special emphasis on passing new campaign finance laws. McCain was a maverick and an underdog, two qualities with broad appeal. Comparing himself to the hero of the *Star Wars* movies, he cast himself as Luke Skywalker, regularly evading the superior forces of the Death Star.

Furthermore, McCain was a maverick and underdog with a heroic past. He had been a Navy pilot who survived five years of torture and mistreatment as a North Vietnamese prisoner of war. There were stories about how some of his fellow senators found McCain confrontational and inflexible. Yet even these seemed only to help him politically. McCain, many voters said, was not a typical Washington politician. He was not a scripted political clone. He seemed, rather, a blunt reformer who spoke his mind without consulting an opinion poll or a focus group.

On primary day in New Hampshire, McCain did not simply beat Bush; he crushed him by an 18-point margin.

Among McCain's fans were some of the reporters covering him. Not that journalists started to wear McCain campaign buttons or cheer at his speeches. In fact, they could be quite rough on him. When he used the word "gooks" to describe his former North Vietnamese captors, reporters covering him pounced on his apparent insensitivity, and McCain quickly apologized. When he said during a debate that if his own daughter ever sought an abortion he would discuss the matter with her, reporters immediately realized that this anti-abortion candidate had given a pro-choice answer. "We really got in his face about that," Bob Kemper of the *Chicago Tribune* recalled.

Still, the reporters covering McCain liked him. One veteran political reporter who differed with McCain on almost every public policy issue admitted in a private conversation with me, "I would never vote for him, but I love the guy."

What reporters liked was McCain's style. He seemed candid, open, authentic—the antithesis of the programmed, controlled, and managed politician. McCain called his campaign van "the Straight Talk Express," and as it rolled along the highway he was always available and always on the record—holding what amounted to a continuing rolling press conference across America. So it was no surprise that in the post–New Hampshire euphoria some stories echoed the predictions of the senator's campaign aides that the momentum that had built up would propel McCain to the Republican nomination. To some reporters on the campaign trail, McCain was a good story, a good guy, and, after his win in New Hampshire, a genuine political phenomenon.

The campaign trail is a bizarre domain that manages to be at the same time self-contained and chaotic—a mass of glaring lights, bulky cameras, shouting crowds, quick flights on chartered aircraft, and a long string of indistinguishable hotel rooms. On the very day of the Virginia speech, for instance, the McCain entourage flew from Virginia Beach to North Dakota, then to Washington state, and finally on to California for the night so the candidate could begin campaigning there in the morning.

In conditions like these, it is no wonder that reporters begin to rely on each other. Who else could possibly understand what they are going through? Thrown together on airplanes and buses, in hotels and restaurants, journalists on a presidential campaign discuss their work with each other regularly—no, incessantly—from morn until sometimes early the next morning. Inevitably, they influence each other. Hence the references to them as a herd, usually called "the pack," with its tendency to funnel all thought into one channel.

It is not that political reporters become like sheep, mindlessly following each other. What is likely to happen instead is that some assumptions evolve into a certain story line—a narrative.

Every campaign has a narrative, though it is rarely discussed and often not recognized at the time. It does not consist of specific events; it is rather the prevailing mind-set surrounding the campaign, and it always transcends mere politics, invading the realms of history, psychology, and myth.

The McCain narrative jelled in New Hampshire. On primary night, in the crowded bar of the Wayfarer Hotel outside Manchester, abetted by that which abets those who gather in crowded bars, reporters molded it into shape, and it went like this: the American people are hungry for someone just like John McCain, not just because he is candid, not just because he makes himself the butt of his jokes, but precisely because he is willing to take on the big boys. He is not going after just the right-wingers. He is even challenging the Republican establishment that anointed Bush.

THE REPUBLICAN BATTLE

But that Republican establishment was no paper tiger. It went right to work, and no faction worked harder for Bush than the religious conservatives who had been a potent force in the Republican Party since the 1970s, when the Reverend Jerry Falwell of Lynchburg, Virginia, had founded the Moral Majority. Motivated by intense opposition to abortion and to the decades-old U.S. Supreme Court decision banning organized prayer in public schools, the church-based movement also fought against legal recognition of homosexuality and what it considered improper material in movies, television shows, and popular music.

The religious right seemed unlikely to become a truly mass movement; if nothing else, its staunch opposition to abortion in virtually all circumstances was out of synch with most voters as measured in scores of public opinion polls. But, like many another determined minorities, it had worked itself into a position of strength. The Reverend Pat Robertson, founder and leader of the Christian Coalition, had run for the Republican presidential nomination in 1988, and the Christian Coalition built on the political organizations he had formed then to take control of some state and county Republican committees.

At first glance, the alliance between the religious right and Governor Bush was a peculiar fit. Pat Robertson had lost the 1988 nomination battle to then–vice president George Bush, Governor Bush's father. The elder Bush had never been a favorite of the religious conservatives. Nor did son George W. seem to be singing in their choir. He was opposed to abortion, but did not promise immediate action to ban it. He did not say much about school prayer, and he let slide several chances to condemn homosexuality. Nonetheless, he got the early and enthusiastic backing of both Robertson and Falwell.

So it was no accident that the day after his New Hampshire loss, Bush spoke at Bob Jones University in Greenville, South Carolina—the state with the next primary. A fundamentalist college, Jones is firmly allied with the religious right, and by appearing there that day, Bush signaled his allegiance to the movement. It helped. With strong support from Robertson and from Christian conservative voters, on February 19 Bush defeated McCain in the South Carolina primary by 11 percentage points. This did not simply stop McCain's momentum; it knocked askew his victory strategy, which from the start had been based on a victory blitz that included South Carolina.

But Bush's association with Bob Jones also hurt him. For years, the university had been racially segregated, and even after it reluctantly admitted black students in the 1980s it forbade interracial dating. And while its current senior officials had not repeated the anti-Catholic statements of their predecessors, they had not publicly refuted them.

The next contest was in Michigan, home to relatively few fundamentalists but to many Catholics. It made no difference that many of those Catholics were Democrats. Michigan, like Virginia, had an "open" primary system; any registered voter could vote in either party's primary.

In Michigan, both campaigns benefited from recorded religious-based telephone messages to targeted voters. Pat Robertson was responsible for the anti-McCain messages, including recorded telephone messages calling former New Hampshire senator Warren Rudman, a McCain co-chairman, a "vicious bigot" who attacked religious conservatives. The McCain campaign then responded with its own "Catholics for McCain" message repudiating Bush for his speech at Bob Jones. Bush asked Robertson to stop the calls before the Michigan vote took place, but on February 22, primary day in Michigan, McCain trounced Bush. Publicly, Bush said he regretted not speaking out against Bob Jones University's intolerance during his speech there, apologizing even to Cardinal John O'Connor of New York.

Despite this embarrassment, Bush may have benefited from the Jones speech in South Carolina, and he was now in the better political position heading toward the Virginia primary. Even if McCain were to win there, he would be about to confront what *Boston Globe* columnist Thomas Oliphant called the nation's first "essentially national primary" the following week. That would be "Super Tuesday," March 7, when eleven states, including California, New York, and Ohio, would hold their primaries. Together, those states would choose almost two-thirds of the 1,034 delegates a candidate needed to win at the Republican National Convention. Thanks to the Michigan vote, McCain may have regained political momentum. But to run in so many states at once required a great deal of money and the political organization money can buy. Bush had much more of both.

Furthermore, out of either obstinacy or confusion, McCain had gotten himself into one of those political thickets from which it is hard to escape. He had announced that because of a scheduling conflict, he would not take part in a California candidate debate sponsored by the *Los Angeles Times*. Bush aides in California were encouraging speculation that McCain was writing the state off, or at least not giving it proper respect. His announcement was not the main reason McCain was trailing Bush by 20 points in a respected California poll. But it didn't help.

Worse, from McCain's perspective, Bush was leading in the Virginia polls by roughly the same margin as he was in California. McCain had little choice but to try to shake up the political situation. To use one of the football metaphors political reporters find so appealing, he had to "put the ball in the air."

McCain did just that. He attacked Falwell and Robertson where they live. Virginia Beach is Robertson's hometown, and it is only about thirty miles from Chesapeake, home to Robertson's Regent University and his religious broadcasting empire. On Sunday evening, February 27, McCain's aides gave the television reporters covering the campaign a hint of what was to come, making sure that the television correspondents told their bosses about it, the better to get a preview on the morning news programs.

The print press was not alerted until the morning of February 28, on the short flight from Washington to Virginia Beach. But, it did not take long for reporters to realize that they were in for quite a day.

"It was electrifying," said David Barstow of the *New York Times*. "You knew you were seeing a potentially historic moment for the Republican Party, a major candidate sticking it to Christian right leaders and in their home turf at a very pivotal moment. There was an excited atmosphere on the plane, like you knew there was going to be a fight. You could see his [McCain's] brain trust all buzzing. [Gary] Bauer was on the plane, so there was a sense of . . .

he's coming for this? You knew McCain was taking an enormous gamble on the speech."

THE SPEECH

On the face of it, covering a speech seems easy. Usually, when a candidate is about to give a major speech the campaign staff hands out copies of the text well before speech time, so reporters can read the speech before it is delivered. Often they write their stories beforehand, though the careful journalist will insert the words "in remarks prepared for delivery," just in case the candidate gets cold feet, gets lost, or dies before actually making the speech. Furthermore, some candidates—and McCain was definitely one of them—are what is known in the trade as textual deviates; they ad-lib or omit, depending on the audience or their moods. So listening to the actual speech is a must.

Because of television, the major campaign speech has become something of a rarity. The political imperative for today's candidate is to get to as many media markets as possible; it is not to discuss public policy in detail, traditionally the purpose of a major speech. If a candidate is going to unveil a new proposal or make a new attack on his opponents, he or she is more likely to do it at a televised candidate debate or in a commercial than from the podium of an auditorium or a hotel ballroom. The very strangeness of the situation surrounding the McCain speech might have intensified that electricity in the air that Barstow and others felt.

So, no doubt, did the tension caused by today's twenty-four-hour news orgy. Almost everybody who is interested knows the essence of a news story hours before the evening newscasts and a day before the morning papers arrive at their doorsteps. Because the world has the capacity to know "what happened," reporters often feel a burden to tell more than simply what happened. They feel they have to tell why it happened, and what the consequences will likely be.

A few minutes after 7:00 Monday morning, the network news programs were reporting that McCain, as Anthony Mora put it on ABC's *Good Morning America,* was planning "to attack Christian Coalition founder Pat Robertson." At just about the same time, Ann Curry said on NBC's *Today Show,* "McCain will accuse Robertson of putting his own personal ambition above the interests of conservative causes."

So the political world knew it was in for a lively day even before John McCain entered the Cox High School gym as the band played the underdog theme "Put Me In, Coach" and the audience (carefully prepped by McCain's advance team) waved light sabers reminiscent, or at least symbolic, of Luke Skywalker in the movies. Former candidate and prominent Christian conservative Gary Bauer, who had endorsed McCain after finishing last in New Hampshire, entered with the candidate and sat behind him during the speech.

Here is a transcript of what McCain said:

> Thank you. I want to start this morning by making a few remarks about our Republican Party, the party that has been my political home since I entered public life. I am proud of that affiliation, for I have always been proud of the beliefs of our great party: our belief in personal freedom and personal responsibility; our belief in a strong national defense and vigorous and capable world leadership; our belief in small, but effective government and in fiscal conservatism.
>
> Most important, I believe in our party because underlying all our party's conservative principles is our respect for the nation's greatness and our appreciation for the ennobling political and social values from which our greatness is derived.
>
> Thus, I have always felt quite comfortable describing myself as a proud conservative, a proud Reagan conservative, and as a member of Congress I have compiled the record of a proud conservative.
>
> I have fought many battles for small government and low taxes; for personal freedom and responsibility; for a strong defense of our national interests and values.
>
> I have fought against wasteful spending whether its patrons were Democrats or Republicans. Moreover, I have proudly defended the sanctity of life and the values that make families strong and our country great. I have fought these battles in good times and bad for our party, and I will fight them for as long as I have the strength to fight.
>
> Throughout my presidential campaign I have remained true to our conservative principles. It is conservative to pay down the national debt, to save Social Security and Medicare. It is conservative to insist on local control of our children's education. It is conservative to expose the pork-barrel spending practices of both political parties. It is conservative to seek to improve the lives of our servicemen and women, and the means with which we ask them to defend us. And it is conservative to demand that America keep its promises to our veterans.
>
> I run for president, my friends, because I believe deeply in the greatness of America's destiny.
>
> We are the world's lantern of freedom and opportunity . . . the bright beacon of hope that our fathers fought to bequeath us and our children were born to inherit. But I know that unless we restore the people's sovereignty over government and their pride in public service, unless we reform our pub-

lic institutions to meet the demands of a new day, and unless we renew our sense of national purpose, we will squander our destiny.

Toward that end, I have called for the reform of campaign finance practices that have sacrificed our principles to the demands of big-money special interests. I have spoken against forces that have turned politics into a battle of bucks instead of a battle of ideas. And for that, my friends, I have been accused of disloyalty to my party.

I am also proud to help build a bigger Republican Party, a party that can claim a governing majority for a generation or more, by attracting new people to our cause with an appeal to the patriotism that unites us and the promise of a government that we can be proud of again. And for that, I have been accused of consorting with the wrong sort of people.

Well, my friends, I have always acted in what I believe to be the best interests of my country. And I always believed that what is good for America is good for the Republican Party.

I don't believe it's loyal to suggest that the Republican Party cannot stand on its own feet and fight for public opinion without six- and seven-figure contributions from people with interests before government but not necessarily ideas to sustain our country's greatness. I don't believe it's loyal to suggest that the Republican establishment is more important to save than a Republican majority. I believe it is the height of foolishness to build a wall around our party in fear that we are so narrowly defined that new faces and fresh ideas in accord with our basic principles will jeopardize our values.

America is more than the sum of its divided parts, and so our party should be.

America is more powerful than its established power centers, and so our party should be.

America is greater than the accumulation of wealth, and so our party should be.

This is my message to my party and my country. It is an honest Republican message that threatens none of our party's principles or the social values of any constituency in our party. On the contrary, it is an inclusive but principled message that trusts in the people to guide our nation in this new century.

I am a conservative, my friends, a proud conservative, who has faith in the people I serve. But those who purport to be defenders of our party, but who in reality have lost confidence in the Republican message, are attacking me; they are people who have turned good causes into businesses.

Let me be clear: evangelical leaders are changing America for the better. Chuck Colson, head of Prison Fellowship, is saving men from a lifetime behind bars by bringing them the good news of redemption. James Dobson, who does not support me, has devoted his life to rebuilding America's families. Others are leading the fight against pornography, cultural decline, and for life. I stand with them.

I am a pro-life, pro-family, fiscal conservative, and advocate of a strong defense. And yet, Pat Robertson, Jerry Falwell, and a few Washington leaders of the pro-life movement call me an unacceptable presidential candidate. They distort my pro-life positions and smear the reputations of my supporters. Why?

Because I don't pander to them, because I don't ascribe to their failed philosophy that money is our message. I believe in the cause of conservative reform. I believe that because we are right we will prevail in the battle of ideas, unspoiled by the taint of a corrupt campaign finance scheme that works against the very conservative reform of government that is the object of our labors. The Republican Party will prevail because of our principles— because that's what it's about, my friends—principles, not special-interest money or empire or ego.

The union bosses who have subordinated the interests of working families to their own ambitions, to their desire to preserve their own political power at all costs, are mirror images of Pat Robertson. Just as we embrace working people, we embrace the fine members of the religious conservative community. But that does not mean that we will pander to their self-appointed leaders.

Some prefer to build walls and exclude newcomers from our support. Apparently, appeals to patriotism can only be heard by card-carrying Republicans, and only certain Republicans at that, not the kind of Republicans who might dissent from the soft-money ethics of a tired party establishment.

Apparently, Republican reformers, Independent reformers, or Democratic reformers, any group that might, like the Reagan Democrats of twenty years ago, be attracted to our cause of conservative reform and national greatness, are too great a threat to the Washington status quo.

That surprises me, since the essence of evangelism is to seek converts. My campaign is bringing new people into the Republican Party every day. I don't apologize for this. No, I wear it as a badge of honor. I will not padlock the Republican Party, and surrender the future of our nation to Speaker Gephardt and President Al Gore.

My friends, we are building a new Republican majority, a majority to serve the values that have long defined our party and made our country great. Social conservatives should flock to our banner.

Why should you fear a candidate who believes we should honor our obligations to the old and the young? Why should you fear a candidate who believes we should first cut taxes for those who need it most? Why should you fear a candidate who wants to reform the practices of politics and government so they fairly reflect your aspirations for your family and country? Why should you fear a candidate who would sign without hesitation a partial birth abortion ban or who would work tirelessly with anyone to improve adoption and foster care choices for those who might be considering the taking of unborn life? Why should you fear a candidate who shares your values?

My friends, I am a Reagan Republican who will defeat Al Gore. Unfortunately, Governor Bush is a Pat Robertson Republican who will lose to Al Gore.

I recognize and celebrate that our country is founded upon Judeo-Christian values. And I have pledged my life to defend America and all her values, the values that have made us the noblest experiment in history.

But political intolerance by any political party is neither a Judeo-Christian nor an American value. The political tactics of division and slander are not our values.

They are corrupting influences on religion and politics, and those who practice them in the name of religion or in the name of the Republican Party or in the name of America shame our faith, our party, and our country.

Neither party should be defined by pandering to the outer reaches of American politics and the agents of intolerance, whether they be Louis Farrakhan or Al Sharpton on the left, or Pat Robertson or Jerry Falwell on the right.

Many years ago a scared American prisoner of war in Vietnam was tied in torture ropes by his tormentors and left alone in an empty room to suffer through the night. Later in the evening a guard he had never spoken to entered the room and silently loosened the ropes to relieve his suffering. Just before morning, that same guard came back and re-tightened the ropes before his less humanitarian comrades returned. He never said a word to the grateful prisoner, but some months later, on a Christmas morning, as the prisoner stood alone in the prison courtyard, the same good Samaritan walked up to him and stood next to him for a few moments. Then with his sandal, the guard drew a cross in the dirt. Both prisoner and guard both stood wordlessly there for a minute or two, venerating the cross, until the guard rubbed it out and walked away.

That is my faith: the faith that unites and never divides, the faith that bridges unbridgeable gaps in humanity. That is my religious faith, and it is the faith I want my party to serve, and the faith I hold in my country. It is the faith that we are all equal and endowed by our Creator with inalienable rights to life, liberty, and the pursuit of happiness. It is the faith I would die to defend.

Don't let anyone fool you about me, my friends, or about this crusade we have begun.

If you want to repair the people's confidence in the government that represents us—join us.

If you want to restore the people's pride in America—join us.

If you want to believe in a national purpose that is greater than our individual interests—join us.

We are the party of Ronald Reagan, not Pat Robertson. We are the party of Theodore Roosevelt, not the party of special interests. We are the party of Abraham Lincoln, not Bob Jones. Join us. Join us.

Join us, and welcome anyone of good faith to our ranks. We should be— we must be—we will be— a party as big as the country we serve.

Thank you, and God bless.

Newspaper Coverage of the Speech

That "God bless" was the starting gun for the race to write stories and prepare broadcast copy.

Some questions would immediately come to the mind of any reporter rushing to file a story on an event like McCain's speech:

- What is the lead here, the most important element or two to begin with? What is the second most important element? The third?
- What importance should be given to the attacks by McCain on specific individuals? How high should they be placed?
- What is the meaning of these attacks?
- How high should I place the obvious political tactics implicit in what McCain has chosen to do, attacking Pat Robertson in his hometown and Jerry Falwell in his home state on the eve of the Virginia primary? And how can I decide what those tactics are?
- What importance should be given to the praise McCain gave to other religious leaders?

Answering questions like these requires more than just being able to read or hear. Reading the political situation is just as important. It is not enough just to report what the candidate said. How he said it, what inspired him, what strategic ends he hoped to accomplish, whether he accomplished them—all these are part of the story, too. In covering a political speech, the twenty-first-century journalist may be expected to serve variously as theater critic, political analyst, and even amateur psychologist, and to do it all between the end of the event and the first-edition deadline.

In Virginia Beach, reporters did not have to deal with the noise and confusion of a common filing room. Instead, the campaign had arranged for rooms at a nearby motel. The reporters got their own rooms, so they could go over the text and their notes in peace and quiet.

But they did not have a lot of time—the campaign plane would leave for North Dakota in just a couple of hours—and with so many reporters trying to call their editors and file their stories at the same time, the hotel's long distance capacity was overtaxed; some reporters had to wait for a dial tone. Barstow of the *New York Times* remembered that he missed the bus to the airport, which had to come back for him and a campaign aide.

"Everybody sort of dashed it off and got on the plane," said Mark Sherman of the Cox Newspapers Washington Bureau. "The next stop was North Dakota, where you couldn't even use your cell phones at the airport. Then by the time we got to Washington State it was past final deadlines for East Coast papers."

Still, almost all the stories were informative and clear. Almost all of the reporters writing on the speech made an effort to place the event in its political context. But there is little doubt that the quality of the coverage was affected by the clock, and by the general tumult of a campaign.

"There wasn't a whole lot of time," Barstow said. "Maybe 45 minutes or less in that hotel. I wanted to convey in the top of the story just how hard a whack this guy had taken at a very important piece of the Republican base, to convey in those first graphs the range of his critique. He was accusing them of many, many sins. Feathering their own nests, hijacking the party. I wanted the story to convey a lot of risks associated with it. The next couple of days there would be a huge question: how's the country going to respond, is this gamble going to pay off?"

Barstow was hardly the only reporter who wanted to get all that into his story, and that is no easy task in forty-five minutes. Earlier in the campaign, reporters might have revisited the story the next day for the traditional second-day thumb-sucker, or penetrating analysis as it is sometimes known. But in this case the next day was primary day in Virginia, Washington state, and North Dakota. The results and what they meant would be the story. There would be no time for looking back.

In general terms, the coverage of McCain's speech by the sixteen newspapers and the AP could be broken down into four categories:

- Some papers depicted the attack against Falwell and Robertson as an attack against the Christian conservative political movement more broadly.
- Some papers depicted the speech as an attack against Falwell and Robertson, but not against the ideas of the Christian conservative political movement.

- Some papers avoided the issue of whether McCain's criticisms were directed at the Christian conservative movement by quoting his remarks about Falwell and Robertson but not trying to characterize or analyze them.

- A fourth group of papers framed their stories around the political tactics and strategy of the speech. Why was McCain giving such a speech? What was he trying to accomplish strategically with this maneuver? Addressing these questions became part of the leads of these stories and the subtext throughout.

We will look at these four approaches one at a time.

THE FIRST APPROACH: SEEING THE SPEECH AS A BROADSIDE AGAINST THE CHRISTIAN RIGHT IN POLITICS

Of those papers that depicted the speech as a broadside against the Christian right, the *New York Post* was the strongest. Reporter Vincent Morris's story was headlined "McCain Launches Holy War in GOP: He Lashes Out at 'Slander' Politics of Religious Right," and read as follows:

> John McCain yesterday delivered a blistering attack on the religious right—dismissing rival George W. Bush as a "Pat Robertson Republican who will lose to Al Gore."
>
> McCain, in a historic declaration of war against the powerful religious right wing of his own GOP, linked the religious right to "slander" politics.
>
> In front of 2,000 students and faculty at Cox HS, McCain claimed Christian conservatives back Bush because he "panders" to the right wing's "self-appointed leaders."
>
> "Neither party should be defined by pandering to the outer reaches of American politics and the agents of intolerance, whether they be Louis Farrakhan or Al Sharpton on the left or Pat Robertson or Jerry Falwell on the right." McCain said.

Morris did not mention Bauer's position on stage or McCain's praise of other religious leaders.

At the *Los Angeles Times,* the lead of the story by reporters T. Christian Miller and Ronald Brownstein took a similar approach, equating the criticisms of Robertson and Falwell to criticisms of the Christian conservative movement overall. Under the headline "McCain Delivers Hard Left to Christian Right," the story began: "In unprecedented language for a serious Republican presidential candidate, John McCain lashed out Monday against leaders of the Christian conservative movement and called George W. Bush a 'Pat Robertson Republican who will lose to Al Gore.'"

But in the second and third paragraphs, the paper tried to address the political implications of the speech, both tactically and in terms of the larger message about the GOP and the Christian conservatives:

> The speech, delivered in the backyard of Robertson's Christian Coalition just one day before Virginia's primary, represented both an escalation of the religious tensions inside the GOP presidential race and an enormous political gamble for McCain.
>
> Christian conservatives have become one of the largest voting blocs inside the GOP, casting as much as a third or more of the primary vote in many states. But McCain, who has seen these voters back Bush by 2 to 1 in South Carolina and Michigan, may be betting he can mobilize independents and moderate Republicans, especially in the Northeast and Midwest, bridling at the religious right's influence in the party.
>
> "I think McCain is looking beyond Virginia . . . to New York, New England and Ohio on how moderate and Catholic voters could unite behind his candidacy," said Scott Reed, Bob Dole's campaign manager in 1996. "The fact that he is trying to move his candidacy back in to the middle as you go into Super Tuesday" on March 7.
>
> With his pointed remarks, McCain is likely to both sharpen the ideological and geographical divisions in the GOP race, and even more important, raise to the surface long-simmering tensions between social conservatives and more secular elements in the GOP.

In the ninth paragraph, the *Los Angeles Times* discussed McCain's effort to distinguish between the two leaders and Christian conservatism in general: "McCain took pains to portray his remarks not as an attack on the religious conservative movement overall but only on a few of its leaders. To underscore that point, he was joined at his speech by Gary Bauer."

A SECOND APPROACH: DISTINGUISHING BETWEEN THE LEADERS AND THE ORGANIZATION

The second general approach to the story was to more clearly highlight the distinction between attacking Falwell and Robertson and attacking the Christian right. Reporters David Jackson and Wayne Slater and their editors at the *Dallas Morning News* were among those who chose this approach. They also suggested in the story's lead that McCain was criticizing Falwell and Robertson not so much because of their ideas as because of their methods and actions. Under the headline "McCain Alleges 'Intolerance' by Religious Leaders," their story began:

John McCain on Monday condemned "self proclaimed" religious leaders Pat Robertson and Jerry Falwell for "political intolerance" that could doom the Republican party in the fall presidential election.

Mr. McCain, speaking a day before contests in Virginia, Washington state and North Dakota, said that GOP rival George W. Bush has aligned himself with these "agents of intolerance"—chiefly with his Feb. 2 visit to Bob Jones University in South Carolina.

"We are the party of Abraham Lincoln, not Bob Jones," Mr. McCain said in Virginia Beach, Va., home of Mr. Robertson's Christian Broadcasting Network and near the headquarters of the Christian Coalition.

After reviewing the most recent religious clashes between Bush and McCain and quoting Bush's response to the speech, in the fourteenth paragraph of their story the reporters mentioned that McCain had tried to make a distinction between Falwell and Robertson and the Christian conservative movement generally: "Mr. McCain also tried to avoid offending religious conservatives, saying before his Virginia Beach speech that he was criticizing only 'a small number of leaders.'"

In the thirty-third paragraph the reporters noted that Gary Bauer was on the stand, and then quoted Bauer:

"If this were an attack on Christian conservative voters, I wouldn't be here," Said Mr. Bauer, founder of the Family Research Council.

In his speech, Mr. McCain said "evangelical leaders are changing America for the better," singling out Charles Colson and James Dobson.

His fight, he said, is with leaders who oppose him "because I don't pander to them, because I don't ascribe to their failed philosophy that money is our message."

The *New York Times* took a similar approach. Reporter David Barstow tried in his story to make a distinction between Falwell and Robertson and the Christian right, a nuance to some, but arguably an important one. His story began:

Taking his presidential campaign to a stronghold of Christian conservatism, Senator John McCain of Arizona delivered a harsh attack today on the "self-appointed leaders" of the religious right, depicting them as intolerant empire builders who "have turned good causes into businesses" while trying to exclude all but "card-carrying Republicans" from the party.

Mr. McCain singled out for criticism two of the Christian right's best-known leaders, Pat Robertson, the founder of the Christian Coalition, and the Rev. Jerry Falwell, the founder of the Moral Majority. He compared Mr.

Robertson to "union bosses who have subordinated the interests of working families to their own ambitions," and he accused both men of trying
to distort his opposition to abortion and "smear the reputations of my
supporters."

"The politics of division and slander are not our values," Mr. McCain said
in a somber address to some 4,000 people who packed a high school gymnasium here only a few miles from the headquarters of the Christian Coalition.
"They are corrupting influences on religion and politics, and those who practice them in the name of religion or in the name of the Republican Party or
in the name of America shame our faith, our party and our country."

In the story's tenth paragraph, Barstow made the distinction clearer:
"In his address—and again in interviews with reporters—Mr. McCain framed
his remarks not as an attack on the Christian right, but as an appeal to religious conservatives to join him in condemning tactics used by Mr. Robertson and Mr. Falwell on behalf of Mr. Bush, his rival for the Republican
nomination."

Barstow's story was the only one with extensive background on how the
McCain camp had decided to take the political gamble of attacking two influential figures in the party. This background made up five paragraphs of the
piece, starting with the twenty-third paragraph. While Barstow mentioned
Bauer's presence in the twenty-eighth paragraph, it did not mention McCain's
praise of other Christian conservative leaders.

Barstow and Bob Kemper of the *Chicago Tribune* were the only two
reporters who noted another possible reason for McCain's anger: Falwell and
Robertson felt threatened by McCain's campaign finance ideas, which would
diminish the influence of their organizations in party politics. Their leads both
quoted McCain's complaint that Falwell and Robertson were turning "good
causes into businesses."

The other reporters covering the campaign did not deal with McCain's
implication that Robertson, Falwell, and other interest-group leaders support the current campaign finance laws because they and their friends are
using the system to make a tolerably good living. Instead, most reporters
used another quote, in which McCain said that the Christian conservatives
opposed him "because I don't pander to them, because I don't ascribe to their
failed philosophy that money is our message." Perhaps they did not deal with
the implication because it was only an implication; McCain never discussed
in detail how campaign finance laws have helped transform politics into a
business.

A Third Approach: Avoiding Interpretation

Still another group of newspapers adopted a third, subtly different, approach. These papers also led with McCain's condemnation of Falwell and Robertson. But they did not then try to characterize one way or the other what McCain might have been implying about religion or about conservatives more generally. Reporters using this approach simply quoted some of McCain's words but avoided trying to interpret or clarify their meaning.

The story run by the Cox Newspapers, including the *Austin American-Statesman* and the *Atlanta Journal-Constitution,* epitomized this approach:

> Arizona Sen. John McCain on Monday tore into evangelists Pat Robertson and Jerry Falwell, accusing them of distorting his positions and smearing his supporters. On the eve of today's presidential primaries in Virginia and Washington state, and caucuses in North Dakota, McCain branded Robertson and Falwell as "agents of intolerance" who could lead Republicans to defeat in November.
>
> "We are the party of Ronald Reagan, not Pat Robertson," McCain said. "We are the party of Abraham Lincoln, not Bob Jones."
>
> McCain compared the televangelists, who are backing Texas Gov. George W. Bush in his presidential bid, to "union bosses."

A Fourth Approach: Focusing on the Tactical Frame

Finally, a fourth group of papers introduced McCain's supposed political tactics into the lead as a frame for the story. This way they were able to avoid the temptation of trying to interpret the meaning of McCain's speech by focusing instead on the motives for it. Under the headline "McCain Attacks Two Leaders of Christian Right," the *Washington Post* story by Craig Timberg and Justin Blum read as follows:

> John McCain denounced Pat Robertson in his hometown of Virginia Beach yesterday for "political intolerance" as the Arizona senator looked beyond today's Virginia primary and sought to tie rival George W. Bush as tightly as possible to the Christian conservative movement.
>
> The sharply worded speech was the latest in a series of increasingly acrimonious exchanges as McCain seeks to portray himself as a mainstream conservative and the Texas governor as a captive to extremists within the movement. McCain also singled out the Rev. Jerry Falwell, based in Lynchburg, Va., as one of the "agents of intolerance."

The strategy, political analysts said, is more likely to bear fruit in next week's "Super Tuesday" voting in 12 states including California, New York, and Maryland than in Virginia, where Christian conservatives are a crucial bloc in the GOP electorate.

Only six of the sixteen papers examined the background of the speech or interviewed McCain's senior staff about the strategy behind it. The *Los Angeles Times* and the *Atlanta Journal-Constitution* quoted campaign director John Weaver, who shares with some reporters a gift for the hackneyed image, calling his boss's attack "the defining speech of the campaign," as well as "a defining moment for the party."

It should come as no surprise that the phrase "defining moment" appeared on the evening news programs of all the commercial television networks. Where would they be without defining moments?

But only Barstow in the *New York Times* reported that the idea for the speech had come from Rick Davis, McCain's campaign manager. Only Barstow and AP political writer Ron Fournier, who wrote an analysis piece from Washington (Mike Glover did the main news story from Virginia Beach), identified the speechwriter as McCain staffer Mark Salter, who had helped McCain write his best-selling book.

Not that the McCain staff was keeping this information secret. Salter, who was on the campaign plane, said he was in constant contact with reporters, and he acknowledged authorship of the speech. So this was not a case of reporters' not knowing a fact. They all knew it; most of them apparently did not consider it important enough to put in their stories.

When I examined sixteen of the leading newspapers[1] and the Associated Press, I found that their coverage could be broken down along the lines summarized in Table 8.1.

TELEVISION COVERAGE

The television news programs attempted to do less in dealing with the political nuances of the McCain speech, but above all, they were first in reporting the story.

The network morning news programs, except for that of CBS, reported on the speech before McCain gave it, characterizing it as an attack on the leaders of the Christian right rather than on the Christian right in general.

ABC's *Good Morning America* singled out Pat Robertson as the target of McCain's speech. Anchor Antonio Mora led into the story by saying, "John

TABLE 8.1

Number of Newspapers Including Various Elements of the Story

Element of the Story	Paragraph Position/ Number of Papers				
	1–5	6–10	11+	No Mention	Total
Religious conservatives versus the two leaders criticized	3	5	7	2	17
Gary Bauer's presence at McCain's side	1	3	11	2	17
Comparison of Robertson and Falwell with union leaders, Farrakhan and Sharpton	7	5	4	1	17
Link between this speech and Bush's Bob Jones speech	2	5	8	2	17
Information from McCain aides about strategy of speech	0	2	4	11	17
McCain's anger at Robertson for Rudman remark	3	3	10	1	17

McCain is targeting a leader of the religious right this morning. . . . He plans to attack Christian Coalition founder Pat Robertson." Then journalist John Yang appeared, reporting from Alexandria, Virginia: "This verbal slugfest continues," said Yang. "[McCain] is expected to say that 'the union bosses who have subordinated the interests of working families to their own ambitions are mirror images of Pat Robertson.' And in the Republican Party, those are fighting words."

Anchor Ann Curry's preview on NBC's *Today Show* focused solely on Robertson, citing McCain's aides as the source of her information: "One day before Republican contests in three more states, John McCain's aides say that he will take on Pat Robertson, the founder of the Christian Coalition, today. They say McCain will accuse Robertson of putting his own personal ambition above the interests of conservative causes."

That evening, television reported the event with tape of McCain speaking and of Bush responding, followed by some political analysis focusing on the likely impact of McCain's speech on his fight for the nomination.

ABC's Peter Jennings led into the story by saying that the day's uproar was an instance of "McCain deliberately getting up and roaring his disapproval at several conservative Christian leaders. It's more a case of McCain trying to undermine his opponent George Bush." He then turned to Linda Douglas, who described McCain's speech as "political war on [the Christian Broadcasting Network's] leader, TV evangelist Pat Robertson." She included two quotes from McCain: first, his assertion about pandering to "agents of intolerance" and second, that Bush is a "Pat Robertson Republican."

CBS anchor Dan Rather led into their story with McCain's criticism of George Bush as aligned with "peddlers of intolerance, division, and smears" and as a "Pat Robertson Republican." CBS reporter Phil Jones then characterized McCain's speech as taking "dead aim at the leaders of the conservative religious right on its home turf" and included a reference to Bush's apology to the head of New York's Catholic Church for speaking at Bob Jones University.

In her report for NBC, Anne Thompson went so far as to describe the contest for the Republican nomination as "now a holy war," with "McCain today making a bold attack on the leaders of the religious right, comparing them to the lightning rods of the left." She first cut to McCain's "agents of intolerance" clip, then to his statement that "division and slander are not our values," and finally to his criticism of George Bush as a "Robertson Republican." Thompson also included quotes from pollster John Zogby and conservative columnist Cal Thomas.

The next morning, television news was still focused on the speech. *Good Morning America* carried an interview with conservative analyst and co-director of the conservative Empower America, Bill Bennett, discussing the "Republican religious war."

The CBS *Early Show*, in previewing the Virginia primary that day, recounted McCain's "attack on two prominent leaders of the Christian right, Pat Robertson and Jerry Falwell, branding them agents of intolerance."

NBC's Lisa Myers continued the network's holy war image, reporting, "In a dramatic play for Republican moderates, John McCain brought his holy war to Washington state, where moderates have battled the Christian right for years." Myers reran several clips from the speech, including McCain's statements that his party was the party of Ronald Reagan and that Bush was a Pat Robertson Republican. She also included Bush's response.

At the end of that hectic day after McCain's speech, the political significance of the speech and of the stories about it remained uncertain. They would not remain uncertain for long.

THE SEQUEL

The Tuesday primaries turned out not to be the only reason reporters could not revisit the speech story the next day. The other reason was that McCain had gotten himself in trouble in one of his fabled rolling press conferences on the Straight Talk Express. Perhaps in a bad mood after a sparsely attended morning event, McCain began to elaborate on his feelings toward Robertson and Falwell as he was being interviewed by Barstow of the *New York Times*. The story in Wednesday morning's paper created a bit of a journalistic stir.

"Senator John McCain intensified the battle over the political power of the religious right today as he accused Pat Robertson and the Rev. Jerry Falwell of having an 'evil influence' over the Republican Party," began Barstow's March 1 story from Bakersfield, California. After citing Bush's Virginia primary win, in paragraph four Barstow continued: "But Mr. McCain's statements today, following his attack on the leaders of the Christian right on Monday, seemed to continue if not escalate his effort to marginalize what has been an important segment of the Republican party for two decades."

The *Times* ran the story on page 18 because the big political story of the day was Bush's sweep of Tuesday's primaries and caucuses. But the "evil influence" quote still shook things up, both in the campaign and in the press corps. Television analysts subjected it to the quasi-Talmudic parsing for which they are renowned. The next morning, the presumably neutral (as a Democrat) George Stephanopoulos said on ABC's *Good Morning America* that McCain's rhetoric now had "a bitter edge" and was "going too far."

McCain's staff was certainly unhappy about the story. Yes, McCain had said what Barstow reported, but it was during one of the rolling press conferences on his bus. Campaign aides maintained that the campaign regulars knew McCain spoke casually from his seat on the Straight Talk Express, treating his seat on the bus more like a chair in the corner tavern than a campaign podium. His casual conversation was one of the reasons so many reporters liked McCain; he could be both funny and candid, even mildly outrageous, during those sessions, just as they themselves were at a real corner tavern. So the regulars gave him a pass when his rhetoric got sloppy. "It's part of the lighthearted, and frankly, optimistic way we try to conduct this campaign," McCain said on CNN that evening, referring to his penchant for casual chit-chat that often includes hyperbole.

But Barstow did not see it as lighthearted. "I started asking him about how he squared his frequent remarks about how 'I'm not running to tear anybody down, I'm not doing the politics of personal destruction' with the speech. I mean, he really left them full of bullet holes. And he got really pissed."

Not, Barstow said, at him for asking the question, but at Falwell and Robertson the more he thought about them: "He said, 'These guys are evil.' He was clearly really exercised. I'm thinking, wow, this sounds harsh, and I kept circling back about it, asking, are you serious? In a span of ten to fifteen minutes he repeats 'evil' I think six times. These were not jokey quotes, nor a jokey tone of voice."

At first, Barstow wasn't quite sure what to do with the information. Before the interview, he, like the other campaign reporters, thought they had their story for the day: early in the morning, McCain had announced that he would participate in that *Los Angeles Times* debate, after all, by satellite from New York. But when Barstow got off the bus, he called his editors and told them about the conversation. Together they decided that McCain's comments deserved a separate story.

There were three other reporters on the bus during that interview, none of whom thought McCain's comments were newsworthy. Perhaps they thought he was just kidding around. But Barstow pointed out that one of the others was from the *Los Angeles Times,* who of course was preoccupied with the debate story, as was the wire service reporter on the bus. The third reporter, Barstow said, was from a San Francisco radio station, and he was mostly interested in interviewing McCain about AIDS.

Only four reporters could fit into the Straight Talk Express. Most had to follow in a separate press bus, with reporters taking turns between the two vehicles. The informal arrangement that emerged was a kind of floating press pool, in which the reporters on the Straight Talk Express shared any news-worthy quote from the candidate with their colleagues on the other bus. That way no one would miss a big story.

Most of McCain's staff sat on the other bus as well. Staffer Mark Salter later remembered: "We always knew there was a bit of a risk" in the constant, on-the-record status of the campaign bus. "We would shuttle as many reporters as possible into the small cabin in back [of the bus] while the rest sat with us, or in another bus. Often the only [staff] guy in there would be [campaign chief Mike] Murphy, and we knew McCain was using his colorful euphemisms. He had done that throughout."

No one, Salter said, ever thought of whispering to McCain that a new-comer, and one from the *New York Times* at that, had entered the inner sanc-tum, and that perhaps he should speak more prudently. "It wouldn't have done any good," Salter said.

Most newspapers either ignored McCain's statement, or put it well down in their stories. For instance, it was in the sixth paragraph of the Associated Press story, which then immediately quoted McCain's reference to his words as "a light-hearted attempt at humor." The exceptions were the *San Francisco*

Chronicle, which led by saying that McCain had "ramped up his talk against leaders of the religious right," and the *New York Times* in the article by Barstow.

McCain never complained, at least in public. "I said it," he told *Brill's Content* editor Steven Brill, agreeing that whatever he said was reportable.

THE AFTERMATH

John McCain lost his gamble. The primaries held the day after the Virginia speech marked the beginning of the end of his candidacy. In Virginia, Christian conservatives made up some 20 percent of the vote according to exit polls, and they overwhelmingly voted for Bush, who got 53 percent of the vote and all 56 delegates. McCain got 44 percent. Worse from McCain's perspective, Bush won in North Dakota and even in Washington state, where a long history of moderate, independent-minded Republicanism should have helped McCain.

If anything, McCain hurt himself by his attack on Robertson and Falwell. There may be enough moderates left in New York, Connecticut, Massachusetts, and Vermont to help a Republican who criticizes the leaders of the religious right. But in California, Ohio, and Washington, they were outnumbered by conservatives—including religious conservatives—who turned out in force.

It is unlikely that these voters would have been any less angry at McCain had every news organization made clear his distinction between attacking Robertson and Falwell and attacking the religious right movement. The voters in every constituency tend to gather round their flag when one of their own is criticized. No recently successful Democratic candidate has gone out of his way to assail even the more extreme leaders of the African American community, the environmental movement, organized labor, or feminism.

On Super Tuesday, McCain won the moderate states of Connecticut, Massachusetts, and Vermont. But Bush won California, Ohio, and even New York. For all practical purposes, Bush wrapped up the nomination. Two days later, McCain held a press conference at his home in Sedona, Arizona, to announce that he was dropping out of the race.

DISCUSSION QUESTIONS

1. Was there a right way to cover this speech? How would you have covered it and interpreted what McCain meant by it?

2. How does analysis in political campaign reporting serve the public? How can it hurt?

NOTE

1. The newspapers studied were as follows: the *Atlanta Journal-Constitution,* the *Boston Globe,* the *Chicago Tribune,* the *Dallas Morning News,* the *Fort Worth Star-Telegram,* the *Los Angeles Times,* the *New York Post,* the *New York Times,* the *(Norfolk) Virginian-Pilot,* the *Pittsburgh Post-Gazette,* the *Providence Journal-Bulletin,* the *San Antonio Express-News,* the *San Diego Union-Tribune,* the *San Francisco Chronicle,* the *Washington Post,* and the *Washington Times.*

Appendix

McCain Attacks Two Leaders of Christian Right

CRAIG TIMBERG and JUSTIN BLUM, staff writers

John McCain denounced Pat Robertson in his home town of Virginia Beach yesterday for "political intolerance" as the Arizona senator looked beyond today's Virginia primary and sought to tie rival George W. Bush as tightly as possible to the Christian conservative movement.

The sharply worded speech was the latest in a series of increasingly acrimonious exchanges as McCain seeks to portray himself as a mainstream conservative and the Texas governor as a captive to extremists within the movement. McCain also singled out the Rev. Jerry Falwell, based in Lynchburg, Va., as one of the "agents of intolerance."

The strategy, political analysts said, is more likely to bear fruit in next week's "Super Tuesday" voting in 12 states including California, New York and Maryland than in Virginia, where Christian conservatives are a crucial bloc in the GOP electorate.

All 3.7 million registered voters are free to cast a ballot in Virginia today as long as they sign a pledge not to participate in another party's nomination process, but analysts expect Republican voters to dominate. The winner will take all 56 of Virginia's delegates to the national GOP convention this summer.

McCain, speaking to more than 2,000 students and supporters at Cox High School in Virginia Beach, said Robertson was at the "outer reaches of American politics." The comments came in response to Robertson's description of McCain campaign chairman Warren B. Rudman, who has criticized some Christian conservatives, as a "vicious bigot" in telephone messages before the Michigan primary last week.

McCain also kept up attacks on Bush for speaking at Bob Jones University in South Carolina, a fundamentalist Christian college that bans interracial dating and is critical of Catholicism. On Sunday, Bush apologized for appearing there without distinguishing his views from those of the university.

"We are the party of Ronald Reagan, not Pat Robertson," McCain said in his 20-minute speech at Virginia Beach. "We are the party of Theodore Roosevelt, not the party of special interests. We are the party of Abraham Lincoln, not Bob Jones."

McCain said he supported Christian conservative voters and praised some of the movement's leaders—saying, "I stand with them"—in between lines critical of Robertson and others. The senator compared Robertson to "union bosses who have subordinated the interests of working families to their own ambitions" and to

---

Washington Post, February 29, 2000, page A1. Copyright © 2000 the *Washington Post* Company.

Nation of Islam leader Louis Farrakhan and the Rev. Al Sharpton, a civil rights activist.

"Neither party should be defined by pandering to the outer reaches of American politics, and the agents of intolerance, whether they be Louis Farrakhan or Al Sharpton on the left, or Pat Robertson and Jerry Falwell on the right."

Dennis Peterson, McCain's Virginia campaign executive director, said it was a message intended to resonate beyond the state and that the location—in the Hampton Roads area, where Robertson's Regent University, Christian Broadcasting Network and Christian Coalition are based—would maximize news coverage.

"We've created a big television studio. That's all this is," Peterson said moments before more than a dozen television cameras beamed the speech across the nation.

Robertson was in Mexico, but Christian Coalition Executive Vice President Roberta Combs denounced McCain's remarks.

"Christian Coalition will rise above this transparent effort to divide one American from another on the basis of religion," she said.

Falwell, through a spokesman, declined to comment.

Bush, campaigning in Washington state, which also has its Republican primary today, accused McCain of "playing to people's religious fears." Bush said the Arizonan "has taken to needless name-calling. I'm a problem-solver. He's a finger-pointer."

In Virginia, Bush's key supporters responded to McCain while accusing him of making phone calls that described Bush as "anti-Catholic," a charge the McCain campaign denied.

"There's nothing even Christian or even decent about anything like this," Virginia Gov. James S. Gilmore III (R) said on CNN. "He didn't tell the truth about the fact that his campaign was calling into Michigan, into Roman Catholic homes in Michigan and now into Virginia doing these things. The 'Straight Talk' bus got tipped over."

Sen. John W. Warner (R-Va.), a Bush backer who has spoken admiringly of McCain, urged him to stop "firing heat-seeking missiles up the tailpipe of everybody."

Earlier in the day, at a rally in Alexandria, Gilmore, Warner and U.S. Rep. Thomas M. Davis III (R-Va.) reminded voters of McCain's efforts to increase flights at Reagan National Airport despite local opposition, and of his vote to increase the tobacco tax, "further increasing the misery and suffering of people in the South-side," Gilmore said.

Mark J. Rozell, a political science professor at Catholic University who has written about the Christian right, said McCain "is banking on hatred of Pat Robertson" to mobilize his own supporters, who include many independents and Democrats.

"It's a risky strategy, because the Christian conservatives are a huge part of the Republican voting base in Virginia," Rozell said.

Christian conservatives have not been the force in Virginia's primary campaign that they were in the Feb. 19 South Carolina primary. Antiabortion forces have distributed fliers urging support for Bush, but Christian Coalition officials said that although they sent out postcards reminding their members to vote, the group did not publish its trademark voter guides. Robertson has not made the calls in Virginia that he did in Michigan, both campaigns said.

Christian conservative Gary Bauer, who quit the presidential race and endorsed McCain this month, appeared with him in Virginia Beach and told reporters that the differences between the candidates on "family issues" are slim.

"There are really minor differences between them," Bauer said. "Either would make a better president than [Democrat] Al Gore."

But the battle over religiously charged tactics heightened.

In an afternoon news conference at Bush headquarters in Richmond, Michael Rowland, 41, of Chesterfield, a member of the local Republican committee, said he received a phone call Sunday night accusing Bush of being "anti-Catholic." Bush officials said similar calls have been made in the Richmond and Virginia Beach area.

Rowland, in an interview, recounted this line from a caller: "Are you aware, as a Roman Catholic, that Governor Bush is very anti-Catholic? He is also a strong supporter of Bob Jones University in South Carolina."

McCain and his campaign officials denied making such calls.

McCain yesterday received the endorsement of prominent Vietnamese Americans in Northern Virginia, including leaders of the Vietnamese, Cambodian and Laotian Voters League, a national group that encourages newly naturalized citizens to vote.

Staff writers David S. Broder, R. H. Melton, Ann O'Hanlon, William Branigin and Spencer S. Hsu contributed to this report.

McCain Rails against Robertson, Falwell

MARK SHERMAN and KEN HERMAN, staff writers

Arizona Sen. John McCain on Monday tore into evangelists Pat Robertson and Jerry Falwell, accusing them of distorting his positions and smearing his supporters.

On the eve of today's presidential primaries in Virginia and Washington state, and caucuses in North Dakota, McCain branded Robertson and Falwell as "agents of intolerance" who could lead Republicans to defeat in November.

"We are the party of Ronald Reagan, not Pat Robertson," McCain said. "We are the party of Abraham Lincoln, not Bob Jones."

McCain compared the televangelists, who are backing Texas Gov. George W. Bush in his presidential bid, to "union bosses."

"Neither party should be defined by pandering to the outer reaches of American politics and the agents of intolerance, whether they be Louis Farrakhan or Al

Atlanta Journal-Constitution, February 29, 2000, page A1. Copyright © 2000 the *Atlanta Journal-Constitution.*

Sharpton on the left, or Pat Robertson and Jerry Falwell on the right," McCain said in a speech to about 1,500 people at Cox High School.

"Unfortunately, Governor Bush is a Pat Robertson Republican who will lose to Al Gore," he predicted.

Bush, campaigning in Bellevue, Wash., accused McCain of trying to turn a political battle into a fractious religious war.

"He is playing the religion card. That is not Reaganesque," Bush said. He said the McCain campaign, as it did in Michigan, is making telephone calls that suggest he is an anti-Catholic bigot.

The calls tell voters of Bush's Feb. 2 visit to Bob Jones University and of anti-Catholic statements made by the school's leaders in the past.

In a letter to Cardinal John O'Connor of New York and other Catholic leaders, Bush said he regrets not condemning the anti-Catholic sentiments associated with the school during his speech at the institution.

McCain said Bush waited too long.

"His words are fine," McCain said. "To me they should have been said three weeks ago."

Bush said Monday he should not be defined by his backing from Robertson, founder of the Christian Coalition, and Falwell, founder of the Moral Majority.

"They're supporters of mine, but I've got all kinds of supporters," Bush said. "What the Republican Party needs is to have somebody who can unite our party."

"Senator McCain is someone who likes to castigate, not someone who likes to lead," Bush said. "It's important to unite our party and lead it to victory."

Monday's sparring came as both candidates battled for 87 delegates available today in Washington, Virginia and North Dakota. Next Tuesday, voters in 12 states will determine the allocation of more than half of the delegates needed to win the Republican nomination.

In addressing the significance of what McCain said Monday, one of his top strategists, John Weaver, said: "This is a defining moment for our party and for our campaign. We're at a fork in the road. The party can choose the well-marked path of . . . exclusion and ultimate defeat, the path George W. Bush is taking with Jerry Falwell and Pat Robertson as his Lewis and Clark. Or we can choose a new path of inclusion that will produce a Republican victory and sweeping majority in November."

In his Virginia Beach speech, McCain mentioned Bush just once by name but made it clear he wants Bush to be tied so closely to the religious right that his nomination would ensure a Democratic victory in November.

In primaries so far, McCain has fallen well behind Bush among Republican voters while picking up unprecedented support from independents and Democrats in states with open primaries.

The March 7 primaries in California and New York are limited to registered Republicans, and McCain is hoping that the numerous moderate Republican voters in those states will reject Bush's ties to religious conservative leaders.

Robertson and Falwell, both based in southern Virginia, have charged McCain's efforts to change campaign finance laws make him a disloyal Republican and they have questioned his commitment to conservative policies.

Roberta Combs, executive vice president of the Christian Coalition, which Robertson founded, called McCain's remarks "a transparent effort to divide one American from another on the basis of religion."

She predicted the group's conservative message would draw record numbers of voters to the polls.

There was no immediate response from Falwell, founder of the Moral Majority.

"They distort my pro-life positions and smear the reputations of my supporters," McCain said, noting Robertson called his national campaign co-chairman, Warren Rudman, a "vicious bigot" in telephone calls to voters.

He said the criticism from Falwell and Robertson "surprises me, since the essence of evangelism is to seek converts."

"My campaign is bringing new people into the Republican Party every day. I don't apologize for this. No, I wear it as a badge of honor," McCain said.

McCain is apparently counting on a belief that many Republicans are tired of the influence of Robertson and other religious leaders in determining their party's nominee.

For McCain, there may not be much to lose. Long before Monday's speech, the religious right was fully mobilized against McCain.

"Their intensity level already is a 10," said McCain campaign manager Rick Davis.

Nevertheless, McCain was careful to confine his remarks to specific leaders in the religious conservative movement.

"This is not an attack on Christian right voters," he told reporters.

At McCain's side was Gary Bauer, the Christian conservative who ended his Republican presidential campaign earlier this month and endorsed McCain.

"If this were an attack on Christian conservative voters, I wouldn't be here," Bauer said.

There also were reverberations from McCain's decision not to take part in a debate Thursday in California. McCain blamed Bush, arguing Bush was initially evasive about accepting the debate invitation.

Given the delay, McCain said, he scheduled events in New York that can't be changed.

Bush said, "I'm sorry that we're not going to have the debate in Los Angeles. I would be glad to spend the entire time on education."

McCain Delivers Hard Left to Christian Right, Republicans: Arizona Senator, in Religious Coalition's Backyard, Takes Conservatives to Task in Blistering Speech

T. CHRISTIAN MILLER and RONALD BROWNSTEIN, *Times* staff writers

In unprecedented language for a serious Republican presidential candidate, John McCain lashed out Monday against leaders of the Christian conservative movement and called George W. Bush a "Pat Robertson Republican who will lose to Al Gore."

The speech, delivered in the backyard of Robertson's Christian Coalition just one day before Virginia's primary, represented both an escalation of the religious tensions inside the GOP presidential race and an enormous political gamble for McCain.

Christian conservatives have become one of the largest voting blocs inside the GOP, casting as much as a third or more of the primary vote in many states. But McCain, who has seen these voters back Bush by 2 to 1 in South Carolina and Michigan, may be betting he can mobilize independents and moderate Republicans, especially in the Northeast and Midwest, bridling at the religious right's influence in the party.

"I think McCain is looking beyond Virginia . . . to New York, New England and Ohio on how moderate and Catholic voters could unite behind his candidacy," said Scott Reed, Bob Dole's campaign manager in 1996. "The fact is he is trying to move his candidacy back into the middle as you go into Super Tuesday on March 7."

With his pointed remarks, McCain is likely to both sharpen the ideological and geographical divisions in the GOP race, and even more important, raise to the surface long-simmering tensions between social conservatives and more secular elements in the GOP.

"This is more than just a throw of the dice," said one senior Bush advisor. "This is a little bit of a burning down of the Republican Party on the way out."

Indeed, after weeks of rising conflict between McCain and religious conservative leaders, the Arizona senator denounced both Robertson and fellow preacher Jerry Falwell in unequivocal terms. "Neither party should be defined by pandering to the outer reaches of American politics and the agents of intolerance," McCain said. "Whether they be Louis Farrakhan or Al Sharpton on the left or Pat Robertson and Jerry Falwell on the right."

McCain added: "We are the party of Ronald Reagan, not Pat Robertson. We are the party of Theodore Roosevelt, not special interests. We are the party of Abraham Lincoln, not Bob Jones."

McCain took pains to portray his remarks not as an attack on the religious conservative movement overall but only on a few of its leaders. To underscore that point, he was joined at his speech by Gary Bauer, a leading religious conservative and former GOP presidential candidate who has endorsed him.

Bush condemned McCain's remarks after a rally in Bellevue, Wash. "It sounds like Sen. McCain has taken to name calling, needless name calling," Bush said. "Ronald Reagan didn't point fingers. He never played to people's religious fears like Sen. McCain has shamelessly done."

Delivered to an enthusiastic crowd of 2,500 at a high school here, the speech represented a dramatic turn for McCain.

Immediately after his victories in Michigan and Arizona last Tuesday, McCain tried to court Republican voters by terming himself a "Reagan conservative" and touting his support for tax reform, budget cuts and banning abortion. With this speech, though, he seemed to be acknowledging that his best hopes rest with moderate voters—Republicans, but also Democrats and independents—cool toward the religious conservative movement.

McCain advisors said the speech marked a new stage for his insurgent candidacy—one that could cast a huge shadow over the remaining weeks of the campaign. "It's the defining speech of the campaign. It's a defining moment for the party," said John Weaver, McCain's campaign director.

In purely political terms, the remarks constitute a gamble of the sort that few presidential candidates ever take. Perhaps the closest recent example was Bill Clinton's criticism in 1992 of a black rap singer named Sister Souljah, who had been quoted after the Los Angeles riots suggesting African Americans should commit violence, not against other minorities but against whites. Clinton, however, chose a target at the periphery of the political world and delivered those comments only after he had clinched the Democratic nomination.

McCain, by contrast, chose the heat of the campaign to target the two most visible figures—Robertson and Falwell—in the movement that has become the single most reliable voting bloc for Republicans in presidential general elections.

After the speech, one senior McCain advisor said the campaign was essentially writing off the remaining Southern primaries, except for the prospect of "cherry-picking" delegates from individual congressional districts in states such as Florida, Tennessee and Georgia. McCain's hope is that by taking such a strong stand against Robertson—an enormously polarizing figure—he can attract voters elsewhere who are socially moderate or simply prefer that the GOP focus on economic issues.

"Bush has already carved out turf as the Confederate candidate," said one top McCain advisor. "He's the candidate of the Deep South, and in staking out that turf he's effectively ceding the rest of the country. This speech puts up a fence around him."

In fact, though, religious conservatives exert a powerful influence in GOP primaries throughout the country, not just the deep South. More than a quarter of GOP presidential primary voters in 1996 classified themselves as members of the religious right in Illinois, Ohio, Florida, Colorado, Oregon, Washington and California. "You cannot win the Republican nomination . . . by kissing off a basic component of the Republican coalition," insisted the senior Bush advisor. One sign of that danger came Monday, when McCain's South Carolina co-chairman quit. Terry

Haskins, speaker pro tem of the state House of Representatives and a Bob Jones graduate, said he was resigning from the campaign in protest over the senator's repeated attacks on Bob Jones University.

Following McCain's decision to skip a *Times*/CNN debate in Los Angeles on Thursday, the speech intensified speculation that the candidate has written off California to focus on New York—both of which will vote, along with several other states, on March 7.

McCain aides, however, emphatically deny that they are abandoning California, saying they have committed to spending more than $2 million on television advertising in the state and will campaign there three days both this week and next. Indeed, senior McCain advisors admit that, given their poor prospects in the South, winning a delegate majority without California will require them to "sweep the table of non-Southern states after California," as one put it.

Still, some in both campaigns read Monday's remarks as a sign that McCain no longer realistically hopes to beat Bush among GOP voters in California—a predominantly conservative bloc whose votes are the only ones that count in the winner-take-all competition for the 162 delegates. Three polls released over the weekend showed Bush maintaining a substantial lead over McCain among California Republicans.

Whatever the delegate result, McCain may also be hoping to win the state's nonbinding "open primary," in which the votes of independents and Democrats will also be counted. Such a victory could allow McCain to argue to voters that he would be more electable in the fall.

At a news conference after his speech, McCain argued that his remarks were directed only against certain people in the upper echelon of the Christian conservative movement, not against grass-roots members.

The speech marked a continued escalation of McCain's conflict with religious conservative leaders over the last month. During the fight in Michigan, Robertson taped a phone message delivered to thousands of homes attacking former Sen. Warren B. Rudman, McCain's national campaign co-chairman, as a bigot who had insulted Christian conservatives.

McCain fired back with taped phone messages to Roman Catholic voters in Michigan attacking Bush for appearing at Bob Jones University in Greenville, S.C., without repudiating its ban on interracial dating and anti-Catholic statements from some of its leaders.

Times staff writer Robert A. Rosenblatt contributed to this story.

The Arizona Senator: McCain Denounces Political Tactics of Christian Right

DAVID BARSTOW

Taking his presidential campaign to a stronghold of Christian conservatism, Senator John McCain of Arizona delivered a harsh attack today on the "self-appointed leaders" of the religious right, depicting them as intolerant empire builders who "have turned good causes into businesses" while trying to exclude all but "card-carrying Republicans" from the party.

Mr. McCain singled out for criticism two of the Christian right's best-known leaders, Pat Robertson, the founder of the Christian Coalition, and the Rev. Jerry Falwell, the founder of the Moral Majority. He compared Mr. Robertson to "union bosses who have subordinated the interests of working families to their own ambitions," and he accused both men of trying to distort his opposition to abortion and "smear the reputations of my supporters."

"The politics of division and slander are not our values," Mr. McCain said in a somber address to some 4,000 people who packed a high school gymnasium here only a few miles from the headquarters of the Christian Coalition. "They are corrupting influences on religion and politics, and those who practice them in the name of religion or in the name of the Republican Party or in the name of America shame our faith, our party and our country." Mr. McCain's remarks came on the eve of another primary day in what has become a bitter battle with Gov. George W. Bush of Texas, a fight that has become increasingly focused on the appeals Mr. Bush made to religious conservatives in winning the South Carolina primary. And while Mr. McCain's statements may cost him votes among the religious right in Virginia, whose contest is one of three to be held on Tuesday, his aides were counting on media coverage to attract more moderate voters in New York, Ohio and California for their March 7 primaries—which are more crucial to Mr. McCain's overall strategy.

Campaigning in Washington State, Mr. Bush dismissed Mr. McCain's remarks, saying, "This is a political game that Senator McCain is trying to play by pitting one group of people against another."

"I'm a problem-solver," he also said. "It sounds like he's a finger-pointer."

Mr. Robertson could not be reached for comment, but the Christian Coalition released a statement saying that the "Christian Coalition will rise above this transparent effort to divide one American from another on the basis of religion."

"Our pro-family message of faith and freedom will draw citizens to the polls in record numbers as we encourage all people of faith to continue their active involvement in the process we call Democracy," it said.

A spokeswoman for Mr. Falwell said he would have no comment.

In his address—and again in interviews with reporters—Mr. McCain framed his remarks not as an attack on the Christian right, but as an appeal to religious con-

New York Times, February 29, 2000, page A1. Copyright © 2000 the *New York Times*.

servatives to join him in condemning tactics used by Mr. Robertson and Mr. Falwell on behalf of Mr. Bush, his rival for the Republican nomination.

As he has for weeks, Mr. McCain today accused Mr. Robertson of slandering his national campaign co-chairman, former Senator Warren B. Rudman, in telephone calls to South Carolina voters, by calling him a "vicious bigot" for criticisms he had made of the religious right. Mr. McCain also suggested that leaders of the religious right might have been behind other calls and e-mail messages to South Carolina voters accusing him of fathering illegitimate children and pointing out that he and his wife, Cindy, have adopted a dark-skinned daughter from Bangladesh.

"Neither party," Mr. McCain said in his speech, "should be defined by pandering to the outer reaches of American politics and the agents of intolerance, whether they be Louis Farrakhan or Al Sharpton on the left, or Pat Robertson and Jerry Falwell on the right."

"Political intolerance by any political party is neither a Judeo-Christian nor an American value," he said.

He later told reporters, "Before South Carolina, I don't think I would have given a speech like this."

McCain aides said the speech was partly intended to re-emphasize Mr. Bush's support from Christian conservatives a day after Mr. Bush wrote to Cardinal John O'Connor of New York that he regretted a speech he gave at Bob Jones University, a bastion of the religious right in South Carolina whose leaders have spoken harshly of Catholics and banned interracial dating.

Mr. McCain referred to Mr. Bush in his speech as a "Pat Robertson Republican who will lose to Al Gore," and later, his aides distributed a packet of campaign materials and news reports that they said showed numerous links between Mr. Bush's campaign and top officials at Bob Jones University.

But a subtext of the speech was Mr. McCain's campaign finance proposals, including limits on advertisements by advocacy groups. Mr. Robertson and anti-abortion advocates have said those restrictions would stifle their influence and were one reason they opposed Mr. McCain.

In his speech Mr. McCain said of them: "They distort my pro-life positions and smear the reputations of my supporters. Why? Because I don't pander to them, because I don't ascribe to their failed philosophy that money is our message."

More broadly, Mr. McCain described his speech as part of an effort to redefine the Republican Party itself, to move it closer to the center much as President Clinton tried to do for the Democratic Party during his 1992 campaign.

"We are the party of Ronald Reagan not Pat Robertson," Mr. McCain said in his speech. "We are the party of Theodore Roosevelt not the party of special interests. We are the party of Abraham Lincoln not Bob Jones. Join us. Join us."

Mr. Bush scoffed at his claims, saying: "Ronald Reagan didn't point fingers. He never played to people's religious fears, as Senator McCain has shamelessly done."

In California, Leslie Goodman, a Republican political consultant who backs Mr. Bush, said of Mr. McCain: "Truly, the prince of candor has turned into the king of media pander. But what he is really doing is confirming to rank-and-file Republicans that he's at war with everybody."

Mr. McCain's aides said the idea of the speech came from the campaign manager, Rick Davis, on a flight on Friday from San Diego to Cleveland. As Mr. McCain's advisers debated whether to stop in Maryland or Virginia, Mr. Davis suggested Lynchburg, Va., where Mr. Falwell is based. The campaign settled on Virginia Beach after it was unable to find a suitable location in Chesapeake, where Mr. Robertson's headquarters are.

On Sunday, Mr. McCain's speechwriter, Mark Salter, began drafting the address, and revisions continued until an hour before the speech. As his bus pulled up to Cox High School, where half the crowd was students, Mr. McCain said he relished the prospect of taking on Mr. Robertson in what one aide described as a "target-rich environment."

But Mr. McCain and his aides took several steps to minimize the chances that some would interpret his words as an attack on all Christian fundamentalists.

They made certain to stud the speech with signposts of Mr. McCain's conservative record—from his eagerness to ban partial birth abortions, to opposition of tax increases, to his admiration for Ronald Reagan. And Mr. McCain was careful to praise several leaders of the religious right, including Chuck Colson, founder of Prison Fellowship, an evangelical group that ministers to inmates. "Let me be clear," Mr. McCain said. "Evangelical leaders are changing America for the better."

He also brought along with him a well-known social conservative, Gary L. Bauer, a former Republican presidential candidate and longtime president of the Family Research Council. "If this were an attack on Christian voters I wouldn't be here today," said Mr. Bauer, who endorsed Mr. McCain shortly after he dropped out of the race.

Still, there was no disguising the extraordinary sight of a major Republican candidate so directly and vehemently denouncing two highly visible leaders from the very wing of the party that for nearly 20 years has been a dominant force in getting Republicans elected.

Asked whether he was concerned that his speech might rupture the Republican Party, Mr. McCain flipped the question around toward Mr. Robertson and Mr. Falwell.

"They've already ripped the party apart with what they did in South Carolina and other campaigns," he said as his campaign airplane left Virginia for North Dakota, Washington and California. "I'm trying to bring the party back together."

Reconciliation was central to the one passage in the speech that brought a hush over the otherwise squirming high school students. Mr. McCain recounted the time he was tied up in "torture ropes" and left in an empty room after his capture in the Vietnam War. A guard, he said, loosened the ropes, then tightened them before his "less humanitarian comrades returned."

Months later, Mr. McCain said, the two of them stood together in the prison courtyard on a Christmas morning. Without uttering a word, Mr. McCain said, the guard drew a cross in the dirt with his sandal.

"That is my faith," Mr. McCain said. "The faith that unites and never divides, the faith that bridges unbridgeable gaps in humanity."

McCain Launches Holy War in GOP: He Lashes Out at "Slander" Politics of Religious Right

VINCENT MORRIS, Post correspondent

John McCain yesterday delivered a blistering attack on the religious right—dismissing rival George W. Bush as a "Pat Robertson Republican who will lose to Al Gore."

McCain, in a historic declaration of war against the powerful religious right wing of his own GOP, linked the religious right to "slander" politics.

In front of 2,000 students and faculty at Cox HS, McCain claimed Christian conservatives back Bush because he "panders" to the right wing's "self-appointed leaders."

"Neither party should be defined by pandering to the outer reaches of American politics and the agents of intolerance, whether they be Louis Farrakhan or Al Sharpton on the left or Pat Robertson or Jerry Falwell on the right," McCain said.

McCain strode into the gym to the underdog anthem "Put Me In, Coach" as his teen audience waved light-sabers in reference to the senator's frequent quip that he feels like Luke Skywalker of Star Wars challenging Bush.

McCain's tough talk came as Bush tried to repair damage from his visit to anti-Catholic, racially biased Bob Jones University with a letter to John Cardinal O'Connor saying, "I deeply regret" failing to speak out against those policies.

But Bush, the one-time GOP front-runner now fighting for his political life, hit McCain for playing the "religious card."

Asked about Robertson and Falwell while campaigning in Washington state, Bush didn't distance himself from them, saying: "They're supporters of mine but I've got all kinds of supporters."

Bush added: "It sounds like Senator McCain has taken to name-calling, needless name-calling. Ronald Reagan . . . never played to people's religious fears like Senator McCain has shamelessly done."

In New York, pro-Bush Gov. Pataki blasted McCain for comparing Robertson and Falwell to Farrakhan and Sharpton.

"You talk about people who are in many instances encouraging violence, have been blatantly racist, anti-Semitic—I'm talking about Farrakhan and Sharpton—and to compare them to the religious leaders of the right is unfair," Pataki said on MSNBC.

But pro-McCain Staten Island Borough President Guy Molinari said: "If the Republican Party has any chance of rebuilding Ronald Reagan's winning national electoral coalition, we must reject the politics of intolerance."

New York Post, February 29, 2000, page 4. Copyright © 2000 the New York Post.

McCain Rips Leaders of Religious Right

BOB KEMPER, *Tribune* staff writer

Risking a rupture within the Republican Party, Sen. John McCain came to the back yard of Pat Robertson and Jerry Falwell on Monday to denounce the two leaders of the Christian right for turning "good causes into businesses" and hijacking the GOP to suit their own ambitions.

On the eve of the Republican presidential primaries in Virginia and Washington, McCain publicly chastised Robertson, founder of the Christian Coalition, and Falwell, founder of the Moral Majority, for distorting McCain's conservative record during the campaign as a way of helping the Arizonan's rival, Texas Gov. George W. Bush.

In attacking Robertson and Falwell, McCain is hoping to motivate independents and moderate elements of the GOP to turn out for him. He risks further alienating some far-right conservatives, but that voting bloc generally has gone to Bush.

"I am a Ronald Reagan Republican who will beat Al Gore," McCain said to the robust applause of about 2,000 students at a high school in Virginia Beach. "George Bush is a Pat Robertson Republican who will lose to Al Gore."

Bush responded by accusing McCain of "shamelessly playing on religious fear."

McCain said Bush's embrace of Robertson and Falwell will only doom the Republican Party in the autumn elections, just as it did in the last two presidential and congressional elections.

The two conservative leaders are polarizing figures, McCain said, likening them to black leaders Louis Farrakhan and Rev. Al Sharpton.

Robertson and Falwell resist McCain's efforts to bring moderate, independent voters and even Democrats into the GOP fold, the senator said, because it would dilute their own power and influence within the Republican Party.

"It sounds like Sen. McCain has taken to name calling, needless name calling," Bush said at a news conference in Bellevue, Wash. "Ronald Reagan didn't point fingers. He never played to people's religious fears like Sen. McCain has shamelessly done."

"I'm a problem solver. It sounds like Sen. McCain is a finger pointer," Bush said.

McCain, who has criticized Bush's campaign appearance at Bob Jones University, a conservative school in South Carolina that bars interracial dating and whose founder has made anti-Catholic remarks, dismissed the regrets Bush offered on Sunday for that appearance.

"Gov. Bush's words were just fine," McCain said. "Unfortunately, they are three weeks late."

Robertson and other conservatives have used advertisements and phone operations in South Carolina and Michigan in recent weeks to raise questions about

---

Chicago Tribune, February 29, 2000, p. 1A. Copyright © 2000 the *Chicago Tribune*.

McCain's conservative credentials, particularly his commitment to the anti-abortion movement, a key issue among conservatives. Robertson also has called McCain's national campaign chairman, former U.S. Sen. Warren Rudman, a "vicious bigot" because of Rudman's past criticism of GOP conservatives.

McCain, who used the word "conservative" 10 times in the opening five minutes of his address Monday, countered those criticisms by emphasizing his support for middle-class tax cuts, paying off the national debt, shoring Social Security and strengthening the military.

"I am a pro-life, pro-family, fiscal conservative, and [an] advocate of a strong defense," McCain added.

"Yet," McCain said, "Pat Robertson, Jerry Falwell and a few Washington leaders of the pro-life movement call me an unacceptable presidential candidate. They distort my pro-life positions and smear the reputations of my supporters. Why? Because I don't pander to them, because I don't ascribe to their failed philosophy that money is our message."

McCain insisted Monday that his attacks on the two religious leaders are not a sign that he is writing off Virginia, where Robertson and Falwell live, or an effort to boost his standing among moderate voters in more critical primary states, such as New York and California.

His complaint, he said, is with the men who ran negative ads and critical phone calls against him in South Carolina and Michigan, not with their followers.

"We embrace the fine members of the religious conservative community," McCain said. "But that does not mean we will pander to their self-appointed leaders."

"We are the party of Ronald Reagan, not Pat Robertson," he said. "We are the party of Theodore Roosevelt—not the party of special interests. We are the party of Abraham Lincoln, not Bob Jones."

The Christian Coalition responded with a statement from Roberta Combs, the group's executive vice president. The group "will rise above this transparent effort to divide one American from another on the basis of religion. Our pro-family members of faith and freedom will draw citizens to the polls in record numbers as we encourage all people of faith to continue their active involvement in the process."

Sen. John Warner (R-Va.), a moderate campaigning for Bush in Richmond, was critical of McCain's remarks. "I have to tell my old friend to pull back on his throttle and quit trying to fire heat-seeking missiles," he said, alluding to McCain's days as a Navy pilot.

Gary Bauer, a conservative activist who abandoned his own presidential bid a month ago and who endorsed McCain although the two differ on a variety of issues, defended McCain's comments.

"If this were an attack on Christian conservative voters, I would not be here today," Bauer said. "I think it is very important that men and women of faith transform politics and not let politics transform them."

The moderate Republican Leadership Council praised McCain for his condemnation of the "agents of intolerance."

"The challenge for both John McCain and George W. Bush now is to focus on a message of inclusion, highlighting issues that affect the daily lives of hard-working Americans," said Mark Miller, the council's executive director.

McCain, talking with reporters on his campaign bus before the speech, gave a whimsical smile when asked why he had chosen to come to Robertson and Falwell territory to launch these attacks.

"I don't think it's confrontational," he said. "It's just things that need to be said."

McCain also defended his decision not to attend a debate in California on Thursday. McCain said he canceled after reading that Bush might not appear at the event.

Tribune news services contributed to this report.

GOP Rivals Place Focus on Religion: McCain Sees "Intolerance"; Bush Says Tactics Divisive

DAVID JACKSON and WAYNE SLATER, staff writers

John McCain on Monday condemned "self-proclaimed" religious leaders Pat Robertson and Jerry Falwell for "political intolerance" that could doom the Republican Party in the fall presidential election.

Mr. McCain, speaking a day before contests in Virginia, Washington state and North Dakota, said that GOP rival George W. Bush has aligned himself with these "agents of intolerance"—chiefly with his Feb. 2 visit to Bob Jones University in South Carolina.

"We are the party of Abraham Lincoln, not Bob Jones," Mr. McCain said in Virginia Beach, Va., home of Mr. Robertson's Christian Broadcasting Network and near the headquarters of the Christian Coalition.

Mr. Bush, campaigning in Bellevue, Wash., accused Mr. McCain of "playing to people's religious fears" to divide voters.

"He is a person who obviously wants to divide people into camps," Mr. Bush said. "The Republican Party needs to nominate somebody who is a uniter, somebody who can not only unite our party and lead us to victory but unite the country."

The exchanges marked the latest clash over politics and religion between the two leading GOP presidential contenders.

A day earlier, Mr. Bush had sent New York City's top Catholic Church official a letter expressing regret for his speech at Bob Jones University, whose leaders ban interracial dating and have espoused anti-Catholic sentiments.

Mr. Bush said in his letter that he "should have been more clear" in disassociating himself "from anti-Catholic sentiment and racial prejudice."

Mr. McCain, who faced fierce opposition from religious conservatives in South Carolina and Michigan, said that he found Mr. Bush's letter sincere but tardy.

"His words are fine," Mr. McCain said. "To me, they should have been said three weeks ago. I think what he did was wrong."

Reassurance

Monday, Mr. Bush repeated his political mea culpa but also sought to reassure religious conservatives that he is not rejecting their support of his candidacy.

"There are a lot of people in our party who happen to be Christians and who are conservative people," Mr. Bush said. "They realize I'm the one person who can lead the country."

As for Mr. McCain's criticism of Mr. Robertson and Mr. Falwell, the governor said: "They're supporters of mine, but I've got all kinds of supporters."

Mr. McCain also tried to avoid offending religious conservatives, saying before his Virginia Beach speech that he was criticizing only "a small number of leaders."

Religious conservatives campaigned vigorously against Mr. McCain in South Carolina, which he lost by 11 percentage points, and in Michigan, where he won with the help of independents and Democratic voters.

In Michigan, some would-be voters heard a taped telephone message in which Mr. Robertson denounced Mr. McCain and referred to Warren Rudman, national co-chairman of the senator's campaign, as a "vicious bigot."

Meanwhile, the McCain camp was also placing calls, issuing a "Catholic voter alert" that criticized Mr. Bush for his Bob Jones University visit.

Explanation

Mr. McCain first denied knowledge of those calls but later acknowledged approving the script. He said he was originally asked whether he had approved phone calls branding Mr. Bush an "anti-Catholic bigot." His campaign's taped message in Michigan did not use that language.

Bush supporters, however, noted that the calls linked the governor to anti-Catholic statements made by Bob Jones University leaders.

Appearing Monday on ABC's *Good Morning America*, Bush strategist Karl Rove accused Mr. McCain of using the Bob Jones controversy to portray Mr. Bush as a bigot. Mr. Rove called the Arizona senator's tactics a "reprehensible attempt to bring religion into American politics in a very ugly way."

Roberta Combs, executive director of the Christian Coalition, said in a statement that Mr. McCain was making a "transparent effort to divide one American from another on the basis of religion." And House Majority Leader Dick Armey, R-Irving, a Bush backer, said the speech was not one "worthy of a Republican presidential candidate."

Mr. McCain, in a response late Monday to accusations that he's dividing the GOP, said: "They've already ripped the party apart by what they did in South Carolina and other campaigns. We're trying to bring the party back together."

Mr. McCain said that religious conservatives have attacked him because of his push to overhaul campaign finances. Their power, he said, would be reduced by such reforms.

"I have spoken against forces that have turned politics into a battle of bucks instead of a battle of ideas," Mr. McCain said. "And for that, my friends, I have been accused of disloyalty to my party."

Speaking at a high school gym, he called himself "a Reagan Republican who will defeat Al Gore," prompting cheering and stomping from his student audience. "Unfortunately, Governor Bush is a Pat Robertson Republican who will lose to Al Gore."

REAGAN COMPARISON

Mr. Bush took issue with the senator for comparing himself with Ronald Reagan, both on the stump and in a new television commercial.

"He invokes the name of Ronald Reagan and yet at the same time plays upon people's religious fears. That's not the politics of Ronald Reagan I remember," Mr. Bush said.

Sen. John Warner, R-Va., who is campaigning for Mr. Bush, also was critical of Mr. McCain's remarks.

"I have to tell my old friend to pull back on his throttle and quit trying to fire heat-seeking missiles up everybody's tailpipe," Mr. Warner said in Richmond, Va.

Mr. McCain and his aides said they still plan to appeal to rank-and-file religious conservatives who may object to their leaders' tactics. The senator was joined on the podium Monday by Gary Bauer, who during his failed presidential bid tried to appeal to religious conservatives.

"If this were an attack on Christian conservative voters, I wouldn't be here," said Mr. Bauer, founder of the Family Research Council.

In his speech, Mr. McCain said "evangelical leaders are changing America for the better," singling out Charles Colson and James Dobson.

His fight, he said, is with leaders who oppose him "because I don't pander to them, because I don't ascribe to their failed philosophy that money is our message."

Mr. Bush focused on education Monday during stops at two Washington community colleges, saying he supports local control, home schooling and taxpayer-funded vouchers to help poor children attend private school.

During his rally in Pasco, Wash., one supporter held up a handmade sign that said, "Catholics for Bush." Another sign read, "I'm a Catholic and I'm for George W. Bush."

The Associated Press contributed to this report.

ABOUT
——— THE AUTHORS ———

JOHN HERBERS spent 24 years on the staff of the *New York Times*. As a reporter there, he covered civil rights, Congress, the Kennedy presidential campaign, urban affairs, and the Watergate years. In 1975 Herbers was named assistant national editor, and in 1977 he became deputy Washington bureau chief. Two years later he requested a return to writing and was named the paper's national Washington correspondent, reporting on national trends in politics, government, and social movements. Herbers began his career at the *Greenwood (Miss.) Morning Star* and then the *Jackson (Miss.) Daily News*. From there he moved to United Press, where he served as Mississippi bureau chief until moving to the *Times*. Herbers is the author of four books, including *No Thank You, Mr. President*.

J. D. LASICA is the director of content for iVendor, a Silicon Valley startup that offers e-commerce capabilities to major brick-and-mortar retail chains. He is also a columnist for the *American Journalism Review* and the *Online Journalism Review*. Prior to this work, he was senior editorial manager for Microsoft's San Francisco Sidewalk and editor at the *Sacramento Bee*.

JON MARGOLIS, author of *The Last Innocent Year: America in 1964*, left the *Chicago Tribune* early in 1995 after 22 years as Washington correspondent, sports writer, correspondent-at-large, and general columnist. He led the *Tribune*'s coverage of all the Presidential elections from 1976 through 1988 and covered other major national stories, including the impeachment proceedings against President Nixon. Since 1996, Margolis has been a regular contributor to *High Country News*, the Colorado-based biweekly that covers Western resource and environmental issues. He writes the political column for *Northern Woodlands*, a Vermont quarterly, and recently has contributed columns to the *Orlando Sentinel* and the *Atlanta Journal-Constitution*. He has also served on the adjunct faculty at Lyndon State College.

STANLEY MEISLER is a former foreign correspondent for the *Los Angeles Times*, a position in which he covered Nairobi, Mexico City, much of Latin America, Toronto, Paris, and the United Nations from 1967 to 1996. He was then a foreign affairs reporter in Washington, D.C., until 1998. Before joining the *Times*, Meisler worked as a reporter for the Associated Press from 1954 to 1964. He is currently an author and contributor to various journals and magazines, including *Smithsonian, Foreign Affairs, The Atlantic Monthly, Foreign Policy,* and the *Columbia Journalism Review*.

GENEVA OVERHOLSER has held newspaper jobs at several levels, including reporter, editorial writer, top editor, and ombudsman, and has free-lanced from such places as Kinshasa and Paris. She began her career as a reporter for the *Colorado Springs Sun*. She then served on the editorial board of the *New York Times* and was deputy editorial page editor for the *Des Moines Register*. She was editor at the *Register* from 1988 to 1995, after which she spent four years as ombudsman for the *Washington Post*. Currently Overholser writes as a columnist.

JACK NELSON, chief Washington correspondent for the *Los Angeles Times*, has covered every president since Richard Nixon and every presidential campaign since 1968. He began his career as a reporter with the *Biloxi (Miss.) Daily Herald*. He later reported for the *Atlanta Constitution*, until becoming Atlanta bureau chief of the *Los Angeles Times* in 1965. Nelson has stayed with the *Times* ever since, filling several positions, including a twenty-two-year stint as Washington bureau chief. Nelson has co-authored six books and has lectured at colleges and universities throughout the country.

ALICIA C. SHEPARD is currently serving as teaching assistant for Gene Roberts at the University of Maryland's College of Journalism, while she pursues a master's degree in journalism. She is also senior writer for the *American Journalism Review*. Her specialties are ethical issues, explanatory stories examining journalistic events, and the newspaper industry. Shepard began her career in Washington, D.C., with Scripps League Newspapers, where she spent five years covering various aspects of the federal government. She next joined the *San Jose Mercury News*, where she wrote about city government and the courts. After five years abroad on a sailing and writing venture with her family, Shepard returned to the Washington area to write and pursue her degree in journalism.

JAMES M. PERRY joined the *Wall Street Journal* in 1977 and worked there as a political reporter until his retirement in 1997. His journalism career began at the *Hartford Times*, and he then joined the *Philadelphia Bulletin*. In 1962 he moved to Washington, D.C., to work for the *National Observer* (the Dow Jones weekly) and began reporting on national politics. It was when the *Observer* folded that Perry joined the *Journal*. Perry has written six books, including two about the press: *Us & Them: How the Press Covered the 1972 Election* and, most recently, *A Bohemian Brigade: The Civil War Correspondents—Mostly Rough, Sometimes Ready*.

Project Consultants

JAMES W. CAREY (academic adviser) is CBS Professor of International Journalism at the Columbia University Graduate School of Journalism. From 1979 to 1992 Carey was dean of the College of Communications at the University of Illinois, Urbana–Champaign. Prior to that, he held the George H. Gallup Chair at the University of Iowa. He has held the National Endowment for the Humanities Fellowship in Science, Technology, and Human Values, and is one of twenty elected fellows of the International Communications Association. In addition to over a hundred essays, monographs, and reviews, Carey has published two books: *Media, Myth and Narratives: Television and the Press* and *Communication as Culture.*

JIM DICKENSON (editor) spent nearly thirty years as a political reporter, editor, and columnist for the *Washington Post,* the *Washington Star,* the *National Observer,* and United Press International. He covered every presidential campaign from 1964 to 1988, as well as the White House, Congress, and the Watergate scandal. In 1991 Dickenson was a media consultant in Belgrade to a consortium of Yugoslav-American businessmen investing in Yugoslavia. He helped train reporters and editors for its proposed news operation and news programs. He is the author of *Home on The Range: A Century on the High Plains* and is currently working on a book about the final battles of World War II in the Pacific, as well as his memoirs.

CLEVE MATTHEWS (copy editor) is a retired newspaper journalist, radio network news director, and journalism professor, who keeps his hand in by teaching retirees and taking on selected writing and editing jobs. He spent nine years at the *St. Louis Post-Dispatch* and twelve years at the *New York Times.* He left the *Times* Washington bureau in 1971 to serve as the first news director at National Public Radio, where he helped create the program "All Things Considered." For seventeen years he taught journalism, first at Wichita State University, then at Syracuse University's Newhouse School. He took a leave from Syracuse when he was named the first Atwood Fellow at the University of Alaska in Anchorage. Matthews has taught a variety of media and public issues courses at the College for Seniors at the University of North Carolina at Asheville. He is the co-author of *Ethics for the Media* (with William Rivers).

RICHARD ROTH (academic adviser) is associate dean of the Medill School of Journalism at Northwestern University. He is also an associate professor at the school and the faculty adviser for the student chapter of the Society of Professional Journalists. Before joining Medill, Roth spent seven years as a tenured faculty member and adviser to the student newspaper at DePauw University (Greencastle, Ind.). As a practicing journalist, Roth was editor-in-chief of the *Terre Haute (Ind.) Tribune-Star* for six years. He also spent eleven years reporting for the late *Buffalo Courier-Express.*